Women and the Misogyny of Religion

Women and the Misogyny of Religion

R R Choudhary

MD PUBLICATIONS PVT LTD
NEW DELHI
www.mdppl.com

Published by :

MD Publications Pvt Ltd
"MD House", 11, Darya Ganj,
New Delhi-110 002
Phone : +91-11-45355555
E-mail : contact@mdppl.com
Website : www.mdppl.com

ISBN : 978-81-7533-295-9

Published and Printed by Mr. Pranav Gupta on behalf of **MD Publications Pvt Ltd** at Printext, New Delhi.

PREFACE

Misogyny is hatred or contempt of women or girls. Misogyny comes from Greek *misogunia* from *misos* "hatred" and *gynç* "woman". It is parallel to misandry-the hatred of men or boys. Misogyny is also comparable with (but not the same as) misanthropy which is the hatred of humanity in general. The prefix miso-, meaning 'Hatred' or 'To hate' applies in many other words, such as misandry, misocapny, misogomy, misarchy and misoxeny.

Frequently, the term misogynist is used in a looser sense as a term of derision to describe anyone who holds an unpopular or distasteful view about women as a group. Misogyny is a negative attitude towards women as a group, and so need not fully determine a misogynist's attitude towards each individual woman. The fact that someone holds misogynist views may not prevent him or her from having positive relationships with some women. Conversely, simply having negative relationships with some women does not necessarily mean someone holds misogynistic views. The term, like most negative descriptions of attitudes, is used as an epithet and applied to a wide variety of behaviors and attitudes.

Traditional feminist theorists propose many different forms of misogyny. In its most overt expression, a misogynist will openly hate all women simply because they are female. Other forms of misogyny may be less overt. Some misogynists may simply be prejudiced against all women, or may hate women who do not fall into one or more acceptable categories. Subscribers to one model, the mother/whore dichotomy, hold that women can only be "mothers" or "whores." Another variant is the virgin/whore dichotomy, in which women who do not adhere to a saintly standard of moral purity (Abrahamic) are considered "whores".

Many religions and philosophies contain what could be called misogyny. St. Paul insisted that women cover their heads and should not talk in church. The Ten Commandments could be inferred as referring to wives as property. In Islam, a woman receives half as much inheritance as a man and her witness is worth half as much in court. In Hinduism, the Code of Manu makes women incapable of ever being independent. At times in Indian history, it was customary for a woman to be pushed onto the funeral pyre of her husband. There is, of course, wide disagreement as to whether these various teachings are misogynistic. Every major religion's texts were written at a time when women were regarded as little better than talking cattle. Their words and commands reflect this, plainly and bluntly.

I am very grateful to Mr. Pranav Gupta, Director of MD Publications Pvt Ltd, New Delhi, for his kind cooperation and support for this book.

R R Choudhary

Contents

1

Women and the Misogyny of Religion

An Introduction

Misogyny is hatred (or contempt) of women or girls. Misogyny comes from Greek *misogunia* from *misos* ("hatred") and *gynç* ("woman"). It is parallel to misandry—the hatred of men or boys. Misogyny is also comparable with misanthropy which is the hatred of humanity generally. Marcus Tullius Cicero reports that Greek philosophers considered misogyny to be caused by gynophobia, a fear of women. In the late 20th century, feminist theorists proposed misogyny as both a cause and result of patriarchal social structures. *Misogyny* is sometimes confused with the similar looking word—*misogamy*—which means "hatred of marriage", hence the following error.

Any doubt he may have ever cherished in his *misogamic* breast concerning a woman's creative capacity. —*Pall Mall Gazette, 7 January 1889*

An example of correct use, from the same period is:

He... walked the banks apart, a thing of *misogyny*, in a suit of flannel. —*Herman Charles Merivale, Faucit of Balliol, 1882*

A clearer example of the sense, also from the same era but using the related word misogynist, is provided by Thackeray.

Confound all women, I say, muttered the young *misogynist. —William Makepeace Thackeray, The Virginians, 1878*

In the second act of *The Importance of Being Earnest*, Oscar Wilde humorously has Miss Prism referring to Dr Chasuble as a *womanthrope*, but intending *misogynist* or *misogamist*: You should get married. A misanthrope I can understand—a womanthrope, never! *—Oscar Wilde, The Importance of Being Earnest, 1895.*

Occasionally writers play on the similarity of sound between *misogyny* and *miscegeny* (mixed-race marriage). This psychosocial analysis of the murder of a white civil rights activist by her mulatto lover (Joe Christmas) is replete with themes of fate, free will, sociopathy, family violence, *misogyny, miscegeny,* and isolation versus community. *—Karl Kirkland, 'On the Value of William Faulkner to Graduate Medical Education', 2001.*

Misogyny comes into English from the ancient Greek word, *misogunia,* which survives in two passages. The earlier, longer and more complete passage comes from a stoic philosopher called Antipater of Tarsus in a moral tract known as *On Marriage* (*c.* 150 BC). Antipater argues that marriage is the foundation of the state, and considers it to be based on divine (polytheistic) decree. Antipater uses *misogunia* to describe Euripides' usual writing—*tçn en to graphein misogunian* ("the misogyny in the writing").

However, he mentions this by way of contrast. He goes on to quote Euripides at some length, writing in praise of wives. Antipater doesn't tell us what it is about Euripides' writing that he believes is misogynistic, he simply expresses his belief that even a man thought to hate women (namely Euripides) praises wives, so concluding his argument for the importance of marriage. He says, "This thing is truly heroic." Euripides' reputation as a misogynist is known from another source. Athenaeus, in *Deipnosophistae* or *Banquet of the Learned,* has one of the diners quoting Hieronymus of Cardia who confirms the view was widespread, while offering Sophocles' comment on the matter.

Euripides the poet, also, was much addicted to women: at all events Hieronymus in his Historical Commentaries speaks as follows,—"When some one told Sophocles that Euripides was a woman-hater, 'He may be,' said he, 'in his tragedies, but in his bed he is very fond of women.'" —*Athenaeus, Deipnosophists, 2nd/3rd century.*

Despite Euripides' reputation, Antipater is not the only writer to see appreciation of women in his writing. Katherine Henderson and Barbara McManus consider he "showed more empathy for women than any other ancient writer", citing "relatively modern critics" to support their claim. The other surviving use of the original Greek word is by Chrysippus, in a fragment from *On affections,* quoted by Galen in *Hippocrates on Affections.* Here, *misogyny* is the first in a short list of three "disaffections"—women (*misogunian*), wine (*misoinian*) and humanity (*misanthrôpian*).

Chrysippus' point is more abstract than Antipater's, and Galen quotes the passage as an example of an opinion contrary to his own. What is clear, however, is that he groups hatred of women with hatred of humanity generally, and even hatred of wine. "It was the prevailing medical opinion of his day that wine strengthens body and soul alike." So, as with his fellow stoic, Antipater, misogyny is viewed negatively, a disease, a dislike of something that is good. It is this issue of conflicted or alternating emotions that was philosophically contentious to the ancient writers. Ricardo Salles suggests the general stoic view was that, "A man may not only alternate between philogyny and misogyny, philanthropy and misanthropy, but be prompted to each by the other."

Misogynist is also found in the Greek—*misogunçs*—in *Deipnosophistae* (above) and in Plutarch's *Parallel Lives,* where it is used as the title of Heracles in the history of Phocion. It was also the title of a play by Menander, which we know of from book seven (concerning Alexandria) of Strabo's 17 volume *Geography,* and quotations of Menander by Clement of Alexandria and Stobaeus that relate to marriage.

Menander also wrote a play called *Misoumenos* or *The Man*

(She) Hated. Another Greek play with a similar name, *Misogunos* or *Woman-hater*, is reported by Cicero (in Latin) and attributed to Atilius. The context is worth quoting in full, because it deals directly with matters. It is the same with other diseases; as the desire of glory, a passion for women, to which the Greeks give the name of *philogyneia*: and thus all other diseases and sicknesses are generated. But those feelings which are the contrary of these are supposed to have fear for their foundation, as a hatred of women, such as is displayed in the *Woman-hater* of Atilius; or the hatred of the whole human species, as Timon is reported to have done, whom they call the Misanthrope. Of the same kind is inhospitality. And all these diseases proceed from a certain dread of such things as they hate and avoid. – *Cicero, Tusculanae Quaestiones, 1st century BC.*

The more common form of this general word for woman hating is *misogunaios*.

- There are also some persons easily sated with their connection with the same woman, being at once both mad for women and women haters. – Philo, *Of Special Laws*, 1st Century.
- Allied with Venus in honourable positions Saturn makes his subjects *haters of women*, lovers of antiquity, solitary, unpleasant to meet, unambitious, hating the beautiful, – Ptolomy, 'Of the Quality of the Soul', 2nd century.
- I will prove to you that this wonderful teacher, this woman-hater, is not satisfied with ordinary enjoyments during the night. – Alciphron, 'Thais to Euthyedmus', 2nd century.

The word is also found in Vettius Valens' *Anthology* and Damascius' *Principles*. In summary, Greek literature considered misogyny to be a disease, an anti-social condition, in that it ran contrary to their perceptions of the value of women as wives, and of the family as the foundation of society. These points are widely noted in the secondary literature. To talk on the immense topic of "Women and World Religions" is an impossible task - we could be here for a few days at least. In the time allotted, I will focus on an area that is of particular personal interest, which is concerned with what could be termed women's "official" roles in various religious traditions. My intent is to present vignettes from different time periods, rather than a historical overview or facts and figures.

As a scholar and teacher in Religious Studies, I understand my role to be one that fosters understanding of religions that differ from those of mainstream Western culture. In this connection, I do have some concern with the term "World Religions", which has been accepted as referring to those religions, both numerous and of sufficient influence, that have had an impact beyond their original borders. I do believe that the contours of this definition are fading, because of both the migration and the displacement of peoples, so that today there is an increasing co-mingling of many religions, other than those labeled "World Religions." In addition, this term does not take into consideration the indigenous peoples of many countries. In beginning this talk, I would like to acknowledge the wisdom and the contribution of spirituality made by the native peoples of Canada. I am not including a discussion of the role of women in their traditions.

This is because until white contact, women were respected in native traditions in their tribes and nations. Women had specific roles as, e.g., elders, members of judging circles, and keepers of the hearth. Their work was vital to the continuance of the circle of life. There was no division whereby women were regarded as inferior or deficient. In this respect, native women differed from certain other traditions that I would now like to examine. I will start by addressing three religions where claims are made that in their beginnings, women were accorded recognized roles or significant participation in their religions. One final word of introduction -throughout my presentation, I will defer to the knowledge of women scholars who have a greater depth of understanding of their own traditions than I do.

ISLAM

There is a strong claim made by modern Islamic women that, at the time of the prophet Muhammad, women actively were engaged in the early community. Women frequented the mosque, celebrated feast days and were present at Muhammad's discourses (Ahmed: 72]. As Leila Ahmed observes:

> Thus the hadith narratives [narratives of the Prophet's conduct and sayings – after the Quran the most important guide to Islamic tradition] show women acting and speaking out of a sense that they were entitled to participate in the life of religious thought and practice, to comment forthrightly on any topic, even the Quran, and to do so in the expectation of having their views heard. (Ahmed: 72)

There is also the example of Khadija, the Prophet's first wife, who was a wealthy widow and a businesswoman, fifteen years, his senior, who proposed to him. She was Muhammad's first convert and supported his efforts to spread the revelations from Allah. Aisha, one of Muhammad's widows, not only participated in battles, but contributed approximately 2,000 *hadiths* which described the behaviour of the Prophet in prayer and the recitation of Quranic *suras* (chapters) – thus providing evidence for the arbitration of disputed readings. To quote Leila Ahmed again: "After all, how many of the world's major living religions incorporate women's accounts into their central texts or allow a woman's testimony as to the correct reading of a single word of a sacred text to influence decisions?" (Ahmed: 73). *Sura* 33: 35 of the Quran explicitly states that the Quran is addressed to both men and women:

> For Muslim men and women,– for believing men and women, for devout men and women, for true men and women, for men and women who are patient and constant, for men and women who humble themselves, for men and women who give in charity, for men and women who fast (and deny themselves), for men and women who guard their chastity, and for men and women who engage much in Allah's praise, – for them Allah has prepared forgiveness and a great reward.

So what happened to change this seemingly egalitarian situation (which, however, was not without ambiguities, which I will discuss later). There are a number of explanations given. One would be the gradual formalization of legal and moral/

theological thought and the introduction of *Shari'a* – the regulative code of life – as well as the establishment of *madrases* (schools of learning). It would seem that women were excluded from these developments.

Another reason offered is that with the spread of Islam to areas of the Byzantine Empire, there were encounters with societies where women were more restricted in their roles and rights. It was in societies such as Syria, Iraq, and Persia that the upper-class women in particular were veiled (similarly to Greek and Roman women), a custom which Islam adopted. It is the issue of the veil today which has become, (unfortunately), the principal focus of discussion of the Western preoccupation with the oppression of Muslim women. Yet it would seem that Muhammad did not insist on the veiling of all women. It was his wives, as proclaimed by the Quran (*Sura* 33: 54), who, when speaking to other men, should remain behind a curtain (*hijab*). The only ordinance for women is that, in public, women should dress modestly (*Sura* 24: 31).

Over the centuries, however, it appears the message of the Quran, which provided women with a measure of religious/social freedom (which are not separate in Islam), has not been universally acknowledged, and it is only today, that educated Muslim women, who study the Quran and *hadith* are reclaiming their status of equivalence.

BUDDHISM

Claims are also made that Buddhism is a religion where women were treated equally in that Buddha (563–483 BCE) established both an order of monks and an order of nuns. He also allowed that women had the same capacity as men to achieve the Buddhist ideal of freedom from suffering and rebirth (*nibbana/nirvana*). In that Buddhism in India started as part of a protest movement against the hierarchical form of Brahmanical Hinduism, it afforded woman a measure of personal autonomy unknown in the wider culture.

In the Buddhist scriptures, there is evidence that there were many women in the early community who became realized beings (*arhats*) and who were respected as teachers. Names such as Khema, Sona, and Nanda are mentioned. But there is also evidence in the texts of some ambivalence on the part of Buddha towards women. First, there is the fact that the institution of the order of nuns took place five years after the establishment of the monks' order. It occurred only because of the insistence and persistence of his aunt, Mahaprajapati, who had raised him. When the Buddha accepted her pleas, he stipulated eight special rules that the nuns would have to accept. These included not just the fact that the nuns should bow down to any monk, whatever his age, but that they could not admonish a monk for his conduct or views – though monks were permitted to act in this way toward nuns.

Perhaps it could be said that, theoretically, on a spiritual plane, women were equal to men, but the residual effects of the cultural attitudes regarding the inferiority of women became evident in the special rules of conduct. (There are those today who question the authenticity of these statements, viewing them as later interpolations.) Whatever the explanation, after the Buddha's death, and the process of an institutionalized monasticism of the male Buddhist order, the role of nuns gradually receded in importance. They do not appear to have played any role in the redaction of the scriptures, or to have made commentaries on them insofar as can be discerned from documental evidence. The *Therigata,* a book of hymns of the early nuns, is one of the few records that remain of their words. The nun Sangha describes her situation:

> Home I have left, for I have left my world.
> Child I have left, and all my cherished herds.
> Lust I have left, and ill will too is gone.
> And ignorance have I put far from me.
> Craving and the root of craving overpowered,
> Cool I am now, knowing Nibbana's peace.

Nancy Auer Falk states that the negative effects of the special rules became most pronounced in the days of the great universities and the royal patrons who built their own fame through these foundations. She continues to say that these "discriminatory rules implied that the men deserved richer offerings, the more elaborate buildings, and the greater opportunity to share in court and in public confrontations". Karma Lekshi Tsomo, a contemporary Buddhist nun, observes that since that time, monks have held superior status and greater authority, both within the institution and in society.

And it is perhaps for this reason that the nuns' orders disappeared, dependent as they were on donations for their existence. While they initially flourished, after the third century CE, their fortunes waned and there is a continuing paucity of evidence regarding their survival. They eventually disappeared from India, but the lineage of ordination for nuns was transmitted to China, where it has continued and has become a source for the restoration and flourishing of nuns' orders today. Within Theravada Buddhism, which is the form of Buddhism that professes to have remained closest to the original teachings of the Buddha, including the establishment of the order of nuns, there has been a resurgence of interest in the ordination of women.

This interest comes, however, not just from Buddhist women in countries such as Sri Lanka, Thailand, Burma, and Korea, but from western women who have become adherents of Buddhism. (This interest in Buddhism by western women is not confined to the Theravada school of Buddhism but to Tibetan and Zen Buddhism as well.) Because of the transmission of the Theravada lineage of ordination to China, and thence eventually to Taiwan, it was possible for an extraordinary event to occur. Though it was not the first or the last contemporary ordination of *bhikkunis*, in February, 1998, an International Full Ordination Ceremony was held in Bodhgaya, India, sponsored by Fo Kuang Shan, Taiwan's largest monastery. As Karma Lekshe Tsomo reports: "At this week long ceremony, 132 nuns were fully ordained, including fifty nuns from the Theravada tradition" (Tsomo: 13).

There is also today a flourishing International Association of Buddhist woman called Sakyadita (Daughters of the

Buddha). With its worldwide membership, this association meets every two years – the next one will take place in Taiwan in June. This association provides dramatic evidence of the diversity of participants – both nuns and laywoman from all schools of Buddhism, East and West. It also indicates the strong interest that contemporary Buddhist women have in reestablishing an almost forgotten heritage. Some of these women are also concerned with changing the older hierarchical structures. All however, are attempting to repair the traditional Buddhist neglect or disregard for the equivalence that they believe was there in the beginnings of Buddhism.

EARLY CHRISTIANITY

There is strong evidence that during the first century and a half of Christianity women were active in various ministries of the early community though not on the same scale as men. The evidence is basically to be found in the Epistles (especially those of Paul) and Acts of the Apostles/disciples. Women taught, preached, presided at the table ministry, and supervised the house churches where these latter services took place. The epistles of Paul name women as co-worker (Prisca, Romans 16:3); as sister (Appia, a leader of a house church; Philemon 2); as deaconess (Phoebe, Romans 16:1); and apostle (Junia, Romans 16: 6-8). In Acts 2:17, Luke remarks that both sons and daughters will prophesy, and he also mentions the four prophetess daughters of Philip (Acts 21:9). In 1 Corinthians 11, Paul's statement on the gift of prophecy can be assumed to address both men and women.

To take a specific example from these citations, Phoebe is referred to by Paul as *diakonos* and *prostatis* in Romans 16:1. Many translators have downplayed these terms, referring to her simply as a co-worker, but when these terms are used with reference to males, they indicate, firstly, a role of ministry, and secondly, a position of authority. It is only within the last thirty years, with the work of scholarly women pioneers (e.g., Eleanor McLaughlin and Elisabeth Schüssler Fiorenza) that this knowledge has come to the forefront of public awareness, as women have searched for authenticating their claims of women for access to ministry, especially in those churches that appeal to tradition as reasons for the exclusion of women.

In the second and third centuries, however, the culturally dominant Hellenistic household codes, as evidenced in 1 Timothy 9-15, began to be implemented. In this code, women were exhorted to be submissive to their husbands, and basically were confined to the private rather than the public sphere. Yet, the issue of women's leadership roles remained a controversial issue for the next two centuries. As Eleanor McLaughlin wrote: "The texts written to justify male leadership record the sad demise of the original Christian version of oneness in Christ" (1979:57). This is not to say, however, that women completely disappeared from the early Church, despite growing attempts to deprive them of ministry.

Many, by "denying their sex" and remaining virgins - an act regarded as one of becoming spiritually a male - chose to be ascetics, anchorites and martyrs. In the early medieval period, they became abbesses, even of double monasteries, and exercised authority over men. Yet these developments took place at the same time that writings of certain of the Patristic writers, e.g., Tertullian (c.160-220 CE), had taken a decidedly misogynistic turn. Women became identified with Eve as temptress, and as the origin of evil - a development that has continued to haunt Christianity and Western culture.

MEDIEVAL PERIOD

Hildegard of Bingen (1098-1179) is a vibrant example of the learning and authority that medieval women nuns were able to achieve, despite their exclusion from ecclesiastical office and cathedral school education. Again, her vast erudition and spirituality have only become widely known because of contemporary women's scholarship. Hildegard was an extraordinary woman, founder of her own monastery (although never formally named abbess). Her learning - including a basic understanding of Latin - was vast. She wrote on theology, medicine and science, composed poetry and music, and was both a visionary and prophetess. She has been accorded the title of Doctor of the Church, one of the few women thus honoured. She has also been described as the "Dear Abby of the twelfth century". (There are approximately three hundred of her letters still extant.)

Among her correspondents were two popes, archbishops, bishops, monks, abbesses, magistrates, congregations, and people from all strata of society. Hildegard's visions were different from the experiences of later women mystics. There was no trance or ecstasy - she remained fully conscious, but suffused, as it were, with divine light. As she wrote in response to a request from a cleric:

> Father, I, a poor little woman, am able to expound upon the question you asked me, because I have looked upon the True Light, and I am sending you the answer I saw and heard in a true vision - not my words, I remind you, but those of the True Light.

"The poor little woman" self-description is an example of the humility formula by which many learned women and mystics defused any charges of presumption levelled at them. Hildegard's knowledge came from God alone, who had privileged her. This permitted Hildegard to teach and prophesize because she believed that the church had fallen into lax times and the clergy were not doing their job properly so a mere woman had to step in. Basically then, she supported the hierarchical church, though she viewed it as in dire need of reform. Yet, as Barbara Newman observes:

> Had she voiced any genuine heresy, that is, doctrinal errors in matters pertaining to the faith, there is no question that she would have been promptly silenced, her books condemned, and her unusual activities brought to a swift and if need be violent end.

The status of learned women such as Hildegard began to change in the late twelfth and thirteenth centuries. This was mainly due to the foundation of universities. At the same time, as a result of increasing reform, the clergy were required to become celibate. Thus, the developing academic culture was one from which women were prohibited, with the "temptress syndrome" and the intellectual inferiority of women being cited as reasons. The universities were strictly regulated by the papacy, and they became virtual corporations, supervising the admission to the professions, and conferring degrees in theology. (It is only in the latter half of the twentieth century that women again were able to obtain graduate degrees in theology in Vatican-approved universities. I believe that Mary Daly was the first American woman, who was not a nun, to do this.)

It is an interesting fact to observe that with this official banishment of women from studying philosophy, theology, and the sacred scriptures in Latin, a new movement arose. Confined to nunneries or living as anchorites, thousands of women, such as Julian of Norwich (b. 1342), Catherine of Siena (b. 1347), and Teresa of Avila (1515–1582) became mystics. Though the forms of mysticism varied, most were expressive of a divine human love relationship, often expressed in highly erotic imagery. It was a way for women to claim direct divine inspiration and communication - thus by-passing to some extent clerical regulations of learning.

They thus had a voice and a wide following. These women mystics, however, were under strict supervision of priestly spiritual advisors who acted both as watchdogs for heresy and as interpreters (often amenders) of their writings. A fascinating observation is that with the gradual return of women to university education from the eighteenth and nineteenth centuries - initially in the humanities - mysticism diminished as a significant form of religious expression. (Perhaps a footnote should be added that mysticism did not resonate with Protestantism.)

HINDUISM

There is an intriguing incidence of women mystics in Hinduism though they began to appear at an earlier period from those just described in Christianity. (As yet, no influence of Hinudism on Christianity has been established.) Most women mystics in India were part of the groundswell of a devotional movement called bhakti. This movement began in southern India around the seventh century with the innovation of a strong attachment to a personal god. Vijaya Ramaswamy (1992) interprets bhakti as an anti-Brahmanical and egalitarian protest, which supported the development of heterodox practices, in particular the rise to prominence of non-literate, low-caste people who used the vernacular to express their emotional relation to the divine. Knowledge was thus no longer the sole prerogative of male Brahmin priests or ritual specialists for whom women had come to represent the supreme obstacle to enlightenment.

The code of stridharma (literally "duty of the wife"), as elaborated in the laws of Manu (Manusmriti) or the Dharmasastras (written around the beginning of the first millennium BCE) were the codified regulations designed to keep erratic female behaviour and desire under strict control. By a girl, by a young woman, or even an aged one, nothing must be done independently, even in her own house. In childhood, a female must be subject to her father, in youth to her husband, when her lord is dead to her sons, a woman must never be independent.... Though destitute of virtue or seeking pleasure [elsewhere] or devoid of good qualities, a husband must be constantly worshipped as a god by a faithful wife. (Manusmriti, v, 147-8; v. 154)

The development of bhakti marked a break in the monopoly of these regulations - women were no longer solely dependent on an earthly husband as her god figure for the attainment of moksa (enlightenment). Without any intermediary, a woman could now seek solace and salvation in a relationship of which the specifications were determined by god alone. The earliest recorded of these exceptional women, Karaikkal Ammaiyar, is purported to have lived in South India in the 6th century CE. In the intervening centuries, women sants/saints have existed in both the North and South of India. They have emerged from different levels of the social strata (varnas and jatis), and they have been devotees of different gods - the most prominent being Siva and Krishna (as an avatar of Visnu).

Female followers of the Divine Mother in the guise of the goddesses Kali or Durga, and thus regarded as embodiments of the divine feminine energy Shakti, while not as numerous, are also in evidence. What is most unusual about many of these women, however, is that their marital status is most irregular in comparison to the ideal wife, or pativrati, as she is depicted in Hindu mythology as the pure, devoted, and deferential consort-wife of a god, e.g., the heroines Sita, Parvati. Thus, the respect as well as the genuine reverence accorded these extraordinary women bhaktas, whose mystical poetry remains renowned and recited even to this day, is something of an anomaly, as they seem to have flouted the model of an ideal Hindu wife. Even today, while their saintly conduct is eulogized, and their songs fervently sung - their spirituality is praised, but their renunciant lifestyle is not recommended as a model to be imitated.

Perhaps some background information is in order to help appreciate this phenomenon. The earliest scriptures of Hinduism are known as the Vedas which date from approximately 1,500 BCE. These scriptures and hymns reflect a sacrificial priestly cult. Yet there is evidence that women of the upper caste were not excluded from these srauta rituals. Women are also named as seers or rishis, i.e. composers of certain hymns in the Vedas (e.g., Gosha, Apala, Lopamudra). In addition, there is evidence that women were educated and teachers. In the Brihadaranyaka Upanishad, (First Adhyaya, Brahmana 8), there is a famous debate between the sage Yajnavalkhya and Gargi on the nature of the absolute (Brahman/Atman), at the end of which Yajnavalkhya recognized Gargi as having attained the highest spiritual knowledge.

Yet gradually women were excluded from these roles both as educators/sages or ritual officiants (purohits). They were assigned to perform domestic rituals (grhya) only. The study of the Vedic scriptures, the performance of sacrifices, and the renunciate life of a wandering ascetic (sannyasin) became solely the domain of men. The bhakti movement, specifically with regard to women, was a protest against such conditions. These female devotees, as Kinsley observes, "found a way out of ... painful situations by emphasizing their devotion to god. Renouncing marriage and life in the world generally, they directed their passions to heavenly consorts" (1980: 92). Perhaps the most famous of these *bhaktas* was Mirabai, a woman of the Rajasthani ruling class who lived from 1498 to 1546. Her love for Krishna also surpassed her familial/marital obligations, and she became a wandering renunciate, abandoning all (dharmic) duties and responsibility.

In one of her poems, she describes her passionate love for the god Krishna:

> Friend, the dark one's glance is like love's dagger.
> It struck me, and I grew restless; I lost all sense of my body.
> Pain spreads through my body, my mind is intoxicated.
> I have found a few friends - all of them are mad.
> Now I know well who he is - the one who wanders the groves?
> But chakor [partridge] loves the moon; the moth by the lamp is burnt,
> The fish dies without water - dear indeed is such love.
> How can I live without seeing (him), my heart is not at rest.
> Go to him and say: Mira is yours. (Kishwar and Vanita, 1989)

Today, in India and the Indian diaspora, there are many groups of women who congregate to honour the revered *bhaktas* and their beloved gods. Their poems are sung or recited in both temples and household ceremonies. Thus, their influence remains strong, and Vasudha Narayanan celebrates their legacy: "Women saints live today through the songs, dances, reform movements, and spiritual quests of twentieth-century women". Though there have always been certain renowned women, it was only in the twentieth century that education became widely available for women in Indian history. As a result, there are now groups of women who recite the Vedas (*rshikas*) and perform Vedic sacrifices. Begun in the state of Maharasthra approximately fifty years ago, this movement is spreading, and there are now five organizations that train women to become ritual specialists. These women are also from all communities and castes. As Narayanan observes: "From women composers of Vedic hymns, it has taken a full thirty-five hundred years to come to women reciters of Vedic hymns".

There is also, however, another significant development for women in India. The number of women gurus, or spiritual advisers, has dramatically increased. Some are also operating in both Europe and America with large followings of Hindus and non-Hindus. Generally, they follow the *bhakti* model, but many, who are devotees of the Great Goddess, in her various manifestations, are recognized as realizations of Shakti, the divine feminine power. All of these developments mark a watershed in the place and role of women in Hinduism.

Indeed, there is a movement by women scholars of Hinduism (e.g., Kumkum Sangari) as well as Hindus themselves to question the orthodox Brahmanical, upper-caste textual tradition, viewing it as simply one purportedly dominant strand of the multiple approaches in Hinduism – and questioning whether it needs to be emulated by women. Narayanan, for one, advocates that it is instead time to listen to "The voices, actions, and rituals of these women, these performers, these goddesses, ignored and muffled in the past". They are representatives of a dynamic element within the manifold of the Hindu tradition that is transforming the contemporary development and understanding of Hinduism.

JUDAISM

Until very recently, Jewish women did not have access to training in colleges or seminaries where they could acquire the relevant scholarship to study the Bible, rabbinics and theology. This had been the preserve of men. Many women cite the Breslau conference of Reform Judaism in 1846 as marking the beginnings of a development to bring equality to women in all aspects of the tradition, though it was not until 1972 that Sally Priesand was the first woman to become a Reform rabbi, with the Conservative and Reconstructionist branches following this momentous change in the following decades. (My discussion of Judaism will focus mainly on the North American context.)

Today in Judaism, there are women in all branches of Judaism – Orthodox, Conservative, Reconstructionist, and Reform, many of whom identify them as feminist, who are striving to reclaim their roles in the Jewish heritage. A contemporary Jewish woman scholar Tikva Frymer Kensky, while she acknowledges that the Bible is a "patriarchal document from a patriarchal society", claims that theologically, in the early Judaism of Biblical times, there was an ideology of equality in the sense that there was no essential hierarchical division between men as sacred and women as profane, and that both male and female were made in God's image and thus were spiritually of equal dignity and worth in the eyes of God. Their respective roles were regarded as complementary, and both were necessary for the maintenance of society.

Yet, as the roles of women came to be socially constructed, women's human contributions appeared to be of less significance. At the same time, Frymer Kensky acknowledges that, as a result of contemporary studies by women, the Biblical text, when "read with non-patriarchal eyes, is much less injurious to women than the traditional readings of western civilization", especially when compared to the then contemporary civilizations such as Assyria. This is not to say that outstanding women were absent from the Biblical texts. There were strong women such as Bathsheba, Yael, and Esther, the matriarchs Hagar, Tamar, Miriam, and Rahab.

There were women identified as prophetesses, Miriam, Huldar, and the judge Deborah. Women, however, did not participate in the public domain. They do not appear to have played a central role in the priestly temple cult, nor in the legal system. Judith Plaskow would assert that there is no history of women's experiences (from their own perspective) or of their presence at foundational events such as Sinai. On her account, "[Women] do not receive the covenant or pass on the lineage". Plaskow wishes to expand the notion of Torah – used in its broad sense of Jewish sources and teachings – so as "to include the history of women, and, in so doing, alter the shape of Jewish memory".

Such an approach is controversial, as is obvious from the responses of the different branches of Judaism. This is because Plaskow's approach also puts into question both Jewish theology and *halakhah* – the sacred laws concerning all conduct. There are those, particularly Orthodox Jews, who would argue that any change to *halakhah* challenges the integrity and identity of Judaism itself. Women today wishing to re-examine *halakhah*, return to post-Biblical Rabbinic Judaism, which slowly emerged from the fifth century BCE onwards.

The interpretations of the Biblical commentators were systematized in the Talmud, which has functioned as the foundation of Jewish law and conduct from the sixth century CE to present times. Judith Baskin, another contemporary woman scholar, assesses Rabbinic legislation as placing women "at a severe disadvantage". (It must be acknowledged, however, that in rabbinic, as in Biblical times, if a woman performed her duties as wife and mother, she was honoured, as men's and women's roles were still viewed as complementary.)

The disadvantage from a contemporary perspective is because women were still exempted from all religious practices of a public nature, and barred from any intellectual undertakings, which would accord them religious recognition. Women's role was a domestic one, where she performed tasks and rituals that maintained the purity of the household. Yet rabbinic Judaism may not have been as monolithic in its early days as it is viewed from today's perspective. Bernadette Brooten (1982) has documented evidence from a number of synagogues in the diasporic Mediterranean area (Egypt and Italy are two examples) where women held significant positions as head or president of the synagogue, as an elder, or leader. This attests that women did hold positions of leadership from the second to the sixth centuries CE.

Though women in Judaism today do not appeal to this precedent, there are many changes that can be discerned in all branches of Judaism where women are engaged in questioning the tradition. In the Orthodox branch, which does not condone women becoming rabbis, there are women working to create new forms of ritual participation for women, such as welcoming ceremonies for newborn females into the community/covenant; conducting Bat Mitzvah ceremonies, celebrating Rosh Hodesh (a new moon ceremony - scripturally identified as a woman's holiday). There are women-only prayer and study groups, with women in leadership roles. There are also those who, while not promoting radical changes to halakhah, have requested that rabbinic authorities review rulings, specifically those that deal with divorce, where women have suffered.

More liberal and progressive elements in Reform, Reconstructionist, and Conservative branches have been effective in requesting that women be included with men in a minyan (the ten people required for a public ceremony, rather than an alternative solution of a separate group of ten women). The other principal demand has been to receive aliyot - the right to pronounce blessings before and after Torah readings, plus to recite the Torah. Women have become rabbis and cantors, as well as presidents of congregations. More radical demands, however, have been made by those such as Judith Plaskow, who believe that the covenant itself needs to be renegotiated. As she states:

> Feminism demands a new understanding of Torah, Israel, and God....It demands an understanding of Israel that includes the whole of Israel and thus allows women to speak and name our experience for ourselves.... It demands new ways of talking about God that reflect and grow out of the redefinition of Jewish humanity.

There are those who baulk at appreciating a notion of God as feminine, arguing that it is not the sex of God that matters (for God is indeed beyond all forms of anthropomorphic identification). Instead, it is the modes of relationship between God and humanity that are of importance, and the aim is to re-establish the right relationship between men and women and God that was there in the story of creation. It is this vision of men and women working together as full covenantal partners that is central to women's contemporary understanding of the Jewish ideal of tikkun olam (repairing the world).

CONTEMPORARY ISLAM

Today, educated Islamic women are returning to the Quran and the hadith to restore their heritage or to question problematic interpretations. Fatima Mernissi observes:

> It is in order to evaluate the depth of the contemporary Muslim's amnesia, which sees equality of the sexes as an alien phenomenon, that we must return to Medina, to its narrow streets where the debate on equality of the sexes raged and where the men were obliged to discuss it but refused to accept it although Allah and His Prophet demanded it.

As I mentioned earlier, there was some ambiguity regarding the role of women in certain Suras of the Quran. Thus, while there are ones that honour women's position: "Wives have rights corresponding to those which husbands have, in equitable reciprocity" (Sura 2:229, as cited by Leila Ahmed), there are others that are more problematic. One of the more controversial is Sura 4:34, an extract of which states: "As for those women whose defiance you have cause to fear, admonish them and keep them apart from your beds and beat them." This is often stated in the context of men being protectors (qawwamun) of women, and thus superior to them. Riffat Hassan, an Islamic scholar takes issue with this interpretation, believing that "a linguistically and philosophically/theologically accurate interpretation" is possible. As she states:

> What is outlined in the first part of the passage [where men are described as protectors of women] is a functional division of labor necessary for maintaining balance in any

society. Men who do not have to fulfill the responsibility of child-bearing are assigned the functions of being breadwinners. Women are exempted from the responsibility of being breadwinners in order that they may fulfill their function as child-bearers. The two functions are separate but complementary, and neither is higher or lower than the other.

A little further on she focuses on the term "daraba," which is generally translated as "beating." She states: "When used in a legal context as it is here, it means 'holding in confinement,' according to the authoritative lexicon Taj-al-'Arus". Hassan believes that it is time for women to question traditional interpretations in this way, to counter the centuries where "Muslim men... have arrogated to themselves the task of defining the ontological, theological, sociological, and eschatological status of Muslim women". She sees her work as contributing to a theology of women within Islam, as she believes that theology is at the root of the problem.

Other women, such as Fatima Mernissi, question the authenticity of certain hadith. The term "isnad" is used to refer to the chain of transmission used to establish a hadith's credibility, which starts with the witness of one of the companions of the Prophet. Al-Burhari, a Muslim scholar, who lived approximately two centuries after the foundation of Islam, was a prodigious collector of hadith. There is one in particular that he attributes to Abu Bakra, a companion of the Prophet, which Mernissi investigates. Abu Bakra is recorded as having heard the Prophet declare: "Those who entrust their affairs to a woman [in the context of political power] never know prosperity". Mernissi finds it strange that Abu Bakra remembered this saying twenty-five years after the death of the Prophet under somewhat compromising circumstances. Also looking at the methodological rules that religious scholars had recommended for authentication of hadith, Mernissi finds that Abu Bakra's own pedigree and record disqualified him as a reliable source. She worries that this misogynistic hadith is presented today as "sacred, unassailable truth", though it was both compromised and fiercely debated. She concludes:

After having tried to set straight the historical record – the line of transmitters and witnesses who gave their account of a troubled historical epoch – I can only advise vigilance when, taking the sacred as an argument, someone hurls at the believer as a basic truth a political axiom so terrible and with such grave historical consequences as the one we have been investigating. Modernist Islamic women scholars such as Ahmed, Hassan, and Mernissi, by returning to the sources, are challenging traditional Muslim views on women as well as the more fundamentalist ones such as were imposed in Afghanistan by the Taliban. The Taliban traces its position and ultra-orthodox reform school of thought in Islam, the Hanbali School of law, which was introduced in the third century after the Hejira, or ninth century CE. Its views came to prominence again, advocated by Ibn Abd al Wahhab, a Saudi Arabian, in the twelfth AH/eighteenth century CE.

The late Fazlur Rahman lamented the Wahhabi movement's tendency "to impose reform under the compulsion of idealism through intolerant and fanatical methods". It is regrettable that the imposition of not just the veil (hijab), but the burqa/chador on Afghan women has come to symbolize the repression of women in Islam at large, not just in Afghanistan, for it clouds other more important issues. As Rosemarie Skaine remarks: "The burqa is part of some Afghan women's total context. The restrictions on women go beyond those of dress. The atrocities committed against the Afghan women cannot be denied". It also needs to be understood that, today, in the larger context of Islam, the veil (hijab) has other implications. Riffat Hassan observes:

> The wearing of the head scarf by a Muslim woman, especially if she is wearing the head scarf as an act of free choice, does not restrict her autonomy as a person. However, total veiling of the body, especially if it is imposed externally, certainly constitutes a serious deterrent to the full and healthy development of Muslim women.

This statement recognizes that, in this century, many educated Islamic women have adopted the veil as a way of professing "their political, economic and cultural emancipation". In many ways, it is a statement of their acceptance of "modernization" (education and the technological revolution) but of their distance from "Westernization," especially feminism as they understand it - but that would be the topic for another paper.

CONTEMPORARY CHRISTIANITY

To do justice to the myriad forms of Christianity that exist in the world today is beyond the bounds of this presentation. In that it is perhaps the most familiar to many present, I will not give it quite as extensive a treatment as other religions. (Again, my survey will emphasize the North American context.) What is intriguing to note as a start is that, from the Reformation onwards, when women claimed the right to preach, they invoked two precedents. Their rallying call was the text from Saint Paul: "There is no longer male and female, for you are all one in Christ Jesus". The other was an appeal to the fact that both the Christian and Hebrew Bible acknowledged women as prophets and that preaching was part of this ministry.

In the second half of the seventeenth century, the Quaker Margaret Fell argued strongly for women's rights to preaching and for leadership roles in her book, *Women's Speaking Justified, Proved, and Allowed of by the Scriptures* (1666). As Rosemary Ruether notes: "For Fell, women's equality with men in the image of God finds its realization in Christ. The female disciples of Jesus as the first witnesses of the resurrection are the foundation of the prophetic community upon whom God's spirit has fallen." The claim by Fell was that women are called to preach equally with men, for God's spirit has fallen upon them as much as upon men at Pentecost.

In North America, in the eighteenth century, where most Christians did not approve of such preaching in public by women, there was an evangelical revival that is known as the Great Awakening. With its emphasis on the personal conversion experience, it was in many ways a definite challenge to established hierarchies, structures, and ministries - and women participated in it as strongly as men. Sarah Osborn (b. 1714) is an example. She established a young women's religious society, the Female Society, which she headed for fifty years. She also began a group of instruction for African Americans - another group who profited from this egalitarian movement, such as the preacher and exhorter, Jarena Lee (b. 1783). In this tradition, the African Methodist Episcopal Church was the first to ordain African American women by the end of the nineteenth century

The legacy of Quaker women who publicly testified and the Baptist women who publicly prayed and exhorted in the Great Awakening was to find full expression in nineteenth century America. The first woman to be ordained a minister was Antoinette Brown. This took place in the First Congregational Church in Butler, New York, on September 15, 1853. Other Protestant denominations followed - Unitarian, Methodist, and Universalist, while some resorted to introducing special ministries for women such as "deaconess." Liberal women, mainly from the Quaker tradition, such as Sarah and Angelina Grimké, Lucretia Mott, and Susan B. Anthony, were joined by rebels from mainstream Protestant religions, such as Elizabeth Cady Stanton (b. 1815) and Matilda Joslyn Gage (b. 1826) - who were active in the suffrage movement.

In the 1890s, Cady Stanton helped organize and directed a women's collective that produced the *Women's Bible* - a commentary on those passages in the Bible that deal with women, as well as on their contemporary interpretation. It was a severe indictment of both the Hebrew and Christian scriptures, especially those aspects that were cited as justification for women's inferiority and subordination. She was particularly scathing with regard to women's submission to clerical authority as well as the lauded self sacrifice that supposedly marked women's redemptive role in the world.

Cady Stanton's work was reissued again in 1974. This seems appropriate for as Susan Hill Lindley has remarked:

The religious questions of nineteenth century radicals really emerged in the last third of the twentieth century. Debates over women's ordination in certain branches of Protestantism once again brought interpretations of key biblical passages, as well as the nature of the Bible and its authority, to the fore. It is not just Protestants, e.g., the Anglican/Episcopalian, however, who have had problems with ordination. Since the Second Vatican Council, convened in the early 1960s by Pope John XXIII, Catholic women's aspirations of being admitted to the priesthood had increased substantially.

They reach their zenith or nadir (depending on how you look at it) when Sister Theresa Kane, in welcoming John Paul II to the United States in 1979, appealed to the Pope that women, or half of humanity, be recognized as worthy of Church ministry. The Pope's response was that the ideal figure for women to imitate was Mary, both virgin and mother of God, who definitely had non designs on ministry (Wills: 104). And there the matter has stood until today. This caused many women to leave the Church or to apply for admittance as ministers of other Christian denominations. Since the 1970s, there has nonetheless been an exponential growth in women studying for theological degrees in most denominations and also being employed as professors and teachers.

There have been complex and critical studies from women who span a spectrum from post-Christian to evangelical feminism, in Biblical studies, ethics, and church history, to name but a few areas of study and research. This renaissance of women's learning brings with it challenges that may well ineluctably alter the nature and course of Christianity. There are also other challenges underway as Latina, Asian and African women work towards their own expressions of theology, as do African-American or womanist scholars in the United States who believe their experience of Christianity differs greatly from that of white middle-class Americans. These women are asking the churches to reflect seriously on the charges of racism and sexism, as well as of other abuses of power.

In Christianity it is obvious that there are many women today working in the trenches for change (and I include in this category the academic study of religion). Women could be appreciated as the life force of countless communities as they undertake various unofficial ministries and positions. The vast majority are not officially recognized, or regarded as having positions of authority. There are the exceptions, such as the ordained ministers in virtually all Protestant denominations, such as the women bishops in the Episcopal and Lutheran Evangelical churches in the States, and such as the former Moderator of the United Church of Canada, Senator Lois Wilson. I believe that the major task of the twentieth century will be to listen to the wisdom and intelligence of women, as they now speak with enthusiasm of their new found knowledge in philosophy and theology.

Women scholars are also undertaking extensive historical studies and uncovering in archives and inscriptions the untold stories if generations of women who have been but footnotes in what has thus far served as the history of mankind. This work represents a significant challenge to Christianity and my hope is that it will receive a response that recognizes its valuable contribution to knowledge. Despite our secular age, religion, in its various guises¸ against the prognostications of the Enlightenment, continues to proliferate. The influence of Judaism and Christianity, particularly in the area of ethics, on many of our public institutions, especially the courts and Parliament, remains strong. To live in the contemporary world, it is, I believe, necessary to have an informed awareness of not just the grounding of our own particular religious allegiances and formation - even if we no longer adhere to them - but also of the other religions in the world which will play a decisive role in the formation of the future.

In addition, I would recommend that particular attention be paid to the role that women are playing in the many of the major religions today - when women's voices are perhaps been heard loud and strong for the first time. Studies of the history of the roles of women in religion will also help to begin to understand the reasons for the relegation of women, despite some promising starts in the earliest stages of different religions, to positions of inferiority. It may also help to clarify the reasons why women's sexual nature began to be regarded as suspect, even contaminating, which led to their rejection from sacred offices and positions of authority. My hope is that the twenty-first century will be an age of insight and of tolerance, where there will be a growing understanding of the ways of all religions, and where the collaborative voices of both wise women and men will prevail.

2

Feminist Theory

INTRODUCTION

Traditional feminist theorists propose many different forms of misogyny. In its most overt expression, a misogynist will openly hate all women simply because they are female. Other forms of misogyny may be less overt. Some misogynists may simply be prejudiced against all women, or may hate women who do not fall into one or more acceptable categories. Entire cultures may be said to be misogynistic if they treat women in ways that can be seen as harmful. Examples include forcing women to tend to all domestic responsibilities, not allowing women to take jobs outside the home, or beating women. Subscribers to one model, the mother/whore dichotomy, hold that women can only be "mothers" or "whores." Another variant is the virgin/whore dichotomy, in which women who do not adhere to a saintly standard of moral purity (Abrahamic) are considered "whores".

Frequently, the term *misogynist* is used in a looser sense as a term of derision to describe anyone who holds an unpopular or distasteful view about women as a group. A man who considers himself "a great lover of women," therefore, might somewhat paradoxically be termed a misogynist by those who consider this treatment of women to be sexist. Archetypes of this type of man might be Giacomo Casanova and Don Juan, who were both reputed for their many libertine affairs with women. Misogyny is a negative attitude towards women as a group, and so need not fully determine a misogynist's attitude towards each individual woman. The fact that someone holds misogynist views may not prevent him or her from having positive relationships with some women.

Conversely, simply having negative relationships with some women does not necessarily mean someone holds misogynistic views. The term, like most negative descriptions of attitudes, is used as an epithet and applied to a wide variety of behaviors and attitudes. As with other terms, the more antipathetic one's position is in regards to misogyny, the larger the number of misogynists and the greater variety of attitudes and behaviors who fall into one's perception of "misogynist". This is, of course, the subject of much controversy and debate with opinions ranging widely as to the extent and breadth of misogyny in society.

Feminist theorist Marilyn Frye argues that misogyny is phallogocentric and homoerotic at its root. In *Politics of Reality*, Frye analyzes the alleged misogyny characteristic of the fiction and Christian apologetics of C.S. Lewis. Frye argues that such misogyny privileges the masculine as a subject of erotic attention. She compares the misogyny characteristic of Lewis' ideal of gender relations to underground male prostitution rings, which share the same quality of men seeking to dominate subjects seen as less likely to take on submissive roles by a patriarchal society, but in both cases doing so as a theatrical mockery of women.

Feminist theology is a movement found in several religions, including Christianity, Judaism, and New Thought, to reconsider the traditions, practices, scriptures, and theologies of those religions from a feminist perspective. Some of the goals of feminist theology include increasing the role of women among the clergy and religious authorities, reinterpreting male-dominated imagery and language about God, determining women's place in relation to career and motherhood, and studying images of women in the religion's sacred texts. Feminists have attempted to counter perceptions of women as morally or spiritually inferior to men; as a source of sexual temptation; as dedicated to childbearing, their homes, and husbands; and as having a lesser role in religious ritual or leadership because of such inferiority or dedication.

Feminist theology attempts to consider every aspect of religious practice and thought. Some of the questions feminist theologians ask are:

- How do we do theology? The basic question of how theologians may go about creating systems of thought is currently being reinterpreted by feminist theologians. Many feminist theologians assert that personal experience can be an important component of insight into the divine, along with the more traditional sources of holy books or received tradition. (The relevance of personal experience to the policies of groups of people is a familiar notion to veterans of the feminist movement.)
- Who is God? Feminist theologians have supported the use of non- or multi-gendered language for God, arguing that language powerfully impacts belief about the behaviour and essence of God.
- Where are women in religious history? Feminist historical theologians study the roles of women in periods throughout history that have impacted religion: the Biblical period, the early Christian era, medieval Europe, and any period of import to a particular religion. They study individual women who influenced their religion or whose religious faith led them to impact their culture. The work of these scholars has helped feminist theologians claim historical figures as their predecessors in feminist theology. For example, Sojourner Truth's "Ain't I a Woman?" speech pointed out, "Where did your Christ come from? From God and a woman. Man had nothing to do with him!" Elizabeth Cady Stanton produced the "Woman's Bible," excising the traditional Christian text of all references she thought contradicted the positions of women's rights.

BAHÁ'Í FAITH

The Bahá'í Faith has as one of its main teachings the principle of the equality of men and women. The Bahá'í teachings suggest that for humanity to advance, that each gender, though not identical in function, must work in unison with each other and allow the healthy functioning of society. The Bahá'í teachings state that gender equality has positive results for everyone, not only women, and require the same academic and spiritual education for both girls and boys.

NEW THOUGHT MOVEMENT

New Thought as a movement had no single origin, but was rather propelled along by a number of spiritual thinkers and philosophers and emerged through a variety of religious denominations and churches, particularly the Unity Church, Religious Science, and Church of Divine Science. It was a feminist movement in that most of its teachers and students were women; notable among the founders of the movement were Emma Curtis Hopkins, known as the "teacher of teachers" Myrtle Fillmore, Malinda Cramer, and Nona L. Brooks; with its churches and community centers mostly lead by women, from the 1880s to today.

Other Religions

In the latter part of the 20th Century, feminism was influential in the rise of Neopaganism in the United States, and particularly the Dianic tradition. Some feminists find the worship of a goddess, rather than a god, to be consonant with their views. Others are polytheists, and worship a number of goddesses. The collective set of beliefs associated with this is sometimes known as theology and sometimes referred to as the Goddess movement.

Gender and God

Others who practice feminist spirituality may instead adhere to a feminist re-interpretation of Western monotheistic traditions. In those cases, the notion of God as having a male gender is rejected, and God is not referred to using male pronouns. Feminist spirituality may also object to images of

God that they perceive as authoritarian, parental, or disciplinarian, instead emphasizing "maternal" attributes such as nurturing, acceptance, and creativity.

J Holland sees evidence of misogyny in the mythology of the ancient world. In Greek mythology, the human race had already existed before the creation of women – a peaceful, autonomous existence as a companion to the gods. When Prometheus decides to steal the secret of fire from the gods, Zeus becomes infuriated and decides to punish humankind with an "evil thing for their delight" – Pandora, the first woman, who carried a jar (usually described – incorrectly – as a box) she was told to never open.

Epimetheus (the brother of Prometheus) is overwhelmed by her beauty, disregards Prometheus' warnings about her, and marries her. Pandora cannot resist peeking into the jar, and by opening it all evil is unleashed into the world – labour, sickness, old age, and death. J Holland also sees evidence of misogyny in the Christian view on the Fall of Man based on the Book Genesis, which according to Christian interpretation brought tragedy and death into the world by a woman.

RELIGION

Katherine M. Rogers in *The Troublesome Helpmate* argues that the Pauline epistles in the New Testament contain texts that have historically been used by some Christian misogynists. The foundations of early Christian misogyny – its guilt about sex, its insistence on female subjection, its dread of female seduction – are all in St. Paul's epistles.

Christian views (attitudes and beliefs) about women vary considerably today as they have throughout the last two millennia, evolving along with or counter to the societies in which Christians have lived. The Bible and Christianity historically have been interpreted as prescribing distinct gender roles, with women often being excluded from church leadership. Until the second half of the twentieth century, institutionalized Christianity was unfavorable to women in pastoral or ecclesiastical office. This traditional stance continues largely unchanged in Roman Catholicism and Eastern Orthodoxy, as well as among "complementarian" Protestants.

Some contemporary writers describe the role of women in the life of the church as having been downplayed, overlooked, or denied throughout much of Christian history. Male leadership was assumed in many spheres of life, not only in the church, but also within government, society, and the family.

As gender roles have shifted in society and in many churches, many Christians have revaluated these positions. Over the last 50 years Christian egalitarians have increasingly argued for equal roles for men and women in marriage, as well as for the ordination of women to the clergy. On the other hand, some Christian conservatives maintain that women and men were created with different roles according to their interpretation of the Bible.

Jesus and Women

Beyond generally accepted social standards which are continually shifting, Christianity sets a moral standard—the attitudes toward and treatment of women by Jesus. There is no recorded instance where Jesus disgraces, belittles, reproaches, or stereotypes a woman. Examples of the manner of Jesus are instructive for inferring his attitudes toward women and show repeatedly how he liberated and affirmed women.

Women in the New Testament Church

From the beginning of the early Christian church, women were important members of the movement. As time went on, groups of Christians organized within the homes of believers. Those who could offer their home for meetings were considered important within the movement and assumed leadership roles. The New Testament Gospels acknowledge that women were among Jesus' earliest followers. Jewish women disciples, including Mary Magdalene, Joanna, and Susanna, had accompanied Jesus during his ministry and supported him out of their private means (Luke 8:1-3).

Although the details of these gospel stories may be questioned, in general they reflect the prominent historical roles women played in Jesus' ministry as disciples. There were women disciples present at Jesus' crucifixion. Women were reported to be the first witnesses to the resurrection, chief among them again Mary Magdalene. She was not only "witness," but also called a "messenger" of the risen Christ.

The letters of Paul—dated to the middle of the first century CE—and his casual greetings to acquaintances offer information about Jewish and Gentile women who were prominent in the movement. His letters provide clues about the kind of activities in which women engaged more generally.

- He greets Priscilla (Prisca), Junia, Julia, and Nereus' sister (Romans 16:3, 7, 15).
- Paul writes that Priscilla and her husband risked their lives to save his life.
- He praises Junia (or Junias) as "prominent among the apostles" (NRSV) or "well known to the apostles" (ESV), who had been imprisoned for their labor. Some theologians understand the name to be that of a woman, suggesting that Paul recognised female apostles in the Church.
- Mary and Persis are commended for their hard work (Romans 16:6, 12).
- Euodia and Syntyche are called his fellow-workers in the gospel (Philippians 4:2-3).

Some theologians believe that these biblical reports provide evidence of women leaders active in the earliest work of spreading the Christian message, while others reject that understanding. The evidence also indicates that these women "ministered" in supporting roles of the church much as the women who followed Christ supported his ministry.

WOMEN IN CHURCH HISTORY

Patristic Age

From the early patristic age, the offices of teacher and sacramental minister were reserved for men throughout most of the church in the East and West. Tertullian, the second century Latin father, wrote that, "It is not permitted to a woman to speak in church. Neither may she teach, baptize, offer, nor claim for herself any function proper to a man, least of all the sacerdotal office" (On the Veiling of Virgins). Tertullian's views on women went further: "The curse God pronounced on your sex still weighs on the world.....You are the devil's gateway...You are the first that deserted the divine laws. All too easily you destroyed the image of God, Adam. Because you deserved death, it was the son of God who had to die·· TheAlexandrian father Origen argued in his commentary on 1 Corinthians 14:34, 35 that female prophets never spoke publicly in the assembly. Similarly, Epiphanius of Salamis claimed that "Never from the beginning of the world has a woman served God as priest" (*Against the heresies*).

John Chrysostom, bishop of Constantinople at the beginning of the fifth century, said of biblical women that they "were great characters, great women and admirable.... Yet did they in no case outstrip the men, but occupied the second rank" (*Epistle to the Ephesians*, Homily 13). Commenting on 1 Timothy 2:11-15, Chrysostom said that "the male sex enjoyed the higher honor. Man was first formed; and elsewhere he shows their superiority.... He wishes the man to have the preeminence in every way." Of women he said that "The woman taught once, and ruined all. On this account therefore he saith, let her not teach. But what is it to other women, that she suffered this? It certainly concerns them; for the sex is weak and fickle, and he is speaking of the sex collectively." (*1 Timothy*, Homily 9).

In early centuries, the Eastern Church allowed women to participate to a limited extent in ecclesiastical office by ordaining deaconesses, whereas in the West the diaconate (as with higher offices) was reserved only for men. A number of minority movements, deemed heretical by the wider church, gave a more prominent place to the ministry of women and in some cases allowed them to participate in the priestly ministry. These include Montanism in the second and third century, the Quintillians and Collyridians in the fourth century, and Priscillianism in the fourth century. These heretical sects provided occasion for the institutional church to condemn the ecclesiastical ministry of women.

Middle Ages

The Roman Catholic Church was the major unifying cultural influence of the middle Ages with its selection from Latin learning, preservation of the art of writing, and a centralized administration through its network of bishops. Historically in the Catholic and other ancient churches, including the Coptic Church, and the Eastern Orthodox Church, the priesthood and the ministries dependent upon it such as Bishop, Patriarch and Pope, were restricted to men. This was ostensibly because the priest when performing the Eucharist stands in representation of Jesus, and because Jesus himself scripturally selected only male Apostles to lead the Church. Notably, Pope Innocent III stated: "No matter whether the most Blessed Virgin Mary stands higher, and is also more illustrious, than all the apostles together, it was still not to her, but to them, that the Lord entrusted the keys to the Kingdom of Heaven" (*Epistle*, 11 December 1210).

Women were allowed to be Deaconesses in the early church. However, the first Council of Orange (441) forbade the ordination of women to the diaconate, a ruling that was repeated by the Council of Epaon (517) and second Council of Orléans (533). These councils are seen by some as evidence that the ministry of women was actively suppressed during the early middle ages. With the establishment of Christian monasticism, other influential roles became available to women. From the 5th century onward, Christian convents provided opportunities for some women to escape the path of marriage and child-rearing, acquire literacy and learning, and play a more active religious role.

Abbesses could become important figures in their own right, often ruling over monasteries of both men and women, and holding significant lands and power. Figures such as Hilda of Whitby and Hildegard of Bingen became influential figures on a national and even international scale. In the later Middle Ages women such as Saint Catherine of Siena and Saint Teresa of Avila, played significant roles in the development of theological ideas and discussion within the church, and were later declared Doctors of the Roman Catholic Church. A major spokesman for the Church in the High Middle Ages (11th through 13th centuries) was Thomas Aquinas, one of the 33 Doctors of the Roman Catholic Church and renowned thirteenth-century theologian. Writings of Thomas Aquinas about women were an opposing influence upon church and philosophical attitudes towards women for centuries.

He began his argument of women and their involvement in the creation story by quoting Aristotle's misogynist view of a woman as being "a misbegotten man." Aquinas reasoned that anything misbegotten or defective should not have existed in the creation story, therefore women should not exist. He viewed women as having been created for man simply to make procreation possible. Men can gain help and support from other men, but the act of procreation requires a woman, he wrote. By arguing that women were created simply to allow continuation of the human race, he attempted to shut down the argument that God made a mistake in creating women. However, according to Aquinas, the female sex cannot represent Christ because women are incomplete human beings.

Post Reformation

The Protestant Reformation, by shutting down female convents within the movement, effectively closed off the option of a full-time religious role for Protestant women. Martin Luther himself taught that "the wife should stay at home and look after the affairs of the household as one who has been deprived of the ability of administering those affairs that are outside and concern the state...." John Calvin agreed that "the woman's place is in the home."

Modern Views

Some 19th century Christian authors began codifying challenges to the centuries-old traditional views toward women both in the church and in society. Only since the 1970s have more diverse views become formalized. Recent generations have experienced the rise of what has been labeled by some as "Christian feminism" – a movement that has had a profound impact on all of life, challenging some traditional basic Christian interpretations of Scripture with respect to roles for women.

There are three major viewpoints in the modern debate. They are known respectively as Christian feminism, Christian Egalitarianism and Complementarianism.

- Christian Feminists take an actively feminist position from a Christian perspective.
- Christian Egalitarians advocate ability-based, rather than gender-based, ministry of Christians of all ages, ethnicities and socio-economic classes. Egalitarians support the ordination of women and equal roles in marriage, but are theologically and morally more conservative than Christian feminists and prefer to avoid the label "feminist".
- Complementarians believe God made men and women to be equal in personhood and value but different in roles. They understand the Bible as teaching that God created men and women to serve different roles in the church and the home. They maintain that men have a responsibility to lead and women have a responsibility to submit to the leadership of men.

Terminology

Although much of the contemporary literature settles on the terms Complementarianism and Christian Egalitarianism, a number of other more pejorative terms are frequently encountered. In complementarian literature, the term "Christian feminism" is sometimes used synonymously with "egalitarianism." In egalitarian literature, the terms "gender traditionalist," "patriarchalist" and "hierarchicalist" are sometimes used with reference to complementarians. Christian egalitarians generally object to being labelled "feminist" or "evangelical feminist", primarily because the term "feminist" is most often associated with secular Feminism, and therefore becomes ambiguous.

In addition, some egalitarians object to the term "Complementarianism" being used to describe "a milder form of the historical hierarchical view." William J. Webb describes himself as a "complementary egalitarian." He defines this as "full interdependence and 'mutual submission' within marriage, and the only differences in roles are 'based upon biological differences between men and women'." The book *Discovering Biblical Equality* uses the phrase "complementarity without hierarchy" to refer to the egalitarian position.

Wayne A. Grudem objects to Webb's use of "complementary" and "egalitarian" together to describe a thoroughly egalitarian position. Calling the terminology "offensive and confusing," he reasons that doing so simply confuses the issues by using the term "complementary" for a position totally antithetical to what complementarians hold. Grudem finds Webb's use of the term "patriarchy" to be especially pejorative because of its connotations in modern society. He also rejects the term "hierarchicalist" because he says it overemphasizes structured authority while giving no suggestion of equality or the beauty of mutual interdependence.

Position Statements

Within conservative Christianity, two organizations have emerged as strong advocates for each opposing view of women. Various prominent theologians have contributed to developing and editing position statements articulating both the Egalitarian and Complementary views:

- Egalitarian View. *Men, Women and Biblical Equality* was prepared in 1989 by several evangelical leaders to become the official statement of Christians for Biblical Equality (CBE). The statement lays out their biblical rationale for equality as well as its application in the community of believers and the family.
- Complementary View. The *Danvers Statement on Biblical Manhood and Womanhood* was prepared by several evangelical leaders at a Council on Biblical Manhood and Womanhood (CBMW) meeting in Danvers, Massachusetts,

in December of 1987. The statement lays out their biblical rationale for male priority and female submission in the community of believers and the family.

CHRISTIAN FEMINIST VIEW

Christian feminism represents the views of the more theologically liberal end of the spectrum within Christianity. In contrast to the more socially conservative Christian egalitarians, Christian feminists tend to support homosexual rights and a pro-choice stance on abortion. The Evangelical and Ecumenical Women's Caucus, a major international Christian feminist organization, values "inclusive images and language for God."

Egalitarian View

Christian Egalitarians' interpretation of Scripture brings them to the conclusion that the manner and teachings of Jesus, affirmed by the Apostle Paul, abolished gender-specific roles in both the church and in marriage. A scripture passage they consider key to the advocacy of full equality of responsibility and authority for both women and men is contained in a Pauline polemic containing three antitheses:

> There is neither Jew nor Greek, slave nor free, male nor female, for you are all one in Christ Jesus.– *Galatians 3:28*

Christian Egalitarians interpret this passage as expressing that the overarching teaching of the New Testament is that all are "one in Christ." The three distinctions, important for Jewish life, are declared by Paul to be invalid in Christ. Therefore, among those "in Christ" there must be no discrimination based on race or national origin, social level, or gender. They respect the natural biological uniqueness of each gender, not seeing it as requiring any dominant/submissive applications of gender to either marriage or church leadership.

David Scholer, prominent New Testament scholar at Fuller Theological Seminary, affirms this view. He believes that Galatians 3:28 is "the fundamental Pauline theological basis for the inclusion of women and men as equal and mutual partners in all of the ministries of the church." Galatians 3:28 represents "the summation of Paul's theological vision," according to Pamela Eisenbaum, professor at Iliff School of Theology, who is one of four Jewish New Testament scholars teaching in Christian theological schools. Christian Egalitarianism holds that the submission of the woman in marriage and womanly restrictions in Christian ministry are inconsistent with the true picture of biblical equality. The equal-yet-different doctrine taught by Complementarians is considered by them to be a contradiction in terms.

Conservative theologian Roger Nicole, a Baptist considered an expert in Calvinism and regarded as one of the pre-eminent theologians in America, is a Christian Egalitarian and also a Biblical Inerrantist. He recognizes that biblical egalitarianism is still viewed by many as inconsistent with biblical inerrancy, although he disagrees. He writes that "the matter of the place of women in the home, in society, and in the church is not an issue that can be conclusively determined by a few apparently restrictive passages that are often advanced by those who think that subordination represents God's will for women."

I believe that most, if not all, of the restrictions on women in society have no basis in Scripture, and that those maintained in the Church are based on an inadequate interpretation of a few restrictive passages, which put them in contradiction with the manifest special concern and love of God for women articulated from Genesis to Revelation. - *Roger Nicole, 2006*

A Baptist theologian, without agreeing with the view, has correctly explained the biblical Egalitarian view this way:

God created men and women equally to bear the divine image. Therefore, in Christ there not only is equality as to one's status before God, but a declaration of equality in all matters, including undifferentiated roles in both the home and the church. Because males and females are equal in Christ, they are both "equal to serve" without any gender-based scriptural qualifications. - *Peter Schemm, 2003*

Alexander Strauch, also a Complementarian author not affirming the Christian Egalitarian position, summarizes the Christian Egalitarian view this way:

According to the evangelical [egalitarian] view, true biblical equality assures that both men and women are full and equal partners in life. The concept of mutual submission and responsibility determines the relationship between men and women in both marriage and the church. Women and men are free to exercise in the church any and all gifts they possess. Men hold no unique, leadership-authority role solely because of their gender. Leadership and teaching in the church is to be determined by spiritual gift and ability, not gender. – *Alexander Strauch*

A limited notion of gender complementarity is held, known as "complementarity without hierarchy."

Complementarian View

The Complementarian position differs theologically and philosophically from Christian egalitarianism in its understanding of the proper roles for men and women. In a 1991 book *Recovering Biblical Manhood and Womanhood*, leading complementarian theologians outlined what they consider to be biblically sanctioned definitions of masculinity and femininity:

"At the heart of mature masculinity is a sense of benevolent responsibility to lead, provide for and protect women in ways appropriate to a man's differing relationships."

"At the heart of mature femininity is a freeing disposition to affirm, receive and nurture strength and leadership from worthy men in ways appropriate to a woman's differing relationships."

The *Danvers Statement on Biblical Manhood and Womanhood*, a position statement adopted in 1988, cites a set of concerns that complementarians have with contemporary philosophies about gender. Among the concerns they express are:

- Cultural uncertainty and confusion over complementary differences between masculinity and femininity.

- Unravelling marriages.
- Increasing attention given what they termed to be feminist egalitarianism.
- Ambivalence about motherhood and homemaking
- Claims of legitimacy for illicit sexual relationships and pornography.
- Upsurge of physical and emotional abuse in the family.
- Emergence of roles for men and women in church leadership seen as nonconforming to Biblical teaching.
- Non-traditional reinterpretation of apparently plain meanings of Biblical texts.
- A growing threat to Biblical authority.

They attribute these ills to the "apparent accommodation of some within the church to the spirit of the age at the expense of winsome, radical Biblical authenticity which...may reform rather than reflect our ailing culture." In contrast to how Christian Egalitarians interpret Galatians 3:28, Complementarians believe that the verse refers only to equal availability of all to salvation. They hold that the writer, the Apostle Paul, is saying that all believers, no matter what their racial, social, or gender status, share the same spiritual status in their union with Christ. They do not believe that Galatians 3:28 or any other scriptures put an end to existing – or forbid any further – privileges or restrictions based on race, class, or gender, as a matter of Christian principle.

Their understanding is that both Old and New Testaments prescribe a male-priority based hierarchy and gender roles in the church, in marriage, and in secular society. These prescribed gender roles only recently have come to be modified by some Complementarians as being "different but equal." Complementarians describe men and women as having "complementary non-overlapping" roles in the church and home. American evangelical writer and minister writer John MacArthur Jr. has this to say about what he terms the modern shift with regard to secular feminism affecting the church.

One of the most devastating, and debilitating, and destructive movements in our day is the "Feminist

Movement." It is changing not only the world but sadly it is changing the church, and as a result the Word of God is being dishonored; opponents are having plenty bad to say about us and God our Savior is being dishonored and shamed. Radical feminism has brainwashed our culture. It has brainwashed our culture to the degree that even the church has fallen victim to this. - *John MacArthur Jr.*

THEOLOGICAL ISSUES

Biblical Authority

In general, all evangelicals involved in the gender debate claim to adhere to the authority of the Bible while the Egalitarians typically argue that the dispute has arisen because of differences in interpretation of specific passages. Nevertheless, Wayne Grudem and other complementarians have accused egalitarians of adopting positions which deny the authority, sufficiency and inerrancy of scripture.

I believe that ultimately the effective authority of Scripture to govern our lives is at stake in this controversy. The issue is not whether we say we believe the Bible is the Word of God or that we believe it is without error, but the issue is whether we actually obey it when its teachings are unpopular and conflict with the dominant viewpoints in our culture. If we do not obey it, then the effective authority of God to govern His people and His church through His Word has been eroded - *Wayne Grudem (emphases original), Evangelical Feminism and Biblical Truth.*

Biblical Hermeneutics

The egalitarian and complementarian positions differ significantly in their approach to hermeneutics, and specifically in their view of biblical history. Egalitarians believe that male and female were created in Genesis 1-2 without a hierarchy of roles, and that male leadership only began at the Fall when God decreed to Eve that her husband would "rule over" her (Genesis 3:16). Throughout the Old Testament era, men continued to rule over women in a "patriarchal" system, which constituted a "compromise" or "accommodation" between sinful reality and the divine ideal. The New Testament moves forward from Old Testament patriarchy, re-instituting full equality of gender roles, principally in Galatians 3:28.

New Testament passages such as Ephesians 5:22-24 which teach submission of wives to husbands are usually understood by egalitarians as a temporary accommodation to first century culture. The Christian egalitarian hermeneutic has received its most systematic treatment by William J. Webb, professor of New Testament at Heritage Theological Seminary, Ontario, and Canada. Webb argues that our main difficulty knows which biblical commands are "transcultural" and therefore applicable today, versus those which are "cultural" and therefore only applicable to the original (first century) recipients of the text. His "redemptive movement" hermeneutic is justified using the example of slavery, which Webb sees as analogous to the subordination of women.

Christians today largely perceive that slavery was "cultural" in biblical times and not something that should be re-introduced or justified, although slavery was

a. Found in the Bible and
b. Not explicitly banned there. Webb recommends that biblical commands be examined in light of the cultural context in which they were originally written. According to the "redemptive approach", slavery and women's subordination are found in the Bible; however the same Scriptures also contain ideas and principles which, if developed and taken to their logical conclusion, would bring about the abolition of these institutions. The result is that egalitarianism will replace biblical "patriarchy."

In contrast to egalitarian teaching, complementarians teach that benevolent male leadership was instituted prior to the Fall in Genesis 1-2 and that the decree in Genesis 3:16 merely distorted this leadership by introducing "ungodly domination." The male leadership throughout the Old Testament (i.e. the patriarchs, priesthood and monarchy) was an expression of the creation ideal, as was Jesus' selection of 12 male apostles and New Testament restrictions on church leadership to men only (1 Timothy 2:11-14).

Complementarians criticize Webb's hermeneutic. Grudem argues that Webb expects Christians to pursue a "superior ethic" to that found in the New Testament, therefore undermining the authority and sufficiency of Scripture. According to Grudem, Webb and some other evangelicals misconstrue the biblical teaching about both slavery and women, and inappropriately confuse the two. He writes that slavery is tolerated in Scripture but never commanded, and in some cases is criticized, whereas wives are explicitly commanded to submit to their husbands, and male leadership is never criticized. Additionally, Grudem believes that Webb's "redemptive-movement" hermeneutic (itself a variation of the "trajectory" hermeneutic commonly employed by egalitarians) ultimately relies on subjective judgments that are incapable of producing certainty about ethical views.

Trinity

The Christian doctrine of the Trinity has become a major focus of the contemporary gender debate, specifically in relation to 1 Corinthians 11:3. In 1977, George W. Knight III argued in a book about gender roles that the subordination of women to men is theologically analogous to the subordination of the Son to the Father in the Trinity. Australian theologian Kevin Giles has more recently responded that complemen-tarians have "reinvented" the doctrine of the Trinity to support their views of men and women, suggesting that some complementarians have adopted a heretical view of the Trinity similar to Arianism. A vigorous debate has ensued, with some egalitarians moving towards the idea that there is "mutual dependence" within the Trinity, including "subordination of the Father to the Son", which must be reflected in gender role relations. Wayne Grudem has countered this by asserting that mutual submission in the Trinity cannot be supported by scripture and chur.ch history.

GENDER AND THE IMAGE OF GOD

Complementarians have traditionally held that Christian ministers ought to be men, because of the need to represent

Jesus Christ, who was the "Son" of God, and incarnate as a male human being. A related position is that while both male and female were made in the image of God, the woman shares in the divine image through the man because she was created out of him, and is his "glory"

For a man indeed ought not to cover his head, for as much as he is the image and glory of God: but the woman is the glory of the man. – *1 Corinthians 11:7*

Christian egalitarians respond by arguing that God is not gendered, and that males and females image God equally and without any differences. In addition, terms such as "Father" and "Son", used in reference to God, should be understood as analogies or metaphors used by the biblical authors to communicate attributes about God in a culture where men had social privilege. Similarly, Christ became a male not because it was theologically necessary, but because first century Jewish culture would not have accepted a female Messiah. Wayne Grudem takes exception to these egalitarian arguments, insisting that Christ's maleness was theologically necessary; he also alleges that egalitarians are increasingly advocating that God should be thought of as "Mother" as well as "Father", a move which he sees as theologically liberal.

RELATIONSHIP BETWEEN ONTOLOGY AND ROLES

Modern complementarians argue that Genesis 1:26-28 and Galatians 3:28 establish the full equality of males and females in terms of status, worth and dignity. Complementary roles in marriage and church leadership, including the primary authority of men and the submission of wives, are not thought to contradict this principle of ontological equality. The equation of role or functional subordination and ontological inferiority is considered to be category confusion.

Egalitarian author Rebecca Merrill Groothuis has abjected to this position. She argues that "woman's spiritual and ontological equality with man rules out the sort of subordination prescribed by gender traditionalists.... It is not logically possible for woman to be essentially equal to man, yet universally subordinate to man on the basis of an essential attribute (i.e., femaleness)."

CURRENT VIEWS BY DENOMINATION

In general, the issues have been what the proper role of women is

a. In marriage;
b. In the church;
c. In society at large. Among the denominations, movements, and organizations that express or have previously expressed a view, there are four main views:

1. Full equality of roles and rights:
   - African Methodist Episcopal Church
   - American Baptist Churches USA
   - Assemblies of God
   - Baptist Union of Great Britain
   - Christians for Biblical Equality
   - Church of the Brethren
   - Episcopal Church USA
   - Evangelical Covenant Church
   - Evangelical Lutheran Church in America
   - The Lutheran Evangelical Protestant Church (LEPC) (GCEPC) in the USA
   - Evangelische Kirche in Deutschland
   - Free Methodist Church
   - Presbyterian Church USA
   - Religious Society of Friends (Quakers) – Quakers have always believed in the legitimacy of women's ministry, with only a few exceptions in the early years. In 1848 at a conference in Seneca Falls, New York, 100 men and women signed a declaration that "all men and women are created equally." Early

leaders of the movement were Quaker, including Lucretia Mott.

- United Church of Canada
- United Church of Christ
- United Methodist Church
- Uniting Church in Australia
- Many others

2. Full secular equality but restricted ecclesiastical roles and privileges:
   - Eastern Orthodox Church
   - Lutheran Church-Missouri Synod
   - Lutheran Church-Wisconsin Synod
   - Orthodox Presbyterian Church
   - Presbyterian Church in America
   - Presbyterian Church of Australia
   - Seventh-day Adventists
   - Roman Catholic Church
   - Many others
3. Restricted roles or rights in both secular and ecclesiastical life:
   - Council on Biblical Manhood and Womanhood
   - Christian Reconstructionism
   - Dominion theology
4. Mixed
   - Southern Baptist Convention's official position is to prohibit females from becoming clergy, and to insist that a wife "graciously submit" to the leadership of her husband. Members of an individual ("local") Southern Baptist church are allowed to vote on matters of business of the church that include the hiring of a pastor. However, many churches that have chosen female clergy as their pastor have been disenfranchised by either local or state Baptist

associations. The vast majority of the congregations tend to hold full secular equality for women.

The above lists are examples and are obviously not exhaustive. It is not always clear which category a church or movement falls into. The Wesleyan tradition and the Holiness and Pentecostal movements, as well as a growing number of contemporary Charismatic churches which draw from them, have increasingly accepted women as leaders on an equal footing with men. Roman Catholicism, addresses the issue from the highest levels, including the Papal Office. For instance, Pope John Paul II has addressed this issue in his 1995, his 1996, and the 1988 Apostolic Letter, for examples.

The Quran declares boldly that, "Men are the managers of women for that God has preferred in bounty one of them over another, and for that they have expended of their property" (Sura al-Nisa´ 4:34)

Taj Hashmi discusses misogyny in relation to Muslim culture, and Bangladesh specifically, in *Popular Islam and Misogyny: A Case Study of Bangladesh.* [T]hanks to the subjective interpretations of the *Quran* (almost exclusively by men), the preponderance of the misogynic mullahs and the regressive Shariah law in most "Muslim" countries, Islam is synonymously known as a promoter of misogyny in its worst form. Although there is no way of defending the so-called "great" traditions of Islam as libertarian and egalitarian with regard to women, we may draw a line between the Quranic texts and the corpus of avowedly misogynic writing and spoken words by the mullah having very little or no relevance to the Quran.

Arthur Schopenhauer has been accused of misogyny for his essay "On Women" (Über die Weiber), in which he expressed his opposition to what he called "Teutonico-Christian stupidity" on female affairs. He claimed that "woman is by nature meant to obey." The essay does give two compliments however: that "women are decidedly more sober in their judgment than men are" and are more sympathetic to the suffering of others. However, the latter was discounted as weakness rather than humanitarian virtue.

Friedrich Nietzsche is known for arguing that every higher form of civilization implied stricter controls on women (*Beyond Good and Evil,* 7:238); he frequently insulted women, but is best known for phrases such as "Women are less than shallow," and "Are you going to women? Do not forget the whip!"

Nietzsche's reputation as a misogynist is disputed by some, pointing out that he also made unflattering statements about men. Nietzsche can easily be interpreted as anti-feminist, believing that women were primarily mothers and opposing the modern notion of women's liberation on the grounds that he considered it a form of slave morality.

Whether or not this amounts to misogyny, whether his polemic statements against women are meant to be taken literally, and the exact nature of his opinions of women, are more controversial. The philosopher Otto Weininger has been accused of misogyny for his 1903 book *Sex and Character,* in which he characterizes the "woman" part of each individual as being essentially "nothing," and having no real existence, having no effective consciousness or rationality.

Weininger says, "No men who really think deeply about women retain a high opinion of them; men either despise women or they have never thought seriously about them." The author August Strindberg praised Weininger for probably having solved the hardest of all problems, the "woman problem."

3

Misogyny and Religion under Analysis

Connections coming from the opposite direction as well: conservative and fundamentalist attacks on women's liberation from oppressive, patriarchal religion can bear interesting parallels to conservative and fundamentalist attacks on atheists who are free from both religion and theism. Mystery of Iniquity quotes Micahel, a fundamentalist who had "questions" about her feminism:

> This question might come across as biting, and I don't want it to, I am honestly curious and I would love it if you answered honestly. How much of your interpretation is simply your preference due to your life experience? I came across your website not through the front page, but as a deeper link through Google, but after a quick glance through a couple of posts, I noticed much of your differences with the bible revolve around its patriarchal tradition. Have you been spurned by a significant man in you life?

It's amazing just how similar this is to what atheists tend to hear from exactly the same sort of religious believer. The entire paragraph could be aimed at atheists by simply changing the final sentence to something along the lines of "Have you been hurt by a church or Christian in your life?" The assumption behind such questions is frequently that people only leave Christianity because of Christians behaving poorly – there's nothing about Christian theology or doctrine that's wrong, so therefore the blame must lie with people. Either the non-believer is to blame, or immoral Christians are to blame. Christianity, being perfect, is absolved of any blame. Above, we have the parallel assumption that there can't be anything wrong with current, patriarchal institutions so therefore some individual men must have done something wrong.

Mystery's gnomic reaction is quite appropriate – and would be appropriate if the situation were about atheism rather than feminism:

> Don't let the "tone" of his comments fool you. There is derision behind that remark. This is such an old, worn-out, put to bed argument about women coming from fundie men that frankly I'm sick of hearing it. And these men wonder why feminists like me are angry. In one stroke he devalues a woman's thought, her arguments, and her reason and blames all of her life experiences and years of education on "being spurned by a man" as if that is the defining moment of her life. And he could tell this from a cursory glance at my posts, he says.
>
> I almost, almost came close to returning to church this weekend that is until Micahel very graciously reminded me why it was that I stopped going. Thank you Micahel for "saving" me from that church hell again.

An atheist could very easily write "This is such an old, worn-out, put to bed argument about atheists coming from religious theists that frankly I'm sick of hearing it. And these Christians wonder why atheists like me are angry. In one stroke he devalues an atheist's thought, their arguments, and their reason and blames all their life experiences and years of education on "being hurt by a Christian" as if that is the defining moment in their life. And the Christian can tell this from a cursory glance at my writing, he says."

Atheism and feminism are connected not simply because secular atheists' critiques of religion are important to feminist liberation. They are also connected because religious theists react to atheism and feminism in similar ways: both are regarded as threats to the status quo, challenges to millennia of religious privilege, and attacks on the ability of traditional religion to continue dominating society. Dismissive, arrogant condescension is but one of the many tactics utilized by religious theists in their effort to shut down dissent, criticism, and challenges.

Astrology is a type of divination based upon the idea that information, usually either about the future or about a person's personality, can be discovered through an examination of "heavenly bodies" - stars, planets, the moon, comets, etc. Read about the different types of astrology and what they are supposed to do. In recent years, there has been quite a lot of (deserved) attention on the Catholic Church's history of covering up priests' sexual abuse of children. Far less attention has been directed towards Protestant churches, in part because their lack of central organization means that there just isn't much information on how widespread the problem is. Now we do have some information and allegations of sexual abuse in Protestant churches may be a little more widespread than in Catholic churches: 260 reports a year in Protestant churches vs. 228 a year in Catholic churches.

Religious groups and victims' supporters have been interested in the figure ever since the Roman Catholic sex abuse crisis hit five years ago. The church has revealed that there have been 13,000 credible accusations against Catholic clerics since 1950 – 228 a year. Protestant numbers have been harder to come by because the denominations are less centralized than the Catholic Church. Some of the only numbers come from three insurance companies – Church Mutual Insurance Co., GuideOne Insurance Co. and Brotherhood Mutual Insurance Co. Together, they represent a large chunk of all U.S. Protestant churches.

It makes sense that insurance companies would want to keep track of such information, since they have so much to lose if allegations of sexual abuse prove true. What's curious, though, is that these insurance companies apparently feel that they have more to lose than the churches themselves – otherwise, the churches would keep better records. Christians like to think of their institutions as important forces for morality in America, but so long as they benefit from structures of unaccountable, closeted power, there will always be abuses. Christians also often claim that because they acknowledge the existence of human sin, they can be more humble and more cognizant of human failings. In practice, though, secular institutions often have far more effective controls and checks against abuse or corruption – there are no priests assumed to be acting selflessly and on behalf of any gods.

The claim that atheists are not humble enough to accept that there are limitations on human understanding, and that we may never get answers to all our questions, is basically the same as saying that atheists believe that nothing is beyond human knowledge. I've debunked that myth in detail already, but here we see the popular move to claim that religious theists demonstrate their humility - and superiority over atheists - by labeling unanswered questions 'mystery.' The suppression of women, one half of the human population, has been a persistent and terrible crime over the course of thousands of years. Pretty much every culture has engaged in this, and at every turn religion has played a significant role in explaining, justifying, and perpetuating these crimes. What, though, can atheism have to say about this?

Agnostic Atheist writes:

Humanity as a whole has struggled with the issue of gender equity in the modern era. Combined with the teachings of the majority of the holy scriptures of today's major religions, progress is slow in coming. Of course, there are nations classed as atheist or secular nations where women are also viewed as second class citizens. However, I should point out that it is not their lack of belief in a deity driving this belief but more the views and traditions of that particular culture. Similarly, theism itself does not classes women as second class citizens but the beliefs of specific theist religions. In fact, one can be a theist and believe in gender equity just as one can be an atheist and believe the opposite. However, despite the fact that there are atheist nations where women are viewed as subjected to men because of their cultural views, it is not a core value of atheism. To be fair, there aren't any "core values" of atheism – but in some ways, that's precisely the point. Secular, irreligious atheism immediately clears away all the detritus of religious superstition and prejudice accumulated over the millennia. On the negative side, atheists are free to fill in any missing spaces with something even worse; on the positive side, though, there is so much that's bad which religion has preserved that there is a lot of good which we can fill in.

This is, in large part, why atheistic critiques of traditional, orthodox religion has long been an important part of feminist liberation. The suppression of women has been aided, justified, and promoted by religious beliefs for millennia – not all religious believers or theists have been misogynists, of course, but the activity complicity and assistance of religion is indisputable. This is why so many of the original women's suffragists were not merely atheists, but very "militant" atheists who engaged in public, direct, and vociferous attacks on organized religion. As an example of just how little has changed, consider this comment made in reaction to proposed measures designed to reduce abortions by increase access to information about birth control:

"There's a utopian view that women ought to be able to have sex any time they want to without consequences – that's the bottom line of all these bills," said Janice Crouse of Concerned Women for America, a conservative group which opposes the measures.

Women are not to be permitted to behave in a manner remotely like that of men. Sex is the topic here, but for traditional religion a lot more has always been involved. Although it might start with sex, of course, there are also always concerns about women working in jobs traditionally held by men, women heading families, women in combat, etc. These attitudes could be defended on the basis of a secular belief system, but in reality it's always religious belief systems that we find at the root of it all. Christianism or Christian Nationalism is analogous to Islamism. Just as Islamists seek to reform society along Islamic, Christianists seek to reform society along Christian lines and force conformity to conservative Christian values, ending church/state separation. As Christian Nationalists, they combine conservative, evangelical Christian theology with extreme American nationalism.

Two important hermeneutical orientations shaping the field of feminist biblical criticism today are social scientific criticism and ideological criticism. The tension between these two critical approaches, a tension which might be helpfully visualized through recourse to a special metaphor: "stepping out" versus "stepping in." While ideological criticism asks the reader to step outside of the ideology of text in order to critique it, social scientific criticism insists that unless we first step into the socio-symbolic world refracted through the text, our readings will be controlled by the unacknowledged projections of modernity's assumptions and worldview.

Given that these two methodologies move in different directions, it is not surprising to find a certain lack of coordination or communication between them. As Claudia Camp has observed, "like much work done in biblical studies today, the study of women vis-à-vis the Bible often takes place in terms of one or the other of two seemingly separate enterprises: the study of women's lives in the ancient historical context or the study of female imagery in the literature of the Bible with little attention to historical context". The ongoing effort to bring these two enterprises into closer conversation. But I will not do so under the pretense of being a disinterested third party, for my own work has been much more concerned with the challenge of "stepping into" an ancient socio-symbolic world in order to glimpse its radical difference than with "stepping out" from the ideology of the text in order to neutralize its continuing authority.

While I appreciate and relish the ways that feminist ideological critics have disturbed and overturned entrenched androcentric reading practices, I am concerned that more attention to the particularity of ancient worlds is needed, especially with respect to the distinct significations of women's bodies and female sexuality in those worlds and seeks to highlight and explore this concern by considering the tension between feminist ideological readings of certain troubling texts - specifically those prophetic metaphors of female sexuality which have been referred to of late as "pornoprophetics" - and the thrust of feminist social scientific work which has been to caution us against the wholesale importation of the cultural baggage that inevitably travels with our own modern notions of "patriarchy."

The question of anachronism in feminist readings of biblical "pornoprophetics" differs from that taken by Robert Carroll who has argued that "without knowing the psychological make-up of the biblical writers it is not possible to evaluate the degree to which their writings may be characterized as misogynistic or otherwise".

Carroll seems to suggest that what is relevant but unattainable here is insight into the psychological make-up of the individuals who produced these texts. But an individual is so much a product of his cultural contexts that what is relevant for the purposes of interpretation is not the psychological makeup of individual writers, but rather the ideological frameworks and socio-symbolic contexts out of which these individuals thought and wrote. But how do we get at these frameworks and contexts? How can we form credible hypotheses about the presuppositions and values of an ancient culture - that is, its ideology?

Ideological criticism itself stresses that its work begins with an "extrinsic" analysis of the socio-economic circumstances under which the text was produced. Only once we understand the social world which produced the text can we move on to an "intrinsic" analysis of the ways in which the text reproduces and promotes particular ideological investments (Yee: 150-1). So ideally, ideological criticism includes and builds upon social scientific criticism. But I would argue that too often, feminist ideological critics falter in this task of extrinsic analysis and too much is assumed at the outset about women's social location and cultural attitudes towards women's bodies in ancient Israel.

STEPPING OUT: IDEOLOGICAL CRITICISM

One of the more influential writers in the current school of "resistant readers" is Cheryl Exum, who helpfully clarifies for us the premises out of which her ideological critical readings proceed. Exum begins with the assertion that in ancient Israel, symbolic production was controlled by men, and that therefore, female characters or feminine metaphors in biblical literature need to be recognized and treated as "male constructs" which reflect androcentric ideas about women and serve androcentric interests (1993: 11).

Even where the authors of a text might have been female or where one finds an ostensibly positive female character or feminine symbol, the world view expressed is that of "the dominant male world view" (1993: 10). Thus the feminist critic "must, of necessity, read against the grain," stepping outside of the ideology of the text in order to subvert that ideology (1993: 11). Those readers who fail to recognize this point risk complicity with the androcentric ideology of the text. Exum's premise about the thoroughly androcentric worldview controlling the production of the biblical texts leads to the thesis, articulated by many feminist critics, that in the Hebrew Bible, woman is always inscribed as the "other," as that which simultaneously defines and threatens the boundaries of a patriarchal order.

This "otherness" of woman is inherent in an androcentric order where woman figures not as "one of us" but as that which, being possessed or not possessed, creates relationships and marks boundaries among "us" (i.e. among men). Further, as an object of male control and competition, woman is always a potential locus of conflict and violence. Thus woman as the "other" is also a symbol of chaos, bearing the meaning of that which is foreign or threatening to the order of things. This argument about woman as a symbol of the threatening "other" within patriarchal thought has found much support in recent feminist ideological readings of the often graphic and disturbing female sexual metaphors found in several prophetic texts.

In the prophetic "marriage" metaphor and other related metaphors of the body politic as a sexually promiscuous woman, the woman's illicit sexual activity represents the nation's sin and sexual violence against her body (public exposure and rape) figure as the deity's "fitting" punishment against "her" for this sin. These texts direct the reader's eye to images of sexually insatiable women, who fornicate with multiple lovers and are then stripped naked and sexually violated in public. Grappling with the disturbing character of these texts, several feminist ideological critics including T. Drorah Setel, Athalya Brenner, the late Fokkelien van Dijk-Hemmes, and Cheryl Exum (1996) have read these images as functionally similar to the modern genre of pornography.

These readers argue that prophetic sexual metaphors have the same function as pornography: the maintenance of male domination through the representation of women as degraded objects of male possession and control. Like pornography, prophetic metaphors of female fornication and sexual violence are products of an androcentric imagination which denigrates female sexuality and degrades women "in order to stress that their sexuality is and ought to be an object of male possession and control". According to these feminist ideological critics, the motive behind this concern with the control of female sexuality goes beyond the patrilineal imperative to guarantee the legitimacy of sons.

Rather, both prophetic and pornographic representations of women's bodies are motivated by "patriarchy's fear of women's reproductive power" and its corresponding needs to control that power, along with its abhorrence of female blood and bodily processes. Thus, undergirding "pornoprophetic" literature is not simply a cultural abhorrence of female sexual transgression, but a cultural abhorrence and denigration of the female sexual body itself. While the term "misogyny" is used sparingly and cautiously by ideological critics, they definitely lean toward the conclusion that the biblical texts encode predominantly negative views towards women's bodies and bodily processes, as is seen most obviously they assert, in the biblical purity codes and in the sacralization of the male penis.

Exum, for example, follows Eilberg-Schwartz in positing an opposition between the signification of the male penis, which in circumcision becomes the symbolic locus for meanings of "covenant, righteousness and wholeness," and that of female menstrual blood, which in the pollution codes becomes a symbolic locus for meanings of "sin, indecency and death". Brenner likewise sees an opposition between the "textual spiritualization of the penis" (1997: 38) in which the male genitalia are euphemistically hidden and protected by biblical law and language, and the graphic exposure of the female sexual organs in both language, and in texts, most especially in the prophets (1997: 31-43).

Mieke Bal's remark on biblical misogyny is quite blunt: For anyone who doubts "that ancient Hebrew society... was thoroughly misogynist..., the books of Laws provide useful reading in their evident contempt for the female body..." (1987: 110). This consensus among feminist ideological critics on biblical attitudes towards the female body has exerted considerable influence upon feminist biblical critics in general. For example, although Renita Weems considers these prophetic metaphors without making a direct comparison with pornography, she reiterates the view that these metaphors reflect a misogynistic cultural orientation that sees women's bodies as "disgusting" and "perceives women's sexuality as deviant and threatening to the status and well-being of men".

STEPPING IN: SOCIAL SCIENTIFIC CRITICISM

The work of ideological critics on prophetic sexual metaphors of sin as female "whoring" and divine retribution as spousal abuse is invaluable at the level of reception as it exposes the damaging effect of these metaphors in their divine validation of patriarchal control of women and sexual abuse, and enables us to resist and reject those effects. These images, as they have been interpreted and used in Jewish and Christian history, are appropriately condemned for their complicity in fostering and reinforcing misogynism through the centuries.

But did these texts emerge from a misogynistic world, or did they help to create subsequent misogynistic worlds? I do not think we can draw any clean and clear lines to demarcate the birth of misogyny in western religions. But nevertheless, someone who comes to this ideological critique of biblical "pornoprophetics" after reading feminist social scientific work on gender in ancient Israel might be surprised by the ideological critic's description of ancient Israel itself as a misogynistic society. In their efforts to reconstruct the social world of pre-monarchic Israel, Carol Meyers and Phyllis Bird have come to the conclusion that ancient Israelite women were not merely the denigrated "sexual property" of all powerful males, but were empowered social actors in their own right.

Their argument begins with a sociological reconstruction of early Israel as an agrarian subsistence economy within which economic production and decision making processes revolved around the domestic family unit and more broadly, the kinship network; this socio-economic system is an example of what Marshall Sahlins called the "familial mode of production". Comparative anthropological studies show that in such contexts, women may "wield significant amounts of power" and "control at least the major portion of important resources and decisions". The centrality of women within the domestic-based, kinship-based social structure is suggested by the archaic term *bet 'em* or "mother's house" which appears in three biblical passages as an alternative designation for ancient Israel's basic social unit, *bet 'ab* or "father's house."

For Meyers, the somewhat startling appearance of the female-oriented term "mother's house" in these predominantly androcentric texts suggests the lingering presence of cultural ways and attitudes from early Israel which located woman at the center of the kinship-based social power network. In light of such arguments about women's social location and power in early Israel, Meyers and Bird have questioned the applicability of the term "patriarchy" to ancient Israel, given that the term evokes assumptions and associations generated by our own experience with modern, capitalistic Western societies which are not transferable to this ancient, agrarian, kinship-based world.

Ancient Israelite women did not possess the kind of social and sexual autonomy which we in the modern world take to be the sine qua non of personal dignity and worth. In the modern world, human value and meaning are predicated upon individual autonomy and bodily self-possession; thus where a modern observer sees persons without the power of self-determination, he or she tends to assume that those persons were coded as inferior beings in that social context. But in the world of ancient Israel, personhood and personal dignity were not predicated upon the possession of bodily autonomy and individual freedom, but rather were defined in terms of one's place within larger corporate structures of family and lineage and by one's contributions to those structures.

In this world, the basic social unit was not the individual but the kinship group, and individual existence was intimately tied to corporate welfare and survival; even in death, one's existence depended upon continuing ties to the family and its land through burial in ancestral tombs. In relation to the material conditions of the familial mode of production, communal orientations to lineage and land defined a world of sacred meaning and order. In such a social world, where the corporate unit rather than the individual is the primary locus of identity, value and meaning, one cannot assume any simple correlations between personal autonomy and social value.

Ancient Israelite women certainly did not enjoy sexual autonomy or self-possession over their own bodies, but this does not mean that women were assumed to be inferior beings or that female sexuality itself was negatively valued. As Meyers concludes concerning gender relations and gender codes in early Israel, "male authority existed in certain spheres but there was no connotation of misogyny, the oppression of females, or the notion of female inferiority" (1988: 187). How does this extrinsic analysis of gender relations and modes of production and gender relations in ancient Israel impact upon the process of analyzing the gender codes encoded in biblical texts? In her reading of Genesis 2-3, Meyers offers an example of how literary analysis can be informed by the sociological picture of relatively egalitarian gender relations which she posits for early Israel (1988: 72-121).

She reads Genesis 3:16, typically translated as "and he [Adam] shall rule over you [Eve]," in light of the historical context of early Israel where corporate survival depended upon women producing as many children as possible. Meyers claims that contrary to the conventional patriarchal reading, Genesis 3:16 was not originally intended as a mandate for male supremacy in general, but rather as a specific reference to male prerogative within the realm of sexuality; "the solution to the need for an increased birthrate in early Israel took the form of a divine ruling that gave men the power to overcome female reluctance". The presence of misogyny behind the production of this text is denied.

THE CONVERSATION

In her explanation of feminist criticism as being, at its best, a form of ideological criticism, Danna Nolan Fewell (1993) characterizes Meyers' interpretation of Genesis 2-3 as naive, but she does not address the credibility of the extrinsic analysis from which Meyers reads, nor does Fewell work carefully to construct an alternative extrinsic analysis which would provide a foundation for a more suspicious ideological analysis of Genesis 2-3 as a profoundly androcentric text. Such lacunae in respect to the work of "extrinsic analysis" is fairly typical of those ideological readings which contend that in the biblical texts women and women's bodies are coded negatively as symbols of the threatening "other" or of chaos. Ideological critics are correct in showing us how, in many ways and in many texts, women and female sexuality figure as volatile boundary markers for the patriarchal order, but they overlook or underplay other significations of female sexuality which are at work in the biblical texts as well.

Clearly, anxiety about female sexual transgression was not the only locus for the construction of cultural meanings of woman's bodies in ancient Israel. Recent archeological finds and renewed attention to related textual evidence have begun to reshape our understanding of the place of the female reproductive body in ancient Israel's religious imagination. The presence of female figurines on the domestic altars (representing either goddesses or more abstractly, the power of fertility itself), and the presence of the feminine symbol of the asherim "trees" at local shrines, in addition to possible worship of Asherah alongside of the national deity (at least in some times and places), suggest a surprising ubiquity of female religious symbolism in ancient Israel. While there is considerable controversy over the interpretation of these feminine religious symbols, their presence suggests at least that in monarchic Israel's religious imagination, the female body served as an icon of sacred power.

The picture of ancient Israel as a world where woman's body could be seen as *sacra* is difficult to reconcile with ideological readings which argue that "pornoprophetic" texts presuppose a cultural abhorrence of female sexuality. So too, sociological reconstructions of relative gender equity in early Israel could potentially disturb the ideological critic's presupposition that symbolic production in ancient Israel was thoroughly controlled by androcentric interests (assuming that is, some relationship between social power and the power of symbolic production). One might argue that there is no necessary tension here between sociological and ideological work on gender in ancient Israel because sociological arguments for relative gender equity apply primarily to pre-monarchic Israel and therefore have little relevance for the study of prophetic texts dating from the monarchic and exilic periods.

As Meyers herself says, social changes precipitated by the emergence of the monarchical state precipitated a marked deterioration in social and symbolic location of women in Israel and Judah over a period of just two or three centuries. The centripetal force of growing monarchic power weakened the power of the lineages and affected a shift from the familial to the tributary mode of production. As power was siphoned away from the kinship networks, the power of the nuclear family unit and the authority of the *paterfamilias* were strengthened. These transformations had a detrimental effect on women's status because the extended kinship network and the domestic-based agrarian economy had been the arenas in which early Israelite women had claimed and exercised their social power. As well, feminine religious symbols, which were important within domestic and local forms of religious practice, were stigmatized as non-Yahwistic as the centralizing state tightened its control.

A historical picture of a more virulent and intensifying patriarchal order is implicit in the ideological critics' analyses of the misogynistic character of many biblical texts. If the politics of state centralization brought about a deterioration of women's social power, and if that historical transformation brought about a concomitant rise in negative and even misogynistic attitudes towards women's bodies and female sexuality, then there is not necessarily any dissonance between the social scientists' view of women's power in early Israel and the ideological critics' reading of latent or overt misogyny in "pornoprophetic" literature. But to account for such a profound shift in cultural values about meanings as fundamental as gender and sexuality, it is necessary to posit that symbolic forms are very closely derivative of the social, political and economic forces in which they are produced, such that ways of thinking are fundamentally created anew with every major shift in the material mode of production.

But it is clear that family religion and ritual practices involving symbols of female fertility did not vanish overnight with the emergence of the monarchy, nor did the value system and the thought patterns rooted in the familial mode of production and lineage-based systems of polity. Traditional patterns of thought persist even in the midst of intense acculturative pressures like statehood, latifundialization, and even imperial conquest and domination. Like mighty trees, cultures have deep roots; these roots are the patterns of language, thought and practice that have been elaborated over time to become part of the cultural core of that people's world. These patterns, which emerge out of a people's imaginative encounter with the material world, with the landscape and climate, with the available means of sustenance and survival given in the environment, and above all, with their own bodies and sexuality, are perpetuated by the intergenerational transmission of knowledge.

Over the centuries, they become so central to that culture's modes of thought and metaphor construction that they cannot be easily eradicated. Indeed, it is easier to cut down the tree than to dig up those roots. The argument for radical social change being accompanied by an intensification of patriarchal social structures and a concomitant rise of misogynism can perhaps be easily applied to Ezekiel, whose obscene language and obsessive fantasies of nymphomania "seem to be fueled by unconscious fear and rage". But Ezekiel's writing emerges in the wake of the cataclysms of total conquest and mass deportation, at a time when the pressing problem of defining ethnic boundaries was addressed by means of an intensified concern with bodily boundaries and bodily pollution.

In this situation, women, whose bodily processes rendered them frequently "unclean," were more and more excluded from the public realm and were coded negatively as symbols of evil. But the same argument is more difficult to apply to prophets from the monarchical period. This period was characterized by ongoing tension and conflict between the traditional kinship-based systems of power and the familial mode of production on one hand, and the trajectories of centralizing state power and its tributary mode of production on the other.

While some texts produced within the monarchical period sought to resolve ideologically the conflicts between the familial and tributary modes of production in favor of the latter, the classical prophets, and especially the eighth century prophets, stood in opposition to the growing power of the monarchy and its efforts to undermine the traditional social and economic systems of power and production.

Hosea, for example, like Amos and Micah, was an advocate for the embattled system of kinship-based power and familial modes of production. His attack on the cultic practices of his day was not an attack upon the fertility religion which had long been an essential component of the world of the bet 'ab (or the bet 'em), but rather was an attack upon the national shrines and the monarchical power structures they sanctified. In his oracles against the monarchy, its royal cult, and its cosmopolitan orientations, Hosea deployed a metaphor of female "whoring" that exploited his culture's fears about autonomous female sexuality. The social body of the nation, he said, was like the sexual body of an adulterous wife ('eshet zenunim) - transgressive and threatening to the order of this society.

Given Hosea's position on the ideological battleground of his day, it seems reasonable to consider his rhetoric within the context of the systems of meaning which were indigenous to the social and ideological world he was defending rather than reading his metaphors in the context of subsequent developments. The prophets' language about Israel as an adulterous woman was spun of many intertwining threads of signification concerning woman, sexuality and gender. One of these threads concerns patriarchy's fear of autonomous female sexuality. But there is another thread at work here that is less often noticed: a symbolic association of the social body with woman's body. And it is this connection between woman and community which is easily hidden or obscured behind ideological criticism's assumption that women in biblical literature always stand as symbols of that which is "other" and threatening to the patriarchal order.

The symbolic association of woman's body with the social body was indigenous to a social world where life revolved around the domestic sphere. Not only the father's body (i.e. Jacob's/Israel's), but the mother's body as well figures in the biblical texts as a symbol for the whole Israelite community. For example in the thrice-repeated "wife-sister" tales, the sexually endangered matriarch figures the vulnerability of the early Israelite community amidst more powerful nations. The trope of woman's body as social body is discernable as well in the Hebrew Bible's three rape narratives where, in each case, the rape of a woman serves as a metonym for war or internecine conflict.

It is likely that this symbolic pattern had deep roots in the religious and cultural imagination of a people whose survival across the generations depended precariously upon the fertility of women's bodies. By the time a remnant of this people suffers through the cataclysmic uprooting of total conquest, deportation and exile, we can see a deformation of this symbolic pattern in the obsessive and misogynistic sexual rhetoric of Ezekiel. Yet even as Judahite culture was overrun by the body-denying philosophical perspectives of Hellenistic culture, a positive valence in this metaphoric complex of Israel as a woman can still be glimpsed in the appearance of heroic female characters - Esther, Judith and Susanna - as "metonymies of community".

Finding itself part of an alien empire, Judean culture grappled with the threat to its cohesion and continuity in part with stories about heroic women who defend their own bodily integrity and/or the nation against invasion or destruction. From Sarah to Susanna, we can see the persistence of a metaphor where woman and woman's body (when both fecund and available only to her husband) are symbols of corporate solidarity, integrity and continuity. From this perspective, the adultery metaphor can be seen as a rhetorical reversal of a deeply rooted and persistent symbol of Israelite cultural identity.

Feminist ideological criticism teaches us to situate ostensibly positive narratives such as those about Esther, Judith or Susanna within a larger frame of patriarchal discourse and its investment in maintaining female subordination. But in turn, social scientific criticism cautions us to attend to the radical differences between ancient and modern worlds, and to investigate the complexities of any language world, tracing its roots down deep into a culture's historical encounter with the material determinants of its existence. In those nether regions of language we find meanings of power which are not only about the power of one social group to dominate another, but also about the powers of life, fecundity, and survival, which find their most obvious material and symbolic locus in the procreative power of women's bodies.

New York City's iconic white morning radio/TV talk show host, Don Imus, rudely awakened a critical mass of "America" when, while describing the Rutgers University women's basketball team (most of whom are black), commented contemptuously on the tattoos on some of the players. Then Bernard Mcguirk, Imus' studio side-kick and producer off-camera, banters that the Rutgers players are "some hardcore hos." Imus rejoins with, "That's some nappy-headed hos there, I'm gonna tell you that now." Imus' pre-emptive defence, in deflection of the unforeseen tsunami of criticisms to come, was that people should get over themselves and not be concerned about "some idiot comment meant to be amusing."

For such "amusement", which not only includes invectives based on ethnicity, race, and gender, but also sexual orientation, Imus, and his doppelganger— drugs and alcohol, earns his networks hundreds of millions of advertising dollars every year. For the uninitiated, in black vernacular the words "ho", "hoe" and "whoe" are all derivation of the word "whore," not unlike the Germanic/Middle-English/Anglo-Saxon "hore" or the Old Saxon/Frisian "hor," or the Gothic "hors," or the Old Norse "horr" and "hor," or the Swedish "Hora," or the Norwegian/ Danish "hore." In black nomenclature "hoe" can mean: someone of loose morals; someone who participates in promiscuous or illicit sexual activity or, depending on the context, "hoe" can be a reference to women singularly or women en masse.

But it was uniquely Imus' "nappy-headed hos" epithet that became "the news" above all the "news" clutter of the U.S. mass media for that week. The following Sunday, I watched with anticipation and, as it turns out, justifiable angst, several of the morning roundtable television "news" talk shows. Of course as status quo and in pro forma most of the talking heads were conspicuously and omnisciously white male "journalist" and commentators discussing, presumably, with authority but certainly with audacity, the African American women's experience as nappy headed "hos". My awe (by which I mean my dread), because I now am numb to the shock of these media phenomena, was that each "news" show allowed the discourse, and thereby the focus, to shift quickly away from Imus' personal responsibility and culpability to the defence of Imus, versus the misogyny of black hip-hop artists.

The argument proffered by these white male "talking head experts" was that rappers and other major black entertainers use terms like "hos" to degrade women incessantly in their music and performances with no condemnation exacted by society or civil rights leaders. I watched hopelessly, helplessly and at times hilariously as white men sat comfortably in-the-round defending other white men's misogynistic behaviour while citing black men as the true social pariah—all at the expense of black women and, for that matter, all women. To be clear, misogyny as I define it here as hostility towards women in the forms of: dehumanization, objectification, chattelization, sexualization and commodification, is detestable and indefensible in any form, whether from black hip-hop artist or a white Don Imus "shock jock".

Indeed, misogyny in black music, dance and film is especially appalling, as it exemplifies a self-perpetuating nihilistic destruction in classic Frierian style of the oppressed oppressing the oppressed. Hip-hop and gangsta rap artist acting out, in exaggerated form, the dominant culture's conspicuous consumption via narcissistic, hedonistic and pornographic behaviour, is abhorrent to me and like-minded black folks. There is no capital in deny that some, not all; black hip-hop/gangsta rap is pornographic. Nonetheless, black hip-hop/gangsta rap misogyny is merely a subgenre of the greater pornographic ideology. Nevertheless, black folks should know better, we should be better and we are better than the images portrayed of us. But to place the origins, the onus, and the omini-oppression of women on black hip-hop artist as the alpha and omega of misogyny is just as racist, sexist and misplaced as Imus.

Absent a contextualized critical analysis of the multi-billion dollar, predominately white- owned pornography industry, and its omnipresent and omnipotent misogyny of all women, any dialogue about hip-hop misogyny is fraudulent. Writing for Z-Magazine in her 1994 essay, Sexism and Misogyny: Who Takes the Rap? Black feminist, author and professor, bell hooks, theorizes that, "The sexist, misogynist, patriarchal ways of thinking and behaving that are glorified in gangsta rap are a reflection of the prevailing values in our society, values created and sustained by white supremacist capitalist patriarchy...[but] young black males are forced to take the "heat" for encouraging, via their music, the hatred of and violence against women that is a central core of patriarchy." As much as black hip-hop and gangsta rap music needs to be called to task for its misogyny, there is a an urgent need to harness and deconstruct the Dr. Frankenstein among us, the creator of this monster—"American" values, as reflected in the way women are generally socialized, portrayed and profiteered.

The inference by the white male moral constabulary is that black hip-hop and gangsta rap culture, as the only purveyors of the exploitation of women, have an unfair special license to be misogynistic, while white people are not allowed such license resulting in a tolling of white freedom of speech and, in turn, the victimization of all of white people. (It's like the classic query, "Why can they say nigger and we can't?"). But what seems omitted from the debate, either in the "news" roundtable discourse or popular white discourse about hip-hop misogyny, is the contribution and predominance of the white male-owned misogynistic sexploitation pornography's to the denigration of women around the world. I argue here that pornography has achieved such normalcy status, mainstream acceptance and international institutionalization that, like the air we breathe, it is invisible and therefore goes unexamined as misogyny. Yet, any cursory examination of gender dynamics reveals the power elitism of white patriarchal media and its entrepreneurial institutions.

And, either by omission or by tradition or both, this patriarchal media gets to define the world, and therefore what is or is not misogynistic, as it sees fit. Consequently, pornography and not hip-hop performance, relative to women and their degradation, gets socially constructed as harmless erotica and not as misogyny as it is filtered through the lens and pens of those employed by white men like, Hugh Hefner, Larry Flynn and Bob Guccione (successfully sued for sexual harassment by Anneka DiLorenzo, a Penthouse Pet, after she proved she was sent out on the road and then pimped to his business associate), who finance, produce and publish pornographic media the likes of: Playboy, Hustler and Penthouse.

It is the unremitting and relentless portrayal of women as anonymous bodies to be poked, prodded, primed, pumped and pommelled that is lost in the analysis of hip-hop misogyny without its parentis—pornography. Anti- pornography activist, Andrea Dworkin, in her 1986 testimony before the Attorney General's Commission on Pornography, testified that pornography portrays women as passive victims, whose only identity is expressed in eroticized degradation, humiliation, and/or violence. I struggle to find the social outrage regarding pornography's contribution to misogyny.

Accordingly, black hip-hop is constructed to become the in locos parentis in substitution for the free pass handed the pornography industry. Although pornography creates a fantasy world of seemingly innocent mutually consenting adults having bawdy sexual adventures, the real-life socialization of the women performing the sexual acts could not be further from the fantasy. Mary Anne Layden, Ph. D., Director for Women's Psychological Health in Philadelphia states in her 1999 essay, If Pornography Made Us Healthy, We Would Be Healthy By Now that: "Most strippers, as with other women who work in the sex industry, are adult survivors of childhood sexual abuse. Research indicates the number is between 60%-80%...The physical and visual invasion of little girl's bodies damages them psychologically and gives them a psychologically unhealthy view of sexuality.

Often as adults they re-enact their childhood trauma by working as strippers, Playboy models, and prostitutes. The men, who, now as customers, physically and visually invade the adult women's bodies, re-enact the role of the perpetrator. These women work in the sex industry because it feels like home." Dr. Layden's research provides real-life victims of the real-life consequences of the society's consumption of pornography and the failure of continuous public debate about pornography. The bridge between pornography and prostitution is structured in the lives impacted by the purchasers, profiteers, pimps and promoters.

Pornography and prostitution often work in tandem in its denigration of women. In a 2005 article examining militarism and women titled, Violence against Women in the Military Martin Donohoe, MD, wrote that: Once in the armed services, recruits become part of a warrior culture. Bellicose military vocabulary is laden with denigrations of feminine traits, and gender slurs motivate men to act aggressively toward women. Until 1999, pornography could easily be purchased by servicemen at US military base commissaries, which ranked among the largest purchasers of hard-core pornography.

Military bases are commonly associated with prostitution, which is tacitly accepted by commanding officers and local authorities. For example, more than 5000 women, mainly from the Philippines and the former Soviet Union, were trafficked into South Korea in the mid 1990s, primarily to work as "entertainers" at bars near US military bases. The use of rape as a weapon of war, including by US soldiers, marks one of the most extreme examples of interpersonal violence. As an institution, U.S. military culture was established long before the influence of black hip-hop or gangsta rap which began in the mid-1970's and late 1980's respectfully, yet society's racist gaze has turned to young black men as a scapegoat for greater ills of society in classic "forest for the trees" myopia.

The width and breath of the residue from pornography may overshadow and foreshadow our worse fears about misogyny. Robert Jensen, of The University of Texas at Austin, School of Journalism in his 2004 essay on Pornography & Sexual Violence wrote: We understand that pornography alone doesn't make men [commit sexual violence], but that pornography is part of a world in which men do it, and therefore the production, content, and use of pornography are important to understand in the quest to eliminate sexual violence...My own studies and reviews of other examinations of content suggest there are a few basic themes in pornography:

1. All women at all times want sex from all men;
2. Women enjoy all the sexual acts that men perform or demand; and
3. Any woman who does not at first realize this can be easily turned with a little force, though force is rarely necessary because most of the women in pornography are the imagined "nymphomaniacs" about whom many men fantasize.

In mainstream films like, Pretty Woman white film makers glorify prostitution where the character Vivian Ward, a streetwalking prostitute—for all practical purposes a "ho"—is played by "America's" beloved sweetheart, Julia Roberts. Where is the white male accountability of this "ho". Pretty Woman would eventually gross $463 million worldwide and was at the time Disney's most successful live-action film. And then there is the stage and film musical of 1978 and 1982, The Best Little Whorehouse in Texas, the title speaks volumes without my commentary. Still, not all institutions have turned a blind-eye to the greater social structural influences of misogyny as the so called "news" media. Amnesty International in a 2005 website press release proffers that: There has been a marked growth of the trafficking of women and girls for forced sexual services throughout the world. Most of the victims come from Eastern Europe - in the Balkans it is estimated that some 60 per cent of trafficked women and girls come from Moldova, one of Europe's poorest countries.

Many victims are lured by promises of work in Western Europe as waitresses or similar but are forced into sexual slavery and many are broken mentally and physically by rape and extreme brutality. And at DePaul University College of Law's International Human Rights Law Institute conference on: Demand Dynamics: The Forces of Demand in Global Sex Trafficking held in October 2003 in Chicago, the IHRLI recognized that demand drives the trade in women and children's bodies and stated that: Trafficking in women, as a broad umbrella concept, encompassed all practices of buying and selling women's and children's bodies. Trafficking, as we understood it included American pornography, temple prostitution in India, military prostitution in the Philippines, street prostitution in Peru, and sex tourism from Europe to Asia. It moved from the micro-"Trafficking within the Family" to the macro-"Trafficking in Women: A Global Perspective."

It exposed mainstream institutions that support and benefit from prostitution: "Military, Government, and Corporate Trafficking in Women." The conference looked at the sex industry as an instrument of the socialization of both men and women..." In 2003, U.S. Attorney General John Ashcoft stated those who traffic in human lives treat [women] as easily expendable and highly profitable. But behind each dollar sign is a human tragedy. In their 1990 essay Femicide: Speaking the Unspeakable and 1992 book, Femicide: The Politics of Woman Killing Drs. Jane Caputi, Jill Radford and Diana E. H. Russell write: An FBI study of 36 sex killers found that pornography was ranked highest in a list of many sexual interests by an astonishing 81 percent. Such notorious killers as Edmund Kemper (the "Coed Killer"), Ted Bundy, David Berkowitz (the "Son of Sam"), and Kenneth Bianchi and Angelo Buono (the "Hillside Stranglers") were all heavy pornography consumers. Bundy maintains that pornography "had an impact on me that was just so central to the development of the violent behaviour that I engaged in."

His assessment is consistent with testimony from many other sex offenders, as well as research on the effects of pornography. Importantly, for this discussion, there is no clear correlation between engaging in pornography and deviant behaviour by most men. I only offer these sources to add balance to the discourse that excludes pornography as misogynist and demonizes black hip-hop culture. Likewise, there is no clear correlation between engaging in hip-hop misogynistic art and deviant behaviour by most men. In defence of all men do not miss the premise. Here the focus is not so much on men's deviance as it is on the silence by the greater culture on women's sexualized exploitation by the white media industrial complex.

On April 21, 1999, one day after the Columbine, Littleton High School shooting masscare, Howard Stern another hugely successful "shock jock," discussed the tragedy on his nationally syndicated morning radio show. Stern reportedly commented: "A bunch of good looking girls go to that school. There were, like, really good-looking girls running out of there with their hands over their heads. Did those kids try to have sex with any of the good-looking girls? They didn't even do that. At least if you're going to kill yourself and kill all the kids, why wouldn't you have some sex." CBS, whose syndication arm Eyemark distributes Stern's weekly television show, said through a spokesman it would not comment on what Stern said. CBS, a member of the white media industrial complex, chose silence over discourse.

And where was the nation's detestation? Did Mr. Stern only see these young women, running terrified from harms way, as sex objects—as "hoes"? Conversely, in the Imus mayhem there was a deluge of "discourse," but it was misplaced, wrong-headed and deflective discourse with no depth of analysis—hence, no real discourse. In no uncertain terms black hip-hop and gangsta rap should cease to desist from its use of misogyny, homophobia, and heterosexism in its performances. However, to single out and demonize black men is to let fester the greater malignancy harming society as a whole—the sexplotiative ideologies of our culture, our values, our media and our business entrepreneurs all to the detriment of women who are dehumanized, objectified, chattelized, sexualized and commodified as result.

So we are all left with the question, "If all women are hos and serve at the pleasure of the patriarch then who are the pimps?" I suggest our society in general and we, each of us, in particular serve as pimps until we begin the work to The wonderful possibilities of The Imus Affair was that this nation may have been poised and positioned for a broader debate on the contributions of sexploitation in the industries of pornography, prostitution and sex trafficking. Alas, the moment was gone when "the news" among all the "news" clutter, trumped Imus' for the week. It reported that yet another woman—Emily Jane Hilscher, also an athlete (with the Virginia Tech equestrian team), not unlike the women athlete's at Rutgers, was singled out as the first person who was fatally shot on Virginia Tech's campus. I wonder how would Howard Stern, or for that matter, Don Imus, or for that matter, Playboy, or for that matter, the world, reference Emily Jane Hilscher—hopefully not as a "ho"!!

Sexist and misogynistic lyrics in gangsta rap music are a serious problem for the African-American community. While sexism and misogyny in no way are restricted to black lyrics or African-American communities, they are prevalent traits of gangsta rap music. The purpose of this critical analysis is not merely to examine sexist and misogynistic lyrics, but to look at a specific group (N.W.A.) for the roots of misogynistic lyrics and attitudes in some forms of black music, to discuss why the black community as a whole does not condemn these lyrics, and to examine how gangsta rappers attempt to redefine black women and their roles in the black community and the larger society.

Misogyny creates a conflict between gangsta rappers and women in which these men struggle to empower themselves. Gangsta rap is their means of this empowerment. The medium of rap music allows them, once empowered, the personal freedom to define themselves, their environments, their lifestyles, and their perceptions of the world. It is as a consequence of this quest for empowerment that the conflict between gangstas and rappers arises. Clearly, what distinguishes the gangsta rapper from other male rappers is not only his misogyny, but also his self-centered view of his community and the world. The gangster rapper seeks to assert himself as a man, as white men are able to do when they become successful. But, in order to do so, he must claim his innocence as a power.

That is, he must appoint himself a victim and adopt a "me against the world" mentality in which he trusts no one and labels himself greatly misunderstood. If the rapper can claim such innocence, then he can adopt a power position in which he can view black women as objects and also use them as scapegoats for his own shortcomings. To gain a better understanding of this conflict, we must go back not only to the beginning of rap music but also to the original influences on the form, and to the social aspects that always have been present in African-American music. The history of today's rap music typically is traced to the South Bronx. It emerged and gained national recognition in 1979 when the Sugar Hill Gang recorded "Rapper's Delight."

However, in The Rap Attack: African Jive to New York Hip-Hop (1984), David Toop traces the origins of rap to even earlier American history:

Rap's forebears stretch back through disco, street funk, radio DJ's, Bo Diddley, the bebop singers, Cab Calloway, Pigmeat Markham, the tap dancers and comics, The Last Poets, Gil Scott-Heron, Muhammad Ali, acappella and doo-wop groups, ring games, skip-rope rhymes, prison and army songs, toasts, signifying and the dozens, all the way to the griots of Nigeria and the Gambia. No matter how far it penetrates into the twilight maze of Japanese video games and cool European electronics, its roots are still the deepest in all contemporary Afro-American music. If rap music can be traced to the African motherland, it should have firm roots in African-American musical traditions like the blues. In "Rap Music and the Black Musical Tradition: A Critical Assessment," Andre Craddock-

Willis examines these connections between rap and blues. He states that most Western scholars describe the "rich oral tradition, the call and response mechanism, the improvisational character, and even the dueling elements of African culture and music"; but the purpose of African-American music is what they so often neglect. He describes African-American music as a way of life that has the ability to communicate in all forms and on all occasions.

Blues and jazz, like rap, were born from the shared experiences of African Americans that include abduction, Middle Passage, slavery, the Southern plantation tradition, Emancipation, Reconstruction, post-Reconstruction, Northern migration, urbanization, and racism (Bell 5). From the pain of the struggle came the creativity that gave birth to artistic expression. Rap music and the blues share several traditional elements. Both forms were created in the midst of African-American struggle, use humor, use narrative and/or documentary forms, have origins rooted in impoverished black areas, and use boasting. In her article, " 'I Can Peep Through Muddy Water and Spy Dry Land': Boasts in the Blues," Mimi Clar Melnick says that boasting is one of the traditional means for the expression of masculinity.

In the history of rap music it is easy to follow the braggadocio style of rappers as they boast of their achievements and status. According to Melnick, the backwoods boaster and the blues singer, in the cleverest possible language, dream of personal greatness in their music. Like the rapper, both follow certain formulas for success. They brag of accomplishments and, in no uncertain terms, establish themselves as heroes. Their boasts provide them with an outlet for aggression and frustration, lend them a means for expressions of protest, and generally are designed to help them "be somebody" with the greatest possible style and color.

The rapper, the blues singer, the backwoods boaster — each seeks status. Whether it is materialized through clothes, cars, liquor, or weapons, his objective is the same: to create a sense of superiority by establishing what Melnick calls the importance of his role in the competitive society. The status of each of these men lies within his identity. Sometimes, to compensate for feelings of inferiority, he blows up his male ego and subjugates others in an attempt to uplift himself. The presence of the boaster in both the blues and gangsta rap suggests that gangsta rappers are perpetrators, not innovators, of misogyny in African-American music. There is a connection between the boaster, misogyny, and powerlessness in gangsta rap.

There is a continual social subplot present in most popular gangsta rap in which the gangsta rapper's bravado aggressively seeks to protect him from the perceived threat of the "bitch" character. Like the "backwoods boaster," whom Melnick describes, the gangsta rapper seeks to verify his personal importance. His male gangsta ego is uplifted and distanced from the female, who is denoted as the "bitch." The "bitch" character in gangsta rap always is depicted as shallow, one-dimensional, and money-hungry. The conflict between the gangsta rapper and the "bitch" character is symbolic of the male gangsta rapper trying to free him from the yoke of white oppression. To do so, he must degrade the "bitch" character for the amusement of his audience: the suburban white teenagers who make up the major buying market for this type of rap music.

Even though it is not the black community that financially empowers these young gangsta rap artists (by funding their hate lyrics), it is the black community that raises and nourishes them. Gangsta rappers constantly try to identify with the inner-city black community and the urban experience. Traditionally, they have been able to preserve their status within their communities because they bring a segment of the black experience to the public. The truth is, however, that once a gangsta rapper becomes successful, he is no longer a part of the world he raps about: He has become a member of the black privileged class. No longer a member of the impoverished class, he now must overcompensate for his wealth in order to retain the acceptance of his community.

Whether one views gangsta rappers as folk heroes or absurd sterotypical images, one must acknowledge that they are capable of dictating images of black women and the black community to the world via the music industry. To gangsta rappers, the black experience is machismo, the gangster lifestyle, and drug use. They portray anti-establishment, high-rollin', shoot-'em-up characters that smoke too much chronic (a very potent strain of marijuana), drink too much alcohol, tote guns, and surround themselves with voiceless women in bikinis or spandex.

There are also hard-core street niggers who never have had anything and just want to rap about their oppressed people; but the one constant element in gangsta rap is the theme of mistreatment of black women. In songs and videos, black women become objects, props that are barely clothed and continually gyrating. Often, many people in black communities, women as well as men, accept these negative images of black women as bitches or sex objects. To such audiences, this degradation of black women is a fair trade, as long as they can see black images on television or hear misogynistic rap songs on the radio.

Gangsta rappers are often quoted as saying that they merely depict life as they see it. A more accurate description of what gangsta rappers depict is a stereotypical fantasy in which black women do as they are told. Perhaps the most ironic observation I can make is that if gangsta rappers were white, the reaction from the black community would be very different. An excuse used by some gangsta rappers to defend their misogynistic actions is that they are merely assuming a stage persona. In "Signifying Rappers," David Foster Wallace and Mark Costello state that the rapper's "masks are many" and that these personae can change frequently, even within an album. A rapper can alternate between hardcore and playful, comic personae. He can be a street-smart trickster or a smooth-talking sugar daddy.

The stage persona theory allows the rapper to disassociate him from his boasting. This gives him the ability to claim himself as a powerless victim who is describing his difficult former life of poverty and violence, thereby deflecting any sympathy from the "bitch" character onto himself. In Paulla Ebron's "Rapping Between Men," she says that the rap performance becomes "a stage where audience and performers actively create themselves and respond to structures of dominance". In their response to these structures of dominance, gangsta rappers appear to believe that they only can make the transformation from boys to men by establishing their domination over women, since, of course, they cannot challenge the dominant white patriarchal power structure, which ironically is where they gain their financial support.

Typically, gangsta rappers use sexist and misogynistic lyrics for three reasons. First, they are selfish and seek to empower only themselves. Second, they put business before art: Songs with misogynistic lyrics sell millions of CDs and tapes. Sales mean money. Money means power. Finally, gangsta rappers reinterpret their experiences into a packageable product that can sell. They peddle half-truths and fantasies that formulate a stereotypical mythology in which all black women are bitches and/or all gangsta rappers live the life of driving sports cars, collecting thong-wearing, gyrating women, and smoking chronic.

The gangsta rap group N.W.A. (Niggers with Attitudes) serves as a good example of the gangsta rapper's quest for empowerment. They burst onto the rap scene in 1989 with their double-platinum album, Straight Outta Compton. At one time the rap group was known as the hardest of the hardcore. Their music consistently has been full of hate, sexism, and misogyny. The group initially consisted of the late Eazy-E (co-founder), Ice Cube (chief lyricist), Dr. Dre (co-founder, rapper-producer), M.C. Ren (DJ), and DJ Yella. They broke up after three albums. Eazy-E, born Eric Wright framed N.W.A.'s opinion of women in the Straight Outta Compton title track when he explained, "Straight Outta Compton is a brother that'll smother your mother."

In the same song he shows no sympathy for a woman who is the victim of a shooting: "What about the girl who got shot? / You think I give a damn about a girl? I ain't a sucka." These lyrics adhere to the street mentality of individualism in which the gangsta rapper separates him from females. Wright and the members of N.W.A. view themselves as "players." They idolize 1970s cult figures like Dolomite, Superfly, and the Mack, who are famous players from that era. N.W.A. member Ice Cube expounds the player's credo when he states in "Gangsta Gangsta" that "Life ain't nothin' but girls and money." This credo is also the credo of the gangsta's predecessor, the blues boaster.

Eric Wright, who died at the age of 31 of AIDS, grew up in a middle-class family in the Los Angeles suburb of Compton. He dropped out of high school, became involved with street gangs, and made a small fortune selling drugs which enabled him to start his music career. The father of seven children by six different women, Wright sought to validate the myth of the "bad nigger." Music columnist Jon Pareles tells how Wright boasted about his contempt for and prowess with women, how he frequently called women "bitches," and how he proudly declared himself a "woman beater". One year after his death, Eric Wright, a man who disrespected and beat women, had songs written in tribute to him by gangsta rappers.

Born O'Shea Jackson, Ice Cube was the chief lyricist of N.W.A. during the group's heyday. He was the first to leave it because of a financial dispute in 1991. Jackson is certainly the most ambiguous in terms of his love/hate relationships with women. During a popular phase of his career, he completed an interview that included photographs of him with his mother. In some photos, they hug and smile in the front yard, like the mother and son next door. Both appear very happy. (In interviews, he also has spoken about being home with his father, hanging out.) Yet, Jackson's music makes understanding his perceptions of women and male-female relationships difficult.

In a March 1990 interview with Fab Five Freddy (134-35), Jackson admits that rappers live blessed lives and should act somewhat like role models. I take this to mean that he believes gangsta rappers should be more responsible concerning their lyrics and their actions. After this statement, however, on one of his albums there appears a sixty-second song continually repeating the word "bitch" (Sager 84). This song is dedicated to the women who would not give him any "play" before his first solo album. Similarly, in Straight Outta Compton he raps an overtly sexist and misogynist song that symbolizes the group's perception of women. The song, written below, is entitled "I Ain't the 1":

I ain't the one, the one that get played like a poop butt
See, I'm from the street
So I know what's up
On these silly games that's played by the women
I'm only happy when I'm going up in 'em
But 'cha know I'm a menace to society
But girls in biker shorts are so fly to me
So I step to 'em
With aggression
Listen to the kid, and learn a lesson today
See, they think we narrow minded
Because they got a cute face, and big behinded
So, I walk over and say, how ya doin'
See, I'm only down for screwin', but you know
You gotta play it off cool
'Cause if they catch ya slippin' you'll get schooled
And they'll get 'cha for ya money son

Next thing you know, you're gettin' their hair and their nails done, for 'em

They'll let you show 'em off
But when it comes to sex, they got a bad cough -
Or headache
It's all give and no take
Run out of money and watch your heart break
They'll drop you like a bad habit

Cause a brotha with money, yo, they gotta have it
Messin' with me though, they gets none
You can't juice Ice Cube, girl
'Cause I ain't the one.
Woman #1: Girl, you gotta get these brothers for all the money you can,
Honey. 'Cause if they ain't got no money, they can't do nothin' for me but get outta my face.

Woman #2: I know what you mean, girl. It ain't no wild thing jumpin' off unless he got dollars.

A classic example of the way gangsta rappers view women, this song exudes paranoia and distrust, and fosters no sense of love or sharing in male-female relationships. It depicts a woman as only interested in a man as an object to provide money for her needs, and as desiring to live on his earnings while she degrades and humiliates him. The rappers' distinction between women and bitches suggests that these men have the power to define what and who women are and the criteria that place women into each particular category. Thus, if a woman shuns the sexual advances of a group member or displeases him in any way, she may be labeled a "bitch." Since male rappers are the overwhelming majority in the rap music industry, women's issues, rights, and concerns are poorly represented.

Jackson obviously does not include his mother in the "bitch" category because she loves him and supports him, unconditionally. Jackson says he does not write about women like his mother "because they aren't the problem." Most importantly, his mother stays in her place (i.e., as she appears in the photos, by his side and at home). Jackson's greatest fear is a woman who will take his money and try to play him, like the money-hungry characters in "I Ain't the 1." Yet, when he tries to clarify his feelings towards all women, it is difficult to take him seriously. In his music we only hear about the "bitch" character; thus, we have no choice but to assume that he perceives all women as bitches. There are no disclaimers in any N.W.A. or Ice Cube music that state that the word "bitch" signifies a specific kind of woman.

Jackson does give women a semblance of voice in Amerikkka's Most Wanted: He shares the microphone with Yolanda Whitaker (Yo-Yo), a female rapper out of Los Angeles, to rap a song that explores sexual stereotypes. (Ironically, Whitaker says she started rapping because she was tired of so many rappers dogging women.) Whitaker's inclusion is an attempt by Ice Cube to be positive, yet her one song is overshadowed by the other sexist and misogynistic songs on the album. Jackson himself proclaims his album to be about "things that need changing." He says, "the radio is full of records about how good everything is. What does that do?"

In deciphering all of this ambiguity we must remember that Jackson, like all rappers, is in the business of selling records. He does not waiver in his decision to sell out all black women in a so-called attempt to chastise a small element within the black community. Yet, since he is one of the most popular and successful rappers in the history of rap music, as long as his beats are funky, he can rap about anything. So why disrespect black women? It is obvious that we cannot trust the stage persona of Jackson, but can we trust the mother-loving son?

Can we trust him when he tells us that "bitches" only refers to women who "strictly" assess men for their economic value? According to Jackson, when a woman selects a man solely based upon economic criteria, she "brings down the community as a whole." He also states that this kind of behaviour eventually leads those who are poor to get money "to impress these women and that generates crime". Empowered by his status as a gangsta rap superstar, Jackson can theorize about the degradation of the black community, yet totally absolve African-American males from responsibility for this abasement.

Andre Young, more commonly known as Dr. Dre, personifies the myth of the bad nigger. In his debut solo album, The Chronic, he is preoccupied with the glorification of chronic ganja and the shoot-'em-up gangsta lifestyle. Unlike the albums by N.W.A. and alumni, there are no songs dedicated solely to the degradation of women. The closest Young comes to all-out debasement is a skit entitled "The Doctor's Office" in which he has a sexual encounter, complete with a banging headboard and a woman who seems extremely sexually satisfied. Young does not greatly emphasize sexism and misogyny in his album, but his public life is full of violence and abuse. A 1991 Rolling Stone article gives a brutal account of Young physically attacking rap show host Dee Barnes. The incident began in 1990 with a segment about N.W.A on her Fox TV rap video show, Pump It Up.

The show crosscut between members of the group dissing their former partner Jackson and a previous interview with him dissing N.W.A. The members of N.W.A. were displeased with Barnes' inclusion of the clip. On January 27, 1991, Young ran into Barnes at a record-release party in Los Angeles, where:

He picked her up and "began slamming her face and the right side of her body repeatedly against a wall near the stairway" as his bodyguard held off the crowd. After Dre tried to throw her down the stairs and failed, he began kicking her in the ribs and hands. She escaped and ran into the women's rest room. Dre followed her and "grabbed her from behind by the hair and proceeded to punch her in the back of the head."

Finally, Dre and his bodyguard ran from the building. Far from denying the attack, the members of N.W.A. insist that, as Ren says, "she deserved it – bitch deserved it." Eazy agrees: "Yeah, bitch had it coming."

Barnes, who first filed charges against Young in February 1991, also pursued a civil lawsuit alleging assault and battery, infliction of emotional distress, and defamation. Barnes states that N.W.A.'s whole philosophy has been that "they're just telling stories, just reporting how it is on the streets.... But they've started believing this whole fantasy, getting caught up in their press, and they think they're invincible. They think they're living their songs". In her opinion, the issue is bigger than just her – one person – getting slapped around: It is a campaign by N.W.A. to promote a Number One album calling for violence against women. Barnes says of N.W.A.: "They've grown up with the mentality that it's okay to hit women, especially black women. Now there are a lot of kids listening and thinking it's okay to hit women who get out of line" (Light 65-66).

Young's violent encounter with Dee Barnes is not an isolated incident. In the past, the rapper has been under house arrest and also has stood trial after being accused of beating up seven New Orleans policemen. His behaviour appears to have become the norm for gangsta rappers. His protégé, Calvin Broadus, more popularly known as Snoop Doggy Dogg, recently was absolved of guilt in a court case involving a gang-related killing which he claims was self-defense.

When they performed together, the members of N.W.A. constantly were accused of glamorizing violence and hatred, and this was their constant defense: They were not advocating anything; they were just reporting what they saw on the streets and setting those reports to Dre and Yella's funky, bass-powered beats. But when questioned about their status as role models, Young has said, "We ain't doing this shit to send out no messages.... We in this shit to get paid...." 100 Miles and Runnin', N.W.A.'s second album, moved the group even deeper into the business of bashing women. Ren says, "Ever since we did 'Just Don't Bite It,' girls tell me how much they like it..."

Arguably the most angry and misogynistic of the West Coast gangsta rappers is Broadus. Broadus was born in Long Beach, California, and nicknamed "Snoop" by his mother. She also gave him the southern twang in his nasal tenor voice. Broadus' parents, as well as his grandparents, were born in Mississippi. The rapper's modest beginnings also include a broken home and his membership in the church choir at Golgotha Trinity Baptist Church, Long Beach.

Broadus began rapping in the sixth grade. He graduated from Long Beach Polytechnic High School, where he was a star on the basketball team. He claims he never joined a gang, though he hung out with gang members and it was from watching them that he obtained much of his subject matter. He was jailed at the age of eighteen for selling drugs. In 1993, aged twenty-two, he was arraigned in the previously mentioned shooting death of a Venice, California gang member. When that particular slaying occurred, the rapper had been released from jail on bail for a weapons-violation charge. Broadus has been in so much trouble he even thanked his probation officer ("Mr. Dwoskin") in the liner notes of his debut album.

Like many other gangsta rap albums, his debut album, Doggystyle, uses humor to discuss or present misogyny. Doggy style is full of bitches, 'hos, hustlers, players, and Mack-daddies. Broadus' credo (repeated frequently) is, "I don't love you 'hos." One of the most disturbing songs on the album is "Aint [sic] No Fun (If the Homies can't [sic] have none)." In its attempt at humor, this is a deceptively rank and vile parody of an R&B loves song. The introduction is a funky R&B groove, sung by a smooth-sounding male vocalist, but quickly drifts into vulgarity, violence, and blatant disrespect for women. Also, in one particular skit on the album, Broadus elucidates his philosophy of women:

> Yeah, niggas be brown-nosing these 'hos, and shit. Takin' bitches out to eat and spending money on these 'hos, you know what I'm sayin'. I treat a bitch like Seven Up: I never have and I never will. I tell a bitch like this: Bitch, you without me is like Harold Melvin without the Blue Notes —You'll never go platinum.

Broadus, Jackson, Wright, and Young use their music to define gender roles, relationships, and social structures. They associate relationships with money and power. There is no mention of love or examples of loving relationships. In fact, these rappers go out of their way to reject the very notion of loving a woman, whose function they perceive exclusively as the fulfillment of their sexual desires.

In the end, this whole argument boils down to the fact that misogyny is ingrained into our culture and we allow it. We buy CDs and go to concerts where gangsta rappers call black women "bitches" and "hos." It is not just black women who are victimized. Since gangsta rappers disrespect our mothers, sisters, and daughters, every black man is a victim. Excuses – "I like the beat," "I don't listen to the words," and "They are only referring to certain types of women" – are not acceptable.

When gangsta rappers disrespect men and women and preach violence and hate to us, we must reject their messages. We cannot buy their CDs, albums, or tapes, or attend their concerts, or appear in their videos, or even support record labels or radio or television stations that advocate gangsta rap in any way. Malcolm X used to preach about the ills of airing "dirty laundry," and that is what gangsta rappers do when they disrespect black women in rap songs. Rap is not just music; it is our African-American culture. It is the way we blacks perceive ourselves, and the way we are perceived by the world. The content of gangsta rap music in its current form is unacceptable. It cannot and should not be tolerated by anyone.

4

Death, Mothers, and the After-life

Two important and influential recent books I would mention especially are *Otherworldly Journeys* by Carol Zaleski and Sogyal Rinpoche's *Tibetan Book of Living and Dying*. Zaleski, a Harvard trained historian of religion, compared medieval and other accounts of post-mortem journeys of the soul with the contemporary literature of NDEs and showed compellingly that visions of the afterlife are based on experience not speculation. Sogyal's book demystifies the obscure symbolic language of the ancient text called the Bardo Thodol (translated usually as *The Tibetan Book of the Dead*).

He shows clearly how the Tibetan "wake" or post-mortem prayers to the deceased person are actually addressed to that person's disembodied consciousness to help him or her navigate through confusing or frightening visions created by his/her own consciousness-a consciousness that goes beyond the body eventually towards further incarnations. The first and most important observation to be made from these two books and the many that they have inspired is that experience beyond the body, either before of after death are of a much greater order and significance than mere energetic discharges and "hallucinations" generated by the brain-a claim that appears increasingly trivial and narrow in its reductionism when evaluated from a religious phenomenological perspective. The disembodied consciousness in these many reports actually encounters other realms, other dimensions, other beings and other states of being. These states include mystical, expanded and often "cosmic" consciousness commensurate with those described in classic texts like R. M. Bucke's Cosmic Consciousness and William James' Varieties of Religious Experience. This is further underlined by a more recent work, Dreamtime and Inner Space by cultural anthropologist Holger Kahlweit. Kahlweit writes that "as far as I am concerned there is no difference between a near death experience and an out-of-body experience". For him they both are versions of the encounter with "other" or "higher" dimensions" described shamanic practitioners as "journeying".

Because of the split and downright antagonism that often exists between those trained in science and those professing particular religions there is often little study of each other's accounts of religious and psychical phenomena, so books like those mentioned are often not known outside a narrow circle of experts or academic authorities. Yet it is worth noting that Carol Zaleski's book has already spawned a whole academic field of research into the phenomenology of "otherworldly realities"-there have been several international conferences to date-while Sogyal's book is now used world-wide to help people who are nearing death prepare for their passing over. My first realization of how important it is to follow a person's consciousness into other realms, in whatever way possible, came when during a psychotherapy session some twenty years ago with a woman who had survived a major car-accident and had gone through a classic NDE during subsequent surgery to save her life.

She was still suffering from manifest PTSD symptoms when she consulted and decided to regress her to the memory of the accident. Not only did she relive the accident and release much buried trauma held in her body but she also proceeded to re-play the experience of watching herself from above as ambulance men pulled her body from the wreckage. She then saw her body taken to the hospital and undergoing surgery. Next she felt herself drifting up to a higher realm and meeting with beings of light that she recognized as deceased members of her family and who told her that her work on earth was not finished and that she must return. She remembered the pain of coming back into her body. Prior to the regression she had not "remembered" any of this.

The session profoundly altered her attitude to death and dying. Indeed what most deeply struck her was the continuity of her consciousness both before and after her "death" and both in and out of her body. Later I was to be reminded of this when reading Sogyal's remark that "birth and death are all in the mind and nowhere else". I have deliberately avoided using any one received picture of other dimensions whether Tibetan Buddhist, Christian, spiritualist, shamanic or other in trying to understand and classify the NDE experiences of my clients, those reported in the clinical literature and my own personal "journeys" into "other realms."

My approach has rather been simply to collect and compare these different descriptions and claims in the spirit of data gathering avoiding rigid or exclusive systems of classification. This is traditionally how the science of religion proceeds: it uses the phenomenological principle of reserving judgement as to the ontological status (i.e. which realm of reality) an experience actually belongs to and simply puts brackets or "parentheses" around the descriptive terms to indicate that it is too soon to decide upon what kind of reality to attribute to it.

This way we can make comparisons and tentative attempts to fit it into difference schemas. For example: is a vision of a "demon" a projection of a person's personal unconscious or a transpersonal denizen of an "otherworld" or "hell"? In other words does this psychic entity that has a "demonic" appearance have an autonomous existence or ontology of its own? We cannot know for sure without addressing all kinds of questions about it origins, context and behaviour. Taking a tentative approach like this avoids what biologist Sir Peter Medawar once called the arrogance of "nothing buttery"-it's nothing but imagination, it's nothing but a hallucination, it's *nothing but* the misfiring of a neural circuit. Reductionism of this kind rarely ventures out of the prison of the closed mind I regret to say. Once we start to study, reports of NDEs, mystical journeys of "the alone to the Alone" (Plotinus), past life reports of meeting higher guides between lives or shamanic accounts of journeys to the Land of the Dead, etc. with the open minded attitude of phenomenology numerous question start to present themselves, not the least of which is whether these states and beings are "real", which is to raise the issue of their ontology. We also find we have to look carefully at our language, which now seems to be booby-trapped with what may be symbols, codes or slippery metaphors. What does "beyond" the body or "beyond" death mean? Is this a spatial picture of another place? How can it be a place if it is not physical? Does that make such a word usage metaphorical? Is it a symbol? If so, then a symbol of what? Here we might consider the tantalizing little dictum of a Sufi master, Al Ghazzali:

The visible world was made to correspond to the world invisible and there is nothing in this world but is a symbol of something in that other world.

The fact is that one of the first assertions that almost all visionaries, mystics, journeyers and NDE survivors make is that their visions are without question of actual existent places or worlds, indeed places or worlds that are manifestly of a non-physical order. It is here that the terminology of "other" or "invisible" or "higher" worlds seems inescapable in describing such experiences. To summarize their claims we have to say that they are positing a referent that is non-physical and yet real. This upsets the Materialist, for whom there is only one reality, namely this one, and at this point he/she must either withdraw from the game or recognize that the greatest minds in the Western tradition have had to face this issue and forgo their assumptions of one-dimensional reality.

When Aristotle, following his master, Plato, tried to summarize the knowledge of his day, he was obliged, after writing the *Physics*, to add another volume, "beyond" *(meta)* the realm of physics, which in Greek became the *Metaphysics*. Plato had already designated a *metaxy* or intermediary world of subtle spiritual forms that were not physical. Indeed, according to the eminent Indian scholar Ananda K. Coomeraswamy, Plato had already been influenced by the teachings of ancient India, for we find Plato's idea clearly expressed in the Hindu Upanishads as follows:

> There are two states for man-the state in this world and the state in the next; there is also a third state, the state intermediate between these two, which can be likened to the dream state. While in the intermediate state a man experiences both the other states, that of this world and that in the next; and the manner whereof is as follows: when he dies he lives only in the subtle body, on which are left the impressions [*samskaras*, Skt] of his past deeds, and of those impressions is he aware, illumined as they are by the light of the Transcendent Self [*atman*, Skt].

This transcendent or intermediary world has been noticed in almost all cultures and traditions in one form or another. Buddhists from Tibet talk of the bardo realm in which many states of the spirit/soul, i.e. bardos, exist between lifetimes on earth. The Spiritualists in their teachings call it the Spirit World, following the great visionary Swedenborg who reported visiting its many dimensions. In his terminology, its "heavens" and "hells" were "states" corresponding to different port-mortem spiritual and moral conditions. (Swedenborg's work has so many parallels with Mahayana Buddhism that it led the Zen master D. T. Suzuki, to call him "the Buddha of the West").

In Celtic tradition the intermediary realm is often called the Middle Kingdom or the Faery World. Australian aborigines call it the Dreamtime, the Sufis of Persia called it the alam al-mithal or Mythic World, which Henry Corbin has dubbed the mundus imaginalis.) Jung called it the collective unconscious, though this term tends to be grossly misunderstood. A good survey of depictions of the "otherworld" (Zaleski's term) from many cultures is to be found in Suki Miller's After Death: How People around the World Map the Journey after Death.

In surveying reports of such journeys in the world religions and innumerable tribal practices Miller and other scholars such as Mircea Eliade have described a common pattern of "ascent", which is to say an ecstatic (from Latin: *ex-stasis*), mystical or out-of body experience wherein the spiritual traveller leaves the physical body and travels in his/her subtle body (or dream body or astral body) into "higher" realms ("higher" because they are of a higher or non-physical vibration, not literally higher.)

For reasons too complex to discuss here, we in the West have mostly lost touch with these "other" or intermediary worlds. The Christian churches only pay them lip service or retail simplistic formulae they don't understand. It is naively thought that we "go somewhere" after death, though descriptions of how and where are mostly stereotypical and ignorant. If there was once a widespread shamanic or spiritual tradition enabling contact with higher realities and the spirit realms in the West it was lost long ago. Some say it disappeared when the Roman Church threw out the Gnostics and the Mystery Schools. Others maintain that in persecuting "witches" in the Middle Ages the Catholic Church successfully suppressed the last folk remnants of indigenous shamanic tradition in Europe.

Fortunately today more and more ministers and priests are taking note of NDE reports and working directly with the realities of "spirit" in transition as Belmont's work eminently shows. In the ancient world the Mystery traditions focused on the stories of divinities such as the Demeter/Persephone, Isis/Osiris, Cybele/Attis diads, or on Mithras or on Dionysus, all of which depict in their stories a momentous death and re-birth through the archetype of the Cosmic Mother. Much was made of these sacred cosmic dramas as models of and as preparations for an individual's eventual death and transition. In fact it seems that the initiates were given a kind of rehearsal of their death by being taken to a dark place-usually a cave or underground chamber-that symbolized the realm of the dead or the womb of the Great Mother.

In the darkness of the mystery the old self died and a new self was reborn with the secret knowledge that it had a spirit or subtle body that was immortal. "He who has seen the Mysteries will not taste death" said one initiate.

The diagram gives a partly symbolic picture of what the intitiate into the Mysteries very likely experienced. The ritual "entombment" vouchsafed for him or her vision of the "otherworld" into which he/she would be reborn. Aeneas' famous descent to visit the Shade of his father Anchises with the Golden Bough at Nemi is a reference to the Mystery of crossing the River Styx (situated not far from Nemi) as a transition into the spirit world. Such "descents" into the Underworld were no doubt preparatory for a hierophany, or showing of the divine in the form of an ex-stasis (i.e. ecstasy), an out of body experience or "ascent" that enabled an encounter with the transcendent realm of divine being. Hence the famous saying of Heraklitos, "The way up and the way down are one and the same".

The intermediary or "otherworld" is multidimensional and is inhabited by a vast range of differing types of beings in subtle form, ranging from angels to demons. Perhaps the most commonly encountered spirits are those of our own ancestors but there are reports of meeting every form of human spirit being from highly elevated masters, Gods and demigods to degenerated sub-human and monstrous forms. Many of these spirits live in clusters, communities, realms or domains of like resonance, held together by ancestral ties, spiritual commonalities, allegiances, or else similarities of karma, whether good or bad.

Some realms are elevated and radiant with light, some dark and hellish. Animals spirits abound in their own realms and every kind of paradisal or hellish landscape may exist, according to the state of being it mirrors for those souls who have condemned or willed themselves to be there (this is Swedenborg's teaching). The reports of NDEs collected by Moody and others show again and again that the disembodied consciousness meets "beings of light" on the "other side" we are calling the intermediary realm. These are frequently ancestors, recently deceased family members who often counsel them and reassure them that their sufferings are over or else, like my client, counsel them that they still have important work to do on earth.

How far these encounters are determined by the beliefs and expectations of those who have "died" has not yet been fully explored, but our knowledge from NDEs is amplified by thousands of past life reports of dying in a previous life and making a similar journey. My own findings and those of colleagues suggest that encounters with ancestors, while being very common are by no means universal. We have also observed thousands of past lives of warriors on battlefields and seen them re-group in the spirit world not with their families so much as with their bands of comrades or councils of warrior elders that they knew on earth. Members of religious communities are more likely to meet with their fellow monks, nuns or sacerdotal communities or with teachers or gurus than return to their spirit ancestors.

Of course NDEs report numerous encounters with "guides" or wise beings of light, which is confirmed by past life therapy. Souls who died in some rebellion or were identified with some cause or movement will re-align with their leaders. The practical importance of these findings, especially for those counselling the bereaved and working with those approaching death is enormous. If only based upon report and not absolute ontological certainty, the overwhelming majority if these reports is that there *is* a world of light or a subtle world beyond this, that in many ways it is a continuity or an extension of this one, but in a non-physical form, and that in it we will encounter beings in their spiritual form usually of a loving and wise nature.

We know that this other world has many dimensions ("many mansions" was Jesus' phrase; the Buddhists talk of *bardos*) corresponding to one's state of spiritual attainment on the earth high or low. Great souls who have journeyed many times and in many lifetimes into and through these realms sometimes leave us their conspectus, their overview *sub specie aeternitatis.* The works of Plotinus are an example of this in the West. Here is the Buddha's report: With the heavenly eye, purified and beyond range of human vision, I saw how beings vanish and come to be again. I saw high and low, brilliant and insignificant, and how each obtained according to his karma, a favourable or painful rebirth.

It is only rare souls that attain the clarity of the Buddha; being able to open their "heavenly eye" (this seems to be a kind of higher consciousness reported by many spiritual voyagers. Compare "the light of Atman or Transcendent Self" quoted in the Hindu Upanishad earlier). Nevertheless many today who practice shamanic "journeying" report the development of clairvoyant powers such as the ability to see other dimensions or realities or to perceive "other lives" and "spirits" in people's auras as well as, in some cases, learning to call spirit beings at will.

The great authority on shamanism Mircea Eliade, called shamans "technicians of the sacred" because of their ability to travel-out of body, ecstatically (= *ex-stasis*), of course-between the worlds, mediating and rebalancing the intercourse between the living and the dead. Because of their facility in travelling through and between these "otherworlds" shamans describe quite sophisticated pictures of the spiritual geography they encounter; this is also true of yogis and great spiritual masters like the Buddha with whom they share these powers. Such voyagers tell, when they move between the various inner worlds or *bardos*, of dark and light forces, of hierarchies or different planes of heavens and hells, of.

It is in fact their job to navigate what Kahlweit calls "inner space", so as to discriminate between hostile or malevolent "spirit" beings and to bring back souls who have either become lost or captive to these destructive powers or more often just stuck in their own negativity or despair. The shaman thus journeys intentionally to various upper or lower realms, deliberately using powers or "allies" from spirits realms to strengthen and help him. Here we hear echoes of the old hero journeys of myth and legend where the spiritual hero (Moses, St John the Divine) may either climb the sacred mountain to receive teachings or descend into hell (Jesus, Aeneas, Dante, Avatars, Bodhisattvas) to encounter or rescue souls that are lost.

In my own practice of regressing clients and students to lost childhood memories, to buried traumas, as well as to their many past lives I have been greatly helped by the cosmographies of the shamans, yogis and the heroes of myth. Their maps of "inner space" have proved invaluable aids in navigating to and from various "otherworld" realities. The journeys I accompany my clients on are not only between physical and psycho-spiritual realms (as, for example, in out-of body or dissociative reactions to trauma, accidents, NDEs etc) but also include the supreme transition from dying in the body to the "afterlife" realms beyond death.

In guiding clients through "past life" realities the re-experiencing of a "past life" death is more often than not the most important part of the journey to be navigated since it may require the release of quite complex psychic or "karmic" imprints such as fear, shame, guilt, grief etc. In working with the post-mortem states the soul inherited from "past lives" I have found the Mahayana Buddhist classification of three realms of Being extremely helpful in locating, rescuing and re-locating lost "soul fragments" (as many writers now call them.) The three "bodies" (*kayas*) or cosmic realms of the Buddha, refer to

1. The highest realm of Pure Light (Amitabha-buddha or Dharmakaya),
2. The intermediary realm of subtle "spirit" forms in all their polarities (heavens, hells etc) which we have already described (Samboghakaya), and
3. The Earth plane or realm of physical or material reality i.e. "this" world (Nirmanakaya).

These different realms or post-mortem "states" we encounter in the past-life journey beyond death help explain how souls or soul fragments frequently get "lost" or "trapped" in different kinds of psychic "limbos". Many report for example, after leaving their "past life body" in a violent death (murder, massacre, catastrophe) that their "past life" consciousness (warrior, refugee, victim) cannot leave the earth but wanders looking for comrades, lost children, family or other villagers. These wandering soul fragments resemble traditional ghosts, who are, like Hamlet's father, "doomed a certain time to walk the earth "They are" spirits, who trapped on the Earth plane; in the East they are traditionally called "wandering ghosts". Equally they are to be found in and around the auras of living human beings, the phenomenon we now call "spirit attachment".

We usually find that these spirits-truly "lost souls"-are in severe post-traumatic shock, unaware they are dead and thus unprepared to "ascend" into "higher" realms of Light or to be welcomed "home" by the ancestral spirits. The intervention of the therapist or the shaman can "awaken" these soul fragments from their self-perpetuating limbos and re-align them with "higher" realms where they find peace and rest or where they can happily re-connect with lost loves ones or other ancestors, much as in classic NDEs.

The second or Intermediary realm is where we find souls trapped not so much on the earth or around persons but stuck in imaginal "hells" or states of severe confusion of their own making. As Swedenborg and more recently Sogyal Rinpoche have observed, the psychic apparatus or "mental body" of a person after death tends to perpetuate whatever state of mind he/she was in before dying. If the dying person in their "past life" dies in despair and loneliness he/she will experience him/herself after death in an exactly similar space of despair or loneliness.

This state, similar to that of the attached earthbound spirit, prevents it "ascending" to happier realms of light or of even being aware of the loving spirit presences that are around it, willing to help and heal. The states-fear, grief, rage at injustice, hatefulness, self-loathing, pride, guilt, sense of failure, resignation etc-are psychological states of "hell" in which the old complexes from the previous life on earth are perpetually and compulsively re-rerun psychically like repeating tape loops, resulting in them being even more deeply imprinted.

Hence the need, according to the Tibetan Buddhists, to counsel the soul after death so that it can let go of its earthly obsessions and experience the joy of deliverance into "the Light" (Amitabha-buddha). If they are not released by prayer, intervention from "higher planes" or self-awareness (which is by no means easy in this "compulsive" state) these "karmic complexes" as I have called them elsewhere, will re-cycle and become the unconsciously inherited psychic patterns (guilt, low self-esteem, compulsiveness, anxiety, depression etc) which will plague future "incarnations" which is to say other states of being. This is symbolically "the wheel of re-birth" in Eastern teaching. Some of Shakespeare's final words summarize this theme:

And my ending is despair
Unless I be relieved by prayer,
Which pierceth so that it assault
Heaven itself and frees all fault
-*The Tempest*

Nearly all voyagers in the inner realms, whether in shamanism, meditation or past life regression have encountered beings of light, whether they call them the ancestors, the Old Ones, angels, Wise Ones or simply the eternal archetypes? These entities belong to the third or "highest" plane of Pure Light, a mystical light of dazzling beauty that pervades and illuminates all Being. Encounter with this Light, as many of the more elaborate NDE reports attest, can lead to a total transformation of the personality.

When it occurs in past life regression it usually marks a phase of the re-alignment of the psyche with its spiritual dimension and the opening of what Jung would call the process of individuation. Others have called this self-realization or self-actualization. It is the end point of the mystical journey of the soul. In Dante's vision of this realm, in the Paradiso the supernal light or "the prime mover" is described as "the love which moves the sun and all the other stars"-l'amor che muove il sole e gli altri stelle.

R. Johanan said: Scripture refers ten times to the death of Moses, as follows: Behold, thy days approach that thou must die; And die in the mount; But I must die; For I know that after my death; And how much more after my death; Before his death; A hundred and twenty years old when he died; So Moses the servant of the Lord died there; Now it came to pass after the death of Moses; Moses My servant is dead.

This teaches that ten times was it decreed that Moses should not enter Eretz Israel, but the harsh decree was not finally sealed until the High Court revealed itself to him and declared: ' It is my decree that you should not pass over,' [as it is said,] For thou shalt not go over this Jordan. Moses, however, made light of this, saying: ' Israel have many times committed great sins, and whenever I prayed for them, God immediately answered my prayer, as it is said, Let Me alone, that I may destroy them; yet what is written there? And the Lord repented of the evil; I will smtte them with the pestilence, and destroy them; what is written there? And the Lord said: I have pardoned, etc. Seeing then that I have not sinned from my youth, does it not stand to reason that when I pray on my own behalf God should answer my prayer?'

And when God saw that Moses made light of the matter and that he was not engaging in prayer, He seized the opportunity to swear by His great Name that Moses should not enter Eretz Israel, as it is said, Therefore (laken) ye shall not bring this assembly, and 'laken' always implies an oath, as it is said, And therefore (laken) I have sworn unto the house of Eli. When, however, Moses saw that the decree against him had been sealed, he took a resolve to fast, and drew a small circle and stood therein, and exclaimed: ' I will not move from here until Thou annullest that decree.' What else did Moses do then? He donned sackcloth and wrapped himself with sackcloth and rolled himself in the dust and stood in prayer and supplications before God, until the heavens and the order of nature were shaken. Said they: ' perhaps, it is the desire of God to create His world anew.'

Whereupon a heavenly voice was heard proclaiming: 'It

is not yet God's desire to renew His world... but, In whose hand is the soul of every living thing, and the breath of all mankindish', and 'man' must surely refer to Moses, as it is said, Now the man Moses was very meek, above all men that were upon the face of the earth. What did God do? At that hour He had it proclaimed in every gate of each of the heavens,2 and in every Court, that they should not receive Moses' prayer, nor bring it before Him, because the decree against him had been sealed.

Now at that hour God hastily summoned the Angel in charge of Proclamations, Achzeriel by name, and He commanded the ministering angels: ' Descend quickly, bolt all the gates of every heaven, because the voice of the prayer threatens to force its way to heaven.' And the angels sought to ascend to heaven because of the sound of Moses' prayer, for his prayer was like a sword which tears and cuts its way through everything, and spares nothing, seeing that his prayer was of the nature of the Ineffable Name which he had learnt from Zagzagel the Master Scribe of the children of heaven. It is to that hour that [the prophet] alludes when he says, And I heard behind me the voice of a great rushing: Blessed be the glory of the Lord from His place; and 'rushing' surely means trembling, and 'great' surely refers to Moses, as it is said, Moreover the man Moses was very great in the land of Egypt, in the sight of Pharaoh's servants, and in the sight of the people.

What is the meaning of, 'Blessed be the glory of the Lord from His place'? When the wheels of the Chariot and the fiery Seraphim saw that God commanded that Moses' prayer should not be accepted and that He did not respect Moses' person, nor grant him more life, nor bring him into Eretz Israel, they exclaimed:' Blessed be the glory of the Lord from His place,' for before Him there is no respecting of persons, great or small. And whence do we know that Moses prayed at this juncture five hundred and fifteen times? For it is said, And I besought (wa-ethhanan) the Lord at that time, saying, the numerical value of 'wa-ethhanan' is this number. Moses said to God: ' Master of the Universe, the labour and the pains which I have devoted to making Israel believe in Thy name are manifest and known to Thee, to what trouble have I gone with them in connection with the precepts in order to fix for them Torah and precepts. I thought, just as I witnessed the woe, so too will I behold their weal; but now that the weal of Israel has come, Thou sayest to me, "Thou shalt not go over this Jordan"; lo, Thou makest of Thy Torah a fraud. Therein it is written, In the same day thou shalt give him his hire, neither shall the sun go down upon it, for he is poor, and setteth his heart upon it; lest he cry against thee unto the Lord, and it be sin in thee. Is this the reward for the forty years' labour that I went through in order that [Israel] should become a holy and faithful people, as it is said, But Judah yet ruleth with God, and is faithful with the saints'?

Sammael the wicked angel, the chief of all the accusing angels, was awaiting the death of Moses every hour, saying, 'When will the time or the moment arrive for Moses to die, so that I may descend and take away his soul from him.' And it is of him that David said, The wicked watcheth the righteous, and seeketh to slay him. There is no one among the accusing angels so wicked as Sammael and there is none so righteous among the prophets as Moses, as it is said, And there hath not arisen a prophet since in Israel like unto Moses, whom the Lord knew face to face.

He was like a man who has been invited to a wedding feast, and looks forward to it, saying: 'When will their rejoicing come that I may share therein.' So, Sammael the wicked was waiting for Moses' soul saying, ' When will Michael2 be weeping and I be filling my mouth with laughter? ' Whereupon Michael replied: ' What, you wicked one, I shall cry, and you laugh!' as it is said, Rejoice not against me, O mine enemy; though I am fallen, I shall arise; though I sit in darkness, the Lord is a light unto me (Micah VII, 8). ' Though I am fallen,' because of the demise of Moses, yet, 'I shall arise,' on account of the leadership displayed by Joshua when he shall have defeated the thirty one kings. ' Though I sit in darkness,' because of the destruction of the first and the second Temples, yet, ' The Lord is a light unto me, in the days of Messiah. Meanwhile there remained unto Moses only one hour. Whereupon Moses said to God: ' Master of the Universe, if

Thou wilt not bring me into Eretz Israel, leave me in this world so that I may live and not die.' God thereupon said to Moses: ' If I will not slay you in this world, how can I bring you back to life in the World to Come? And what is more, you make of My Torah a fraud, for in My Torah it is written by your hand, and there is none that can deliver out of my hand '.

Said Moses to God: ' Master of the Universe, if Thou wilt not bring me into Eretz Israel, let me become like the beasts of the field that eat grass and drink water and live and enjoy the world; likewise let my soul be as one of them.' Whereupon God replied:' Let it suffice thee '. Moses then prayed: ' Master of the Universe, if not, let me become in this world like the bird that flies about in every direction, and gathers its food daily, and returns to its nest towards evening; let my soul likewise become like one of them.' Whereupon God answered: 'Let it suffice thee.' What is the meaning of 'Let it suffice thee '? God said to him: 'you have spoken sufficiently.' When Moses saw that no creature could save him from the path of death, he thereupon exclaimed,' The Rock, His work is perfect; for all His ways are justice; a God of faithfulness and without iniquity, just and righteous is He'.

What did Moses do? He took a scroll and wrote down upon it the Ineffable Name, nor had the Book of Song1 been completely written down when the moment of Moses' death arrived. At that hour God said to Gabriel: ' Gabriel, go forth and bring Moses' soul.' He, however, replied: ' Master of the Universe, how can I witness the death of him who is equal to sixty myriads, and how can I behave harshly to one who possesses such qualities?' Then God said to Michael: 'Go forth and bring Moses' soul.' He, however, replied: 'Master of the Universe, I was his teacher, and he my pupil, and I cannot therefore witness his death.' God then said to Sammael the wicked: ' Go forth and bring Moses' soul.' Immediately he clothed himself with anger and girded on his sword and wrapped himself with ruthlessness and went forth to meet Moses.

When Sammael saw Moses sitting and writing down the Ineffable Name, and how the radiance of his appearance was like unto the sun and he was like unto an angel of the Lord of hosts, he became afraid of Moses and declared: 'Of a surety, angels cannot take away Moses' soul.' Now before Sammael showed himself to Moses, Moses knew of his coming, and when Sammael caught sight of Moses trembling, fear took hold of him, as of a woman in travail, and he had not the effrontery to speak to Moses, until Moses said to Sammael,' There is no peace, saith God, concerning the wicked. What are you doing here? ' He replied: ' I have come to take away your soul.' Moses asked him: ' Who sent you? ' He replied: ' He who created all the creatures.' Moses then said to him: 'You shall not take away my soul.'

Whereupon he replied: 'The souls of all who come into this world are delivered into my hands.' Whereupon Moses said: 'I have greater strength than all who come into this world.' He then asked: 'And wherein lies your strength?' Moses replied: 'I am the son of Amram, and came out from my mother's womb without prepuce, and had no need to be circumcised; and on the very day on which I was born I found myself able to speak and was able to walk and to converse with my father and mother, and I did not even take suck of [my mother's] milk; and when I was three months old I prophesied and declared that I was destined to receive the law from the midst of flames of fire; and [once] when I was walking in the street I entered the palace of the king and removed the crown from his head; and when I was eighty years old I wrought signs and wonders in Egypt and brought forth sixty myriads before the eyes of all Egypt; and I divided the sea into twelve divisions, and I made the bitter waters sweet; and I ascended heaven and trod out a path there, and engaged in battle with the angels, and received the law of fire, and sojourned under God's.

Throne of fire, and took shelter under the pillar of fire, and spoke with God face to face; and I prevailed over the heavenly Familia, and revealed unto the sons of man their secrets, and received the Law from the right hand of God, and taught it to Israel; and I made war on Sihon and Og, the two giants of the heathens to whose ankles the waters of the flood did not reach because of their [great] stature; I caused sun and moon to stand still on high, and I smote them with the staff in my hand and killed them; is there any one amongst mankind who is able to do likewise? Away, wicked one, from here, you must not speak thus, go, flee before me, I will not surrender my soul to you.'

Immediately Sammael went back and reported to God. Whereupon God commanded Sammael, 'Go, and bring Moses' soul.' Straightway he drew his sword from the sheath and placed himself at the side of Moses. Immediately Moses became wroth, and taking hold of the staff on which was engraven the Ineffable Name he fell upon Sammael with all his strength until he fled from before him, and he pursued him with the Ineffable Name and removed the beam of glory [halo] from between his eyes and blinded him. Thus much did Moses achieve? At the end of a moment, a heavenly voice was heard, declaring: 'The end, the time of your death has come.'

Said Moses to God: 'Master of the Universe, remember the day when Thou didst reveal Thyself unto me in the bush and didst say to me; Come now therefore, and I will send thee unto Pharaoh, that thou mayest bring forth My people the children of Israel from Egypt; remember the time when I abode on Mount Sinai for forty days and forty nights, I implore Thee, do not hand me over into the hand of the Angel of Death.' Thereupon a heavenly voice was heard saying to him: ' Fear not, I myself will attend to you and your burial.'

At that hour, Moses arose and sanctified himself like the Seraphim, and God came down from the highest heavens to take away the soul of Moses, and with Him were three ministering angels, Michael, Gabriel, and Zagzagel. Michael laid out his bier, Gabriel spread out a fine linen cloth at his bolster, Zagzagel one at his feet; Michael stood at one side and Gabriel at the other side. God said: ' Moses, fold your eyelids over your eyes,' and he did so. He then said: 'Place your hands upon your breast,' and he did so. He then said: ' Put your feet next to one another,' and he did so. Forthwith the Holy One, blessed be He, summoned the soul from the midst of the body, saying to her: 'My daughter, I have fixed the period of thy stay in the body of Moses at a hundred and twenty years; now thy end has come, depart, delay not.'

Whereupon she replied: 'Master of the Universe, I know that Thou art the God of all spirits and all souls, the souls of the dead and the living are in Thy keeping, and Thou hast created and formed me and placed me within the body of Moses for a hundred and twenty years. And now, is there a body in the world purer than the body of Moses in which there has never been an offensive smell, nor worm nor maggot, nor any kind of vermin; therefore I love him and I do not desire to leave him.' Whereupon God exclaimed: 'Soul, go forth, do not delay, and I will raise thee to the highest heavens and will place thee under the Throne of Glory next to the Cherubim, Seraphim, and other troops of angels.'

Thereupon the soul replied: 'Master of the Universe, two angels, Uzah and Azael, came down from near Thy divine Presence and coveted the daughters of the earth and they corrupted their way upon the earth until Thou didst suspend them between earth and heaven. But the son of Amram from the day Thou didst reveal Thyself unto him at the Bush has had no marital relations with his wife,' as it is said, And Miriam and Aaron spoke against Moses because of the Cushite woman whom he had married; for he had married a Cushite woman. 'I implore Thee let me remain in the body of Moses.' Thereupon God kissed Moses and took away his soul with a kiss of the mouth, and God, if one might say so, wept [as it is said], who will rise up for me against the evil-doers? Who will stand up for me against the workers of iniquity?

And the Holy Spirit said, and there hath not arisen a prophet since in Israel like unto Moses. The heavens wept and said, the godly man is perished out of the earth. The earth wept and said, and the upright among men is no more. And when Joshua was looking for his master and did not find him, he also wept and said, Help, Lord; for the godly man ceaseth, for the faithful fail from among the children of men. And the ministering angels said, He executed the righteousness of the

Lord. And Israel said, And His ordinances with Israel. These and those said He entereth into peace, they rest in their beds, each one that walketh in his uprightness; The memory of the righteous shall be for a blessing, and his soul for the life of the World to Come. Amen. May this be His will? Blessed be the Lord for ever. Amen and amen.

The fascination with death extends far back into human history. Throughout time, people have had obsessions with death and all things related to death and the afterlife. In past times, people would form cults around death gods and figures. Famously, Anubis, Osiris, Hades, and Death (Saint Death) have all had large cult followings. La Santa Muerte (Saint Death), or the personification of death, is currently worshiped by many in Mexico and other countries in Central America. Day of the Dead, November 2, is a celebration for the dead in Saint Death's honor. The ancient Egyptians are most famous for their fascination of death by mummifying their dead and building exquisite tombs, like the pyramids of Giza, for their dead. Many of their deities were death-related, such as: Ammut, the devourer of unworthy souls; Anubis, the guardian of the Necropolis and the keeper of poisons, medicines, and herbs; and Osiris, the king of the dead.

The Greek underworld, Hades, was ruled by the god Hades, and had five rivers that flowed through it. The rivers were: Acheron, river of sadness; Cocytus, river of lamentation; Lethe, river of forgetfulness; Phlegethon, river of fire; Styx, river of hate. The Underworld had attendants who, though not rulers, were important gods and beings. The Furies were female spirits who exacted vengeance against people who committed specific crimes. Keres were female spirits of death and destruction. Persephone was the goddess of the underworld and the spouse of Hades. Thanatos, the god of death, was said to wear dark robes. The Vikings believed that if a warrior died in battle, he would be taken to the Norse afterlife: the hall of Valhöll, in which the warriors would prepare for Ragnarökk, the battle at the end of the world. Rune stones were erected to commemorate particularly brave warriors. Death in one's sleep (a "straw death") was considered dishonorable.

Death-related Holidays:

- Kali Puja in Kolkata, India, in which people light candles in memory of the dead.
- Samhain, a Celtic holiday marked with bonfires in which the spirits of the dead travel to the otherworld. The holiday was later transformed by Christian missionaries into the festivals of Halloween, All Saints and All Souls Day from 31 October to 2 November. The two latter days are celebrated in Mexico as the Day of the Dead.
- Ullambana, a Buddhist festival normally in August stemming from the Ullambana Sutra, which describes a man saving his mother from the underworld by making offerings to the sangha. Today it is celebrated as the Bon Festival of Japan, the Ghost Festival of China, and Vu Lan of Vietnam.

IN CONTEMPORARY WESTERN CULTURE

In the early part of the 20th century, it was common to hold séances at dinner parties. Harry Houdini was known for going to these séances and proving that the medium, the person conducting the séance, was a fraud. A séance is the event where a group of people (3 or more) try to communicate with the dead through one person of the group, the medium. Today there are a number of commenters who have spoken on the fascination people have with death. "If it bleeds it leads" is a phrase related to this, meaning that in the media, the most popular material - as well as most of the material in general - is based on death. For example - death as a topic in the news.

Musician and artist Marilyn Manson often talks and bases his music and artwork around the way people are fascinated with death, as well as fame (in relation). He comments on how people will use death to gain certain immortality in the minds of others (fame). His stage name is a reference to Marilyn Monroe and Charles Manson, one a symbol of fame (and early death) the other of murder. He has further commented that people are willing to die and kill if they know enough people are watching, to gain this immortality or fame. This extends into a social comment on martyrism, television, and the hypocrisy people show between their fascination and thus promotion of death, and their decryment of violence.

A mother is a blessed saintly being in her own world. The Ka'ba is the spirit, meaning, essence, and atlas of the entire reality of the universe; Makka is the same for all places, and the mind for the entire body; so too a mother is the spirit, meaning, essence, and atlas for the smallest unit of a society, i.e., the family; she is its foundation, pillar, essence, and a most important material of the Creative Power. In a home, everything centers on her, enwraps her, and turns into her. As for the mother, she always revolves around her own axis, like the North Star and follows an orbit that extends above the firmaments.

Mothers are beings that are oriented on the Hereafter in this world. The reward they obtain through their role and employment in creation, the imbalance between the pains and trouble they go through, and how they are responded to in return make up the clearest evidence of this fact. There is no need for complicated research to comprehend this; a casual glance at what they sow and what they harvest through-out their entire lifetime, what they go through, and what they find in return suffices. Their faces are as otherworldly as the hours in Paradise, their looks are as profound as those of the angels, and their feelings are as pure as that of any spiritual being.

Like the roses of a blessed land whose water, soil, and air have been brought from realms beyond this one, they are so enviable, so lovely, and so fascinating that, if you look carefully, you will conclude that there is a magic within them that surpasses their material being, the world, and what it contains, that even surpasses the mothers themselves. By probing souls which are sensitive and thoughtful, one is able to find reflections of the sweetest dreams fed by heavenly thoughts within the world of the mother, a world which is always sensitive, caring, and overflowing with affection, and thus reach a melody of pleasure that transcends human imagination.

In their atmosphere we are able to be almost constantly aware of breezes that waft tranquility; this is different at night and different yet again in the day. We can feel the mercy, affection, and poetry of the heavens pour into our hearts... and in this way, we feel as if our horizons have been completely encompassed by angels and spiritual beings. Who knows how many times we can see in the heart of the night a spirit and meaning that comprises the essence of creation reflected in their radiant, charming faces; it descends to the world, transcends all times and locations, and we are able to sense an immense mercy that is rooted in infinity; this gleams out at us through their smiles and their sorrows.

We long to jump into their arms; there is some obscure, vague, yet appealing, motivation to do this. Who knows how many times we have been heartbroken and disappointed, feeling sad and lonely, and then we are able to allow ourselves to rest on their almost magical bosom, which inspires in us hope and a feeling of security. This is a place that is warmer, livelier, and cozier than a nest that has taken wing from a state of rapture to another; we stretch ourselves, made warm by their mysterious whispers. Each time they press us to their bosoms they become a hero of faith that does not expect anything in return; they fall into an almost magical state. Then we are able to straighten up, looking around us in security and confidence, feeling that we can overcome anything. We even feel as if we are able to challenge everybody when we hold them tight.

A mother is as profound as the skies, and she is a mysterious world of emotions where thoughts and feelings number as many as the stars in the sky, boiling and overflowing like rivers of lava or underground springs flowing every which way. She conforms to her fate—be it bitter or sweet—at peace with both joys and sorrow, without any expectations in return, and she feels no resentment toward her baby. She is such a paragon of affection and faith, someone whose nature has been crystallized by divine morals, that neither the troubles that she experiences, which rise up in her throat like the flood of sweat on Judgment Day, nor the faithlessness of her children, which covers her soul like the north wind blowing, giving her the bitterest pain of separation, can make her submit, or make her give up.

There is the story of a mother: "her blood-thirsty son stabs her with several piercing blows and when the knife lightly cuts his own finger he unintentionally shouts out 'Mother!' and she holds on to his arm in return, screaming 'My baby!'" Ever since my childhood, whenever I remember this story, I cannot help but shiver and I try to feel the immensity of a mother's affection through this small drop. Those mothers who believe in eternity and the afterlife possess a spiritual and otherworldly aspect, in addition to their physical and material aspects.

Within the established world of material and spiritual realms, in the world of the body and soul, their hearts have such an incomprehensibly strong bond with their children that even relationships that are considered to be very strong and fundamental by worldly people amount to nothing more than a pale shadow in comparison. However, it would not be that easy to explain this to those who have felt neither any faith nor the delight of eternity within faith. Yes, it would be very difficult indeed to relate how their sincerity remains so deep, how their devotion continues without pause, how their hearts are enthusiastic with love, how their looks pour into us, promising care and trust, and how they overflow with such eternal and otherworldly feelings, even though they grow up in a land of mortality and transience.

Think about it, what a long process of preparation they undergo for us, what insurmountable hardships they have come up against and what things they overcome. What challenges they struggle with, and what dreams and weariness they live with. What reveries and dreams their hearts are filled with, and emptied of, what hopelessness and disappointment they suffer. What hardships and burdens they stand firm against and how many ordeals they undergo. What pains they suffer and how they moan. How many times they cry, screaming out and how many times they console our crying. How many times they overflow with compassion and how many times they are in need of compassion. In short, what valuable things they spend for us and what efforts they make, expecting nothing in return.

If there is someone who hugs, cuddles, kisses, and caresses us, who relieves our feelings of sadness and dejection, who shares our worries, who prefers us to eat in her place, us to be dressed well instead of her, who feels her hunger or fullness when we are hungry or full, who bears unimaginable hardships with a superhuman effort for the sake of our happiness and joy, who shows us the way for our body to develop, our will to strengthen, for our intelligence to become sharp and perspicacious, for our horizons to be oriented on the Hereafter, a person who does all these with-out expecting—openly or secretly—anything in return, that person is none other than our mother.

We spend a significant part of our lives in their embrace and in their atmosphere, a place more beautiful than the feathers of peacocks, more charming than the magical world of flowers, warmer and livelier than beehives, more protective and secure than the best of nests. True, we see, recognize, and learn the joy and excitement of being protected and cared for; we learn its practice and responsibility, its system and method. And whenever our needs and weak-nesses overcome us, along with our feebleness, our shortcomings, and the other things that go wrong in life, we always take refuge in our mother, and try to overcome all the obstacles we have come across with their help. When we take refuge in them, they press us to their bosoms with all the warmth of their hearts, always breathing security and confidence into our hearts at times of distress.

In such cases, I think that almost all of us have felt as if we were listening to a silent poem, a flood of emotions, a breeze of affection coming from their eyes, their smile, and their gestures. In those emotional, dreamy nights and days that we spend with them we are almost continually in a dream of bliss. In the bright daytime, we hear the sweetest melodies of life from their bosoms, like a nightingale's song, and say "this must be real happiness," at least to the extent of our comprehension.

The mother is the most important element of the event of Creation, the most fertile pillar of the world of humanity, and she is the light of our eye. All of us are bent over double before her, feeling an unbearable sense of debt and the heaviest of responsibilities. We bend over double and we are immensely proud of our hunched back. The fountains of Heaven, where angels flit like white doves, provide the water that forges the glowing steel of the mother. If this were not true, could the light of her soul ever dazzle our eyes like that? Not only her light, even her shadow burns the moths it attracts—in my own world, I still have not been able to recover from the shock of the deep emotions inspired by that sublime quality—and her light—now that I sense it better than ever—is a mysterious source of light, enlightening our hearts in the darkness.

A mother is a hero of love who keeps the delicacy and valor in her soul abreast when she is considered in terms of her affection, benignity, and grace; she is soft like a feather, fine and smooth as silk, yet at the same time she is tough and fierce as a lioness when it comes to protecting and caring for her children. Whatever lies under the firmaments above us, her hand is above all these, and the way to Paradise runs under her feet. God has granted such a sublimity and royalty to her that earthly kingdoms are nothing more than mere crowns without status in comparison. Moreover, crowns that rest on heads which have never found a place beneath their mothers' feet cannot be said to have any lasting value.

O sublime and precious being, who is as fine as the spirits, as innocent as the angels, and as profound as the skies; the realm beyond gives you a value above values, and sympathizes with your shyness. The melody of your fame is heard where angels abide, the song of your life rings out at the skirts of the heavens. You have always lived with the blade of emotions impaled through your heart, wearing the jewel of religion as a necklace. All of us are your slaves, and you are an uncrowned sultana who captures us with her net of affection, faith, and sincerity. If everything has a peculiar spirit, an essence of life in this world of existence, then you must be our essence of life.

5

Jewishness and the Uncanny

Like "genocide," the term "Anti-Semitism" is of relatively recent origin, but the phenomenon is not. The essays in this section contribute to the study of anti-Semitism in its earlier as well as its nineteenth- and twentieth-century manifestations. Julius Lester explores the intertwined history of racism and anti-Semitism as rational dimensions of our civilization. "Anti-Semitism and racism are two of the organizing principles of Western civilization," he asserts. He is quick to remind us, however, that rational thought is not necessarily moral, and can serve evil purposes. The fusion of racial and anti-Semitic ideologies in Nazi Germany has deep roots in the Christian world, and Lester sketches the emergence of the early modern conceptions of man out of the sacred world of medieval Christianity, pointing to many of the markers that indicate "the unholy wedding of humanism with the degradation of Africans, Jews, women, Incas and Aztecs." In the modern period, Lester argues, the new and enabling ingredient is capitalism.

"Racism became a cornerstone of modern Western civilization because by suppressing Africans, women and Jews, European man suppressed in himself the human attributes which most threatened that brave new world he was building, a world in which the economic mode changed from feudalism to capitalism." In a powerfully sweeping concluding section, Lester then goes on to link this development with the emergence of the evils of the twentieth-century, which exemplify what Hannah Arendt called the "thoughtlessness" of monstrous injustices, including the effects of slavery, anti-Semitism and the life denying assaults on humanity they entail. We turn from Lester's overview to Frederick A. Busi's study of anti-Semitism in nineteenth-century France. Busi focuses on the thought of Henri-Roger Gougenot des Mousseaux (1805-1876) identifying numerous factors that can be seen as precursors of later anti-Semitic manifestations.

Among them are the economic, religious, and racial features of Gougenot's career that came to be embodied in his main publication in 1869, *Le Juif, le judaïsme et la judaïsation des peoples chrétiens.* Busi shows how Gougenot came to the pessimistic view that Jews, refusing to convert, would need to be exterminated like rats or "noxious microbes...bent on destroying Catholicism." In ways that would become all too familiar later, Gougenot blamed the Jews for myriad ills afflicting France. "What Gougenot did, Busi writes, "was to achieve a clever union of official church and state anti-Jewish animosity with more assertive forms of Judeophobia which could easily be connected to the extreme forms of anti-Semitism?" Gougenot died in 1876, but anti-Semites were borrowing from his work even before then and by the time of the Dreyfus affair in 1894, his influence was widespread, manifesting itself, for example, in the Protocols of the Elders of Zion and the vitriol of the Nazi ideologist Alfred Rosenberg, to justify what Gougenot called "our necessary violences" against the Jews.

Robert Schwartzwald is also concerned with France, through a study of the career of Father Marie-Alain Couturier (1897-1954), whose exemplary refutation of anti-Semitism stands in sharp contrast to the historical strain that Busi traces. Father Couturier's commitment to spiritual and intellectual liberty led him to work with artists for their genius, not their religion. As his life and the century progressed, he came to realize that "a culture of anti-Semitism [was] central to France's own undoing: this and not some presumed Jewish- Masonic-Bolshevik conspiracy, is at the heart of the moral bankruptcy that leads to the collapse of the Third Republic." Schwartzwald follows the evolution of Father Couturier's views from their early rural origins, through his involvement with the Action française and his rejection of it in the face of its collaboration with Hitler's demands.

Father Couturier arrived in New York City in January 1940 and spent the war years in North America. In Quebec in the early 1940's, Schwartzwald writes, "Couturier was particularly effective in helping shift sympathies among Catholics away from Vichy to the Free French by insisting upon the Nazi travesty of Christian principles." And in New York, having suffered rejection by his Dominican brothers, he still refused to succumb to the diminishment of prevailing stereotypes. Father Couturier maintained his Christian integrity by recognizing the potential fascist or racist in each of us and by acting in accordance with his choice of justice over authority and audacity over security. His life stands in sharp contrast to the ideologies of anti-Semitism that preoccupy the other essays in this section.

Susan Shapiro turns our attention to the history of a stereotype, the eternal, wandering Jew, Ahasverus as "a living corpse," an uncanny image. She begins by reminding us of a paradox, that the very success of Jewish assimilation fed the fantasy of perfidious, secret Jewish power. The representation of the Jew remains "unheimlich," unhomey, having no resting place. Taken up by such figures as the Hegelian Karl Gutzkow, the Wandering Jew is understood in both in negative terms, as the doomed rejecter of Christ, or in a positive reading, as pointing toward a final conversion to Christianity. The figure of the Wandering Jew is also taken up by Zionist writers, such as Leo Pinsker and Moses Hess, for whom the establishment of a national home will end the submission to Judeophobia that relegates the Jew to ghostlike status within European cultures. Shapiro then goes on to outline the manifestations and transformations of the image of the uncanny Jew in the twentieth century.

In Freud's 1919 essay, "The Uncanny," the image of the Jew is absent, and Shapiro argues that this absence indicates Freud's transformation of the image into his theorization of the place of the maternal and the death instinct in the experience of the uncanny. Freud thus reads "the uncanniness of the Jew into the very structures of the unconscious within everyman." Finally, in a condensed reading of French critical theory, Shapiro focuses on what Pinsker called the "inseparable companions," Judaism and anti-Semitism, questioning the responsibility of Jewish thinkers who take up such volatile images as the "Jewish Uncanny." In 1838, the left wing Hegelian thinker, Karl Gutzkow, dramatically presented the image of the Jew and Judaism as it was shaped by the "Jewish Question," that is, by the question of whether or not Jews should be politically emancipated and admitted as citizens to the modern nation-state.

In this instance, the question was raised in Germany by Gutzkow in the following terms: Ahasverus [the eternal, wandering Jew] is the tragic consequence of Jewish hopes. There is embodied so painfully in this individual just that which the Jews wish collectively for themselves. There is in Judaism despair because though they would gladly die, they cannot. Certainly, the stubborn clinging to life by the Jews is a tragedy among their misfortunes. A messianic hope, which cannot be relinquished by even the most enlightened and purified Jews, tethers them to a bleak existence.... For Judaism has never had the urge to self-destruction [*Selbstvernichtung*]. It has always been greedy to preserve and maintain itself for a triumphant future. Ahasverus' tragic fate is not his violent and unsuccessful search for death, but rather his exhausted dusk-watch, his outliving of himself, his obsolescence. Time itself always remains young: new peoples arise, new heroes, new empires. Only Ahasverus stays on a living corpse, a dead man who has not yet died.

This image of the Jewish people as a "living corpse" is a representation that haunts the very formulation and rising of the Jewish Question, not only—but especially—in Germany. Can the Jews as a people, as a nation, as a race, and/or as a religion be incorporated into the German nation-state? As indicated by the phrases that describe the Jews as an "Ahasverus..., a dead man who has not yet died," Gutzkow represents the tragedy of the Jews as the prolongation and obsolescence of their existence, not as their "search for death."

The representation of Jews as Uncanny may have been shaped in and through the "logic" of the Jewish Question, but that image has a history which that question both inaugurated and could not contain. We must pay attention not only to the "logic" of arguments, of questions and answers, but to the figural terms that shape and imaginatively locate and make possible this very logic. In order to approach the implication within the Jewish Question of the image of the Jew as Uncanny—that is, as occupying an indistinguishable and undecidable borderline between life and death—I will first rehearse this question in its German and French settings. I do so in order to demonstrate how its very cultural and political "logic" was both produced by the representation of Jews as uncanny others and how the contradictions of this logic further exacerbated the negative character of this image, producing ever more pernicious framings and "solutions" to the Jewish question. The contradictions of Jewish emancipation are very clearly and compactly set forth by Alain Finkielkraut in his book, The Imaginary Jew. I will quote selections from this text so as to frame my treatment of the history of the image of the "Uncanny Jew" in terms of these contradictions.

Finkielkraut describes how, in response to their emancipation in France—and as the "Acts of the Israelitish Deputies" attests—"everything in [Jewish] law that might mark them as strangers to the human community was cast aside." "They acquitted their debt by dejewifying themselves; the law, their law demanded they become mimics, for the advent of emancipation had placed them in France's debt." But what of the transgressors? The visible Jews those who stood out? Who spoke French with a bad accent? Who were nostalgic for the ghetto and rejected integration? And the incorrigibles who persisted in acting as if a Jewish nation might still exist? By unilaterally violating the rules of emancipation, they encouraged anti-Jewish sentiment and placed the safety of their coreligionists at risk; traitors twice over, they were inadequate as citizens of France and as Jews.

For the Israelites, acting Jewish in public could only be seen as a kind of dangerous sabotage.... The man of the past must be rooted out relentlessly: it's a question of life and death. The hunt demands a continual state of alert, for not to pursue him in others is an indirect admission that he still lives within us. The same pattern holds for the Israelite: his regeneration and recovery cannot be regarded as finished until he devotes himself to an undying hatred of traditional Jews. Judeophobia among the assimilated was all the more passionate; their social status was at stake, living as they did under the constant threat of being identified as Jews.... The only good Jew was an invisible Jew. The other, the visible Jew, was an obscene creature, indecent; morality as well as personal hygiene demanded that such an exhibitionist be shunned.

But, ironically, it was precisely this effacement and hidden ness of Jewishness that was most threatening for emancipated European Jewish communities. Again, as Finkielkraut suggests, Assimilation cannot be reduced to a fiasco pure and simple; it should perhaps be thought of as something more ironic, more diabolical yet: as a dreadful misunderstanding. Genocide [in WWII] was not imposed on the Jews in spite of their effort to assimilate, but in response to this very attempt. The more they hid their Jewishness, the more terrifying they became to others. As Jewish appearances gave less and less hint of ethnic background, the evils charged to Jews by anti-Semitic opinion grew worse and worse. Could these men of the Enlightenment ever have imagined that their increasing resemblance to the gentiles would arouse a hatred that ran so deep?... For the myth of Jewish omnipotence to take hold, the people of Zion first had to pass unnoticed, merge with the general populace. It took a Jew without qualities to fit the part of spy or conspirator.... Assimilation thus became a strange kind of trial in which the defendants completely misunderstood the indictment their judges had prepared. Assimilated Jews thought they were being charged with excessively Jewish behaviour, when it was their will to integration that was really the crime: the wary would only weaken their case in the very way they secured their defence. A kind of relentless mechanism had been set in place, turning every protestation of innocence into yet more evidence of guilt.

This pernicious logic is characteristic of the Jewish Question in Germany as well. As Paul Laurence Rose has importantly emphasized, "For nineteenth-century Germans, so unsure of their own 'Germanness,' the Jewish Question was ultimately the German Question. It was, in effect, another way of asking 'What is German': and receiving the satisfying answer— 'whatever is not Jewish.'" The success of the Jew in mimicking the German further threatened the German's ability to define himself as, precisely, not a Jew, ironically making 'jewification' (in a logic of 'contagion') both more pervasive and threatening because invisible, unlocatable and, thus, uncontainable. This contradiction at the heart of the Jewish question represents the two poles between which Jewish identity was stretched in the dialectics of modernity brought on by the enlightenment and emancipation and their aftermath.

Alas, this mimicry did not ultimately empower the subject but, as I have noted, rather, made the Jew who would be emancipated in the modern nation-state even more threatening and threatened. This no-win situation, I suggest, finds its figural condition and expression in the images and metaphors that shape the "Jewish Question." Indeed, the very problematic of Jewish visibility and invisibility were made visible through the imagistic lens by which the Jew was perceived and represented in the religious, philosophical, political, psychological, and aesthetic discourses of French and German modernity in particular. This figural "lens" is, as I have already suggested, that of the "Jewish Uncanny," that is, the representation of the Jew, Jewishness, and Judaism as Uncanny.

The Jewish Uncanny represents the Jew(s) as spectral, disembodied spirits lacking a national home and, thus, as unwelcome guests or aliens wandering into and within other peoples' homes, disrupting and haunting them, making them "Unheimliche," unhomey. Moses Hess wrote of the Jews, as "a soul without a body, wandering like a ghost through the centuries." The image of the already dead, but uncannily still present, Jews was a very prevalent one in discourses from Hegel and Heine to Gans (and other members of the Wissenschaft des Judentums) and Pinsker.

In some versions, the solution to the Jewish Question emphasized the invisibility and, indeed, the disappearance of the Jews, as is the case with Gutzkow, with whose quote I began this essay. Gutzkow writes further in these terms as follows: The Jews wander and find only shelter among you. Yet they have been long amongst us and strive to merge with us. Thus must now be exactly fulfilled the word of Christ that the Jews would wander in error for eternity and they should remain scattered over the whole earth. Pious Christians would fear that emancipation might deny this prophecy of Christ in an outrageous way. But in fact emancipation would for the first time directly split the Jews apart from one another, who until now have simply been scattered, and would fulfill the curse that was foreseen by Christ, namely that the Jews should cease for all eternity to be a people.

Arthur Schopenhauer likewise sought the disappearance of the Jews. He suggested that the solution to the Jewish Question was conversion to Christianity and intermarriage. Note the pronounced resonances with the first quote from Gutzkow with which I opened this essay: Ahasverus, the Wandering Jew, is nothing but the personification of the whole Jewish race… This pettifogging little nation, this John Lackland among the nations, is to be found all over the globe, nowhere at home and nowhere strangers.... It asserts its Jewish nationality with unprecedented stubborness... [but] lives parasitically on other nations... To bring an end in the gentlest manner to the tragicomedy, the best way is for marriages... between Jews and gentiles... Then, in the course of a hundred years, there will be only a very few Jews left, and soon the ghost will be exorcized. Ahasverus will be buried, and the chosen people will not know where their abode was. This desirable result, however, will be frustrated if the emancipation of the Jews is carried to the point of obtaining political rights…

While he opposed giving political rights to Jews, Schopenhauer did support the granting of civil rights to German Jews. One must be careful, however, not to assume that use of the same images of Jews necessitates identical positions on the Jewish Question. Ahasverus, the myth and representation of the Eternal or Wandering Jew, is a shared trope in both Gutzkow's and Schopenhauer's writings and their political stances are very close as well. But others, who use this trope, as I will presently demonstrate, reverse its meaning and its political consequences. Even the negative connotations of Ahasverus, which came to the fore in a series of early 17th-century chapbooks, were not uniformly—although they were most often—adopted.

The "positive" Christian reading of Ahasverus is that he is a sign of Christian faith in the second coming, at which point the Eternal Jew will finally find rest in his embracing of Jesus as Christ and his conversion to Christianity. Ahasverus, thus, is to be preserved as a part of, and a crucial witness to, the truth of Christianity. In its "negative" reading, Ahasverus becomes only the unloving and egoistic Jew who rejected Christ and was, therefore, cursed to wander ceaselessly and to find no rest, which was a sign of the Jew's depravity and anti-sociality. This "negative" Ahasverus is decidedly outside of the bounds of Christianity, the religion of love. Eliminating Ahasverus becomes, in this version, part of the triumph and fulfillment of this love.

The significance of the myth and image of Ahasverus, I suggest, is not only that it was in these writings negatively inflected, but that it was a way of representing the Unheimlichkeit of the Jews as an ancient problem, as a problem of the Jews' essential character, be that essence understood to derive from their national, religious, racial, or psychological character. The living death embodied by the Jews in the figure of Ahasverus—especially when messianic redemption (as in the first Gutskow quote) or Salvation in the second coming is no longer considered part of his myth—is fully negative. Unredeemed "living death" is, potentially, a threat to others in a way that such Uncanniness, a witness to ultimate redemption or salvation, is not. And, further, it is important to note that in all of the instances of Ahasverus cited in the context of the Jewish Question, it is specifically and always the male Jew's spectral "Unheimlichkeit" that is put to rest—

for Schopenhauer through intermarriage, conversion and assimilation, but not through political emancipation.

For other thinkers, the solution to the Jewish Question was precisely to heighten their profile as Jews in their own nation-state. Proposing a radically different position on emancipation than Gutzkow or Schopenhauer, the Zionist, Leo Pinsker, employed a remarkably similar figure to describe the condition of the Jews:

> The world saw in this people the Jews the uncanny [Unheimliche] form of one of the dead walking among the living. The ghostlike apparition of a living corpse, of a people without unity or organization, without land or other bonds of unity, no longer alive, and yet walking among the living—this spectral form without precedence in history, unlike anything that preceded or followed it, could but strangely affect the imagination of the nations.
>
> And if the fear of ghosts is something inborn, and has a certain justification in the psychic life of mankind, why be surprised at the effect produced by this dead but still living nation?... A fear of the Jewish ghost has passed down the generations and the centuries. First a breeder of prejudice, later in conjunction with other forces... it culminated in Judeophobia. Judeophobia is a variety of demonopathy with the distinction that it is not peculiar to particular races but is common to the whole of mankind, and that this ghost is not disembodied like other ghosts but partakes of flesh and blood, must endure pain inflicted by the fearful mob that imagines itself endangered.... It is this fear of ghosts, the mother of Judeophobia that has evoked this abstract; I might say Platonic hatred, thanks to which the whole Jewish nation is wont to be held responsible for the real or supposed misdeeds of its individual members, and to be libelled in so many ways, to be buffeted about so shamefully.

In employing the figure of the "Unheimliche" Jew, the medical doctor Pinsker diagnosed him as in a pathological, but curable, condition as a result of the incurable pathology of European "Judeophobia." Writing just prior to the turn of the century, the Russian Pinsker penned a manifesto in German, calling for the auto-emancipation of the Jews, in the wake of the failure of their emancipation and increasing anti-semitism in Europe. The building of a national home would, finally, put an end to their spectral, haunting diasporic status. Pinsker concludes his argument as follows:

> The Jews are not a living nation; they are everywhere aliens; therefore they are despised. The civil and political emancipation of the Jews is not sufficient to raise them in the estimation of the peoples. The proper, the only solution, is in the creation of a Jewish nationality, of a people living upon its own soil, the auto-emancipation of the Jews; their return to the ranks of the nations by the acquisition of a Jewish homeland..... That we may not be compelled to wander from one exile to another, we must have an extensive, productive land of refuge, a center which is our own..... The international Jewish question must have a national solution.

Ahad Ha 'Am, writing in 1902, about 20 years after Pinsker, drew out some of the implications of Pinsker's views in ways that seem prescient. They echo the contradictions of assimilation found in the writings of Finkielkraut and Rose. Ahad Ha' Am asks:

> Assimilate with the nations? If real assimilation be meant—the assimilation that reaches to the very soul and ends in annihilation—that is a kind of death which does not come of itself, and we do not wish to bring it on by our own efforts. But the surface assimilation which is the panacea advocated by a certain section of Jews can only make matters worse for us. Pinsker himself does not draw this conclusion in so many words; but it is a necessary consequence of the idea just mentioned. For, seeing that the source of anti-Semitism lies in our lack of a concrete national existence, which would compel the other nations to recognize in us a nation equal to themselves in status, it follows plainly that the more we assimilate—the more we imitate our surroundings and whittle away our national distinctiveness—the less concrete and the more spiritual will our national existence become; and the

more, therefore, will the ghost-fear which begets anti-Semitism grow in intensity.... It is fundamental to Pinsker's view that national equality is unattainable so long as we lack the concrete attributes of nationality. A nation which is a nation only in the spiritual sense is a monstrosity which the other nations cannot possibly regard as their compeer; it follows that they cannot recognize its title to demand the same rights as those enjoyed by the real nations.

By either being "completely incorporated into [the fabric of Europe]," which Eduard Gans—a proponent of Wissenschaft des Judentums—calls for, or by resurrecting or regenerating the body of the Jews by planting its seed again within its home soil, as Moses Hess proposes, the Jewish Question would be resolved. Hess, who is often considered the first modern Zionist, elicits the regeneration of the Jews in their national homeland by way of two very striking images. In the first image, "the soldiers of civilization, the French, are gradually sweeping away the dominance of the barbarians; and with their strong Herculean arms will roll off the tombstones from the graves of the supposedly dead peoples and the nations will reawaken once more." In the other image, Hess declared that:

The Jewish nation still preserves the fruitful seed of life, which, like the grains of corn found in the graves of Egyptian mummies, though buried for thousands of years, have never lost their power of productivity. The moment the rigid form in which it is enclosed is shattered, the seed, placed in the fertile soil of the present environment and given air and light, will strike root and prosper. For Hess, this rigid form or husk that needs to be broken is the classical Jewish Reformists' assimilationist desire to become German and, thereby, invisible as Jews. He was concerned as well with the rigidity of the Orthodox. But whereas he thought the rigid husk around the reformists had to be broken from the outside in the final, great cultural calamity in which they would disappear, the Orthodox husk had to be preserved to protect the nationalist seed within until such time as they could one again sow their land and return to life from the grave. The grains of corn in

Hess's second image, buried in Egyptian graves for thousands of years, like the seed that is again planted within its home soil in Hesse's first image, "have never lost their power of productivity." Egyptian mummies and graves signify absolute death and stasis. They also signified, for Hegel, entombment and belief in immortality.

Hegel thought the Jews lacking in belief in immortality and, thus, as failing to undertake—and as incapable of understanding the significance of—mummification. Thus, in locating the Jewish "grains of corn" in the graves of Egyptian mummies—but not as the mummies themselves—Hess makes his thought more compatible with that of Hegel, whose thought Hess admired. Jews may have sojourned in Egypt but, for both Hess and Hegel, they are not Egyptian. For Heinrich Heine, however, Jews are (sometimes) figured as embalmed: "Oh, those Egyptians—their handiwork defies time, their pyramids still stand immovable; their mummies are indestructible as ever. And just as indestructible is the mummy-nation that wanders over the face of the earth, wrapped in its age-old scroll of the law; a petrified piece of world-history—a spectre, which for a livelihood traffics in bills of exchange and old clothes."

The "emphasis on the Egyptian origins of Judaism [in the late 18th and early 19th centuries] suggested to many that the uncanny persistence of the Jewish corpse after the death of Judaism might be attributable to a process of mummification." But Heine (and in this he is more like Hess) also employs more positive images of the uncanniness of Jews and Judaism: "The Jews are a ghost who keeps guard over a treasure which was once entrusted to him. Thus sat this murdered people, this ghost-people, in its dark ghetto, and guarded there its Hebrew Bible." In both images, the Jews are closely connected to their texts: the "age-old scroll of the law" which is connected to death and mummification and the "Hebrew Bible," which it guards as a treasure with its life. This is a typical Wissenschaft des Judentums view as well of the respective value of these texts. The image of the wandering, "Eternal Jew" is made to intersect even more fully with that of the uncanny, ghostly Jew in some of Hess's other writings. Resonating with tropes common in those writings of the Wissenschaft des Judentums, as I have already indicated, and informed by Hegel, in these passages Hess suggests the different directions taken later in the divergent writings of Pinsker and Franz Rosenzweig, both of which, however, are also marked by the association of Jewishness and unheimlichkeit. Eventually, the Jews carried their fermentation into humanity at large. They have been criticized for the fact that most of them, during Christ's lifetime, thought only about the re- establishment of their tiny state and did not rise to the sublimity of the great ideas of Christ... It should, however, not surprise us that the people could not conceive the sublime idea—after all, in our own time, most people do not yet understand this idea. Do not look down in distaste at the "Eternal Jew."

Do not forget that your own hopes for the Second Coming of your own Saviour met with the same fate as the one that befell the Jewish messianic beliefs. It is true that once the Jews gave up their idea of the future, and rejected Christ, they became like a lifeless mummy. Since then the Israelites have been afflicted with the curse of lack of change [Stabilitat]; ghostlike, they have wandered over a world inspired by God, unable to die or to be revived alike. The rejuvenating element of Judaism, the messianic belief, has been extinguished and their quest for redemption, after they had been mistaken in the nature of true salvation, became a barren abstraction.

But did not the same happen to the Christians as far as their belief in the triumph of Christ is concerned? This hope had inspired the middle Ages. But after Christ proved victorious on earth, the Christians pushed their victory from earth to heaven, as they were unable to understand the new age. The rejuvenating idea of the Christian Church was also extinguished: the hope for eternity and for the Resurrection of the Lord occupied in Judaism—as an appendage which is dispensable, which can be subsumed or pushed indefinitely into the future. Although both Judaism and the Jews are regarded by the Christian West as static and unchanging after and because of their rejection of Jesus as the Christ, the Jews are actually the source of movement and change. As Schlomo Avineri explains, As Judaism formed the transition between the Oriental and the Occidental, Judaism possessed within itself an element of movement; it is characterized by a permanent unhappiness about the world as it is, as dissatisfaction with existing conditions, a perennial quest for a better world, an eternal dream of looking for new horizons. This is Jewish messianism as understood by Hess. Against the traditional Christian view, which saw post- Biblical Judaism as a fossilized code of static laws and frozen regulations, Hess sees Judaism as a constant element of ferment, as movement, as the dialectical moment in history. Indeed, Judaism—in a trope that will be repeated in later Jewish thought, most notably, that of Hermann Cohen—is the source of fermentation in the West: The Jews had therefore to become the thorn in the side of Occidental humanity. Just as the Orient needed a Chinese wall, so as not to be disturbed in its static existence, so the Jews are the element of fermentation in Western humanity and have been destined, from earliest times, to force upon it the element of movement and change.

A number of questions arise from these formulations and associations of the Jews and change. Most notably, how does this association transform Hess' understanding of Hegel's dialectic? Guided by the world-historical Spirit [Geist], what has Hess's revised view of messianism—both Jewish and Christian—to do with this transformed view of dialectic? If for Hegel the Jews were an anachronism and associated with a certain stasis—a people living in the present whose historical contribution, however, had already been made and whose epoch was decidedly past—how does Hess' association of the Jews with fermentation change Hegel's system? Is Hess turning it inside out by reassociating the Jews with the messianic dimension—perhaps, even the very medium of the movement—of history itself?

While the above quoted texts are from Hess's The European Triarchy, by the time he writes Rome and Jerusalem, Hess has not only turned Hegel's system inside out, he has reversed its movement in a kind of "messianic" return to the

Jewish state. Hess's Jewish nationalism both extend Hegel's support of Jewish emancipation and turn it on its head, locating it now not in a European nation, but in the Holy lands itself. The Jews are emancipated there not as individuals alone, but as Jews, as a nation. The Jewish "quest for redemption" brings them back most properly not to an other-worldly faith, but to a return to the rebirth of the Jewish nation in their ancient land. It is this that will rejuvenate them from their ghostlike lack of change.

The European Triarchy is worth considering again, now more closely: Do not look down in distaste at the "Eternal Jew." ... It is true that once the Jews gave up their idea of the future, and rejected Christ, they became like a lifeless mummy. Since then the Israelites have been afflicted with the curse of lack of change [Stabilitat]; ghostlike, they have wandered over the world inspired by God, unable to die or to be revived alike. The rejuvenating element of Judaism, the messianic belief, has been extinguished and their quest for redemption, after they had been mistaken in the nature of true salvation, became a barren abstraction.

Here, Hess seems to accept the uncanny, ghostlike and "lifeless mummy" character of the Jews since they "gave up their idea of the future." In this, as I have noted, he seems to repeat some of the tropes of Jewish stasis that both Christianity and the Wissenschaft des Judentums movement associated with post-biblical—especially, rabbinic and medeival—Judaism. In particular, as I have shown, the image of Jewish mummification resonates with that of Heine and, in its association of Egypt and stasis, with Hegel. The inability either to die or be revived aptly describes their location in Hegel's (and others') view of the Jews as both anomaly and anachronism. The Jews, since they rejected Christ, were cursed, as in the legend of the Eternal or wandering Jew. Here this legend is explicitly further elaborated in terms of their ghostliness. However, the context of these remarks is framed first by the exhortation to his Christian readership not to "look down in distaste at the 'Eternal Jew.'"

Why? Because, according to Hess, "the same thing happen[ed] to the Christians as far as their belief in the triumph of Christ is concerned." Hess claims that just as in Judaism "the messianic belief... became a barren abstraction," so in Christianity, "the hope for eternity and for the Resurrection of the Lord... [came to be treated] as an appendage which is dispensable, which can be subsumed or pushed indefinitely into the future." The remarks which frame the close of this paragraph, however, point beyond not only this paragraph and its argument, but even beyond this text to that of Rome and Jerusalem. There, the frame is widened or reframed, now as a redemptive return to the national homeland and away from salvation as a "barren abstraction." This "return to history" is the ferment of the Jews.

It is, as Avineri suggests, "the dialectical moment in history." Pinsker later takes a similar position in his, "Auto-emancipation." And while—like Hegel and unlike Hess, Rozensweig affirms the eternal, stasis-like character of the Jew—Rozensweig also works with the image of the Jew as wandering, ghostlike, and eternal, and emphasizes the Jewish temporal relation to the messianic as always pointing toward redemption. In this later characteristic, Rozensweig's position is like that of Hess' reversal of Hegel on the Jew's contribution to messianism as precisely not past. These are but a very few examples of the image and trope of the "Jewish Uncanny." The Jews are here represented as always already dead but, somehow, and problematically, still apparently present (Schopenhauer) or as apparently dead and buried, but actually awaiting regeneration, resurrection, rebirth, or redemption (Hess or Pinsker). But either way, what appears to be the case is not.

The Jew is on the border between life and death, life in death, death in life. But which one is it? Embedded in this image is this very ambiguity and undecidability. It is as this border-state, this spectral and ghost-like condition, that I think the trope of the "Jewish Uncanny" is both repressed and returns in Sigmund Freud's writings, especially in his 1919 essay, "das Unheimliche" ("The Uncanny"). This may seem an odd suggestion to make as Freud does not explicitly mention Jews as Uncanny in this essay. He even repeatedly states that the Uncanny itself does not have as much to do with uncertainty as to whether something is living or dead, as much as it has to do—in Freud's description of Frederich Schelling's terms—with that which "ought to have remained hidden and secret, and yet comes to light."

Freud draws the reader's attention toward the figure of the Sandman, in E. T. A Hoffman's tale of that name and to the oedipus complex and away from the figure of Olympia, the automaton, and his seeming confusion of her with a living young woman. While there are connections drawn between castration and circumcision in Freud's corpus that trouble the association of the Uncanny and the Jew, this phallic reading takes account only of the oedipal themes of Freud's "das Unheimliche." I agree with some interpreters that we, the readers, have had "sand thrown in our eyes" and that the exclusively oedipal interpretation fails to contain the many different examples which proliferate throughout Freud's essay.

These and other interpreters demonstrate as well that "das Unheimliche" is an uncannily hybrid and heterological text, close interpretations of which unravel Freud's attempt to master the Uncanny in terms of the Oedipal complex. Instead of the predominance of the paternal, I suggest it is the maternal that haunts Freud's essay and that it is the death instinct—rather than the more restricted oedipal economy—that dominates "das Unheimliche." I can only here indicate—because of limitations of space— that it is these two factors, the maternal and the death instinct, which condition the relation of the Uncanny and Jewishness in Freud's essay. While, as I have already noted, Freud explicitly directs our attention away from the question of intellectual uncertainty and from the uncanniness of the borderline living/dead, I think that it is precisely this trope of Jewishness that Freud is both displacing and attempting to reenvision. Writing during WWI, Freud attempts to embed the Jew (and Jewishness) within a universalized male subject, making the Unheimliche (the Uncanny) that which is always already in—and originating from—the Heim, the family, the familiar.

Ameliorating (or exorcizing) the Jewish problem by reading the uncanniness of the Jew into the very structures of the unconscious within everyman, the Uncanny may thereby be seen as generated by the German Heim itself (as both family and nation-state) and not by a stranger, an Ahasverus wandering into and within the Heim from the outside. Especially after WWI, unheimliche others might thereby be reincorporated into the [national] Heim, the Heimat. Specifically, the Jew as the Uncanny other, the haunting ghost, might be put to rest by universalizing the site and origins of the Unheimlich within (and not as split off from, or as outside of) the Heim. Freud's use of the trope of the Uncanny, thus, offers a third response to the "Jewish Question"—not Schopenhauer's conversion and intermarriage of Jews as a way of accomplishing their disappearance nor Pinsker's or Hess's Zionism in which the Jews become ever more visible by either emancipating themselves or by awaiting national redemption at the hands of Europe, and France in particular.

Freud turns the trope of the Uncanny from the Jew to everyman, returning the spectre to its familial origin in the mother's body, her "womb," the first home. The Uncanny is, thereby, displaced from the Jewish male and grafted onto the body of woman, especially as mother. The primary anxiety which produces this sense of "unheimlichkeit" is located in this way not in racial terms, but explicitly in sexual difference. If, as has been argued, the Jew's body was in the fin-de-siecle negatively feminized and, thereby, made other than everyman, this feminine difference was in "das Unheimliche" displaced and reinscribed onto women's bodies.

In this way, Freud reinstituted the male Jews' masculinity, making him capable of the Bildung and Sittlichkeit necessary for full emancipation. And if, as I have suggested, Freud is performing such a covert reincorporation of the Jew within the (national) home, he would hardly flag such a performance. Again, I cannot here more fully make this case, but part of its persuasiveness depends on reading Freud's essay in the context of previous images of the Uncanny Jew as well as those in works of his contemporaries, such as Franz Rosenzweig, which were written as well (even if only in part) during WWI. The Uncanny, the Unheimliche, has consistently been associated with the feminine, with passivity and lack. For Pinsker, it is "the fear of ghosts" that is "the mother of Judeophobia." And, of course, Freud treats the Uncanny as a form of homesickness or nostalgia, of the desire to "return home" to the mother's womb. Both Freud and, especially, Pinsker found the Uncanny unsettling and each in his own way sought to put the Unheimlichkeit of the Jews to rest. Pinsker sought to create a national home for the Jewish people which had "no fatherland of its own, though many motherlands; no center of focus or gravity, no government of its own, no official representation." The Jew, he goes on to say, "homes everywhere, but [is] nowhere at home.... Not only is he not a native in his own home country, but he is also not a foreigner; he is, in very truth, the stranger par excellence.

He is regarded as neither friend nor foe but an alien, of whom the only thing known is that he has no home." For Pinsker, once the ghost is put to rest in the founding of a national Jewish home, the Uncanny disappears. "Home" (Heim) and the "Uncanny" (Unheimliche) are opposing terms. This is not the case for Freud. He puts to rest the Ahasverus myth, in which the Jew wanders into the homes of others from the outside, by locating the origin of the Unheimlich within the home itself. Even the very term "Unheimlich" is understood by Freud to derive from its apparent opposite, that is, Heimlich. As he says, "Thus, heimlich is a word the meaning of which develops towards an ambivalence, until it finally coincides with its opposite, unheimlich. Unheimlich is in some way or other a sub-species of heimlich." That which is secret, geheim, and is considered part of the privacy of the home, the heimich, develops as "something hidden and dangerous" into the uncanny, the un-heimlich.

Freud interprets "Schelling's definitions of the uncanny as something that ought to have been kept concealed but which has nevertheless come to light" as related to the repression of the familiar, of that which originates from within the home, the feminine, the heimliche. Freud, unlike Pinsker, does not eliminate the Uncanny, but relocates it, as I have explained, displacing it from the Jewish male to the woman's body, from Ahasverus to the hearth. In this way, the Uncanny becomes a feature of the experience of every man, including the Jew who, thus, becomes an Everyman and is incorporated into the nation-state, the heim or heimat. For Rosenzweig, as for Pinsker and Freud, the Uncanny is associated with the feminine, passivity, and lack. And yet, Rosenzweig differs significantly from them in his treatment of the Uncanniness of the Jews. Unlike both of these thinkers, Rosenzweig emphasizes the Unheimlichkeit of the Jews.

As a Holy people, they are Uncanny to the nations. This Uncanniness is part of their very witness. The Jewish Question, for Rosenzweig, is formed and answered very differently than for Pinsker. The Jews, according to Rosenzweig, are not a people like other peoples. Jewish roots are genealogical, within the "blood," not within the soil. The Jews are not a land-oriented people. Even the Holy land is not theirs, but God's, the Holy One. He writes, to the eternal people, home never is home in the sense of land, as it is to the peoples of the world who plough the land and live and thrive on it, until they have all but forgotten that being a people means something besides being rooted in a land. The eternal people have not been permitted to while away time in any home. It never loses the untrammeled freedom of a wanderer.... And so even when it has a home, this people, in recurrent contrast to all other peoples on earth, is not allowed full possession of that home. It is only 'a stranger and a sojourner.'... The holiness of the land removed it from the people's spontaneous reach while it could still reach out for it. This holiness increases the longing for what is lost, to infinity, and so the people can never be entirely at home in any other land.

And that land is not theirs but God's. Not a Zionist like Pinsker or Ahad Ha-Am, Rosenzweig sees the Jews as an eternal people precisely because of their uncanniness, living "beyond [the] external life" of the nations, barred from [its] own soil and [its] own language..... The eternal people buy its eternity at the cost of its temporal life.... For this people, the moment petrifies and stands between unincreased past and immovable future....While the myth of peoples changes incessantly... here the myth becomes eternal and is not subject to change.... And so... we see... in the relation to its own history, what we saw before in its relation to language and land, that this people are denied a life in time for the sake of life in eternity. It cannot experience the history of the nations creatively and fully. Its position is always somewhere between the temporal and the holy, always separated from the one by the other. And so, in the final analysis, it is not alive in the sense the nations are alive: in a national life manifest on this earth, in a national territory, solidly based and staked out on the soil. It is alive only in that which guarantees it will endure beyond time, in that which pledges it everlastingness, in drawing its own eternity from the sources of the blood.

As these quotations from the Star of Redemption demonstrate, Rosenzweig incorporates the Unheimlichkeit of the Jews into his view of their role and purpose. As the eternal people, the Jews are God's portion. It is this, and not the Christian explanation of the punishment of the Ahasverus—the Wandering or Eternal Jew—for rejecting Christ, that accounts for their Uncanniness. What is viewed by the nations as central—especially the possession of their own land, everyday language, and national history—is not valued in the same way for Jews. From the perspective of eternity the lives of the nations appear vain and transient. The real home of the Jews is in the Holy, in eternity. All other homes, even that of the holy land, are not fully their own and their inhabiting of these lands can only be partial. And as with the land, so too with language.

As Rosenzweig says, "The holiness of the holy language which the Jew employs only for prayer does not permit his life to put out roots into the soil of a language of its own. So far as his language is concerned, the Jew feels always he is in a foreign land, and knows that the home of his language is in the region of the holy language, a region everyday speech can never invade." Neither Pinsker nor Freud would be satisfied with this revaluation of the Jewish Uncanny. For Rosenzweig preserves just that separateness and otherness of the Jews that they would have erased, the one by normalizing the people as a nation with its own land (Pinsker) and the other by dissolving the racially marked difference of the Jews in terms of a more primary and constitutive notion of sexual difference (Freud). And Rosenzweig does so by interpreting home and heimlichkeit in terms of the Holy and eternity, thereby making the Jews inescapably and purposely Unheimlich.

In this way, he appears to confirm anti-Semitic views of Jews as negatively uncanny, as defined by lack, as not having a national land, language and history. At the same time, Rosenzweig affirms a different sense of the Unheimlichkeit of the Jews, transvaluing it in terms of the difference between the value of the order of temporality and that of the eternal. One understanding of the Uncanny is, at it were, the uncanny mirror image of the other. How does one decide between them? Which image casts the light from which the other gains its reflection, or are both reflections of equal status and truth? Are the Jews a petrified or an eternal people? In a way, Rosenzweig might claim that the Jews are both petrified and eternal, but that only the Jews can understand, through the witness of their lives, their own eternity.

There is an impassable chasm between the view of non-Jews and of Jews on this matter. This is why the Jews suffer in history, even in the modern nation-state, as they fulfill their witness of pointing to the not-yet character of redemption. Anti-Semitism would, thus, seem unavoidable. In the messianic time will anti-Semitism's negative Uncanny be finally understood in light of the Holy and the eternity of the Jews? Or will Jews, having fulfilled their mission, disappear? What are we to make of this complementarity between Jewishness, Judaism, and its supplement or Uncanny double, anti-Semitism? Pinsker seems to have thought that, at least before the making of a national home for the Jews, these two would necessarily coexist. "In this way have Judaism and anti-Semitism passed for centuries through history as inseparable companions. Like the Jewish people, the real wandering Jew, anti-Semitism, too seems as if it would never die. He must be blind indeed who will assert that the Jews are not the chosen people, the people chosen for universal hatred."

Since its formative development with the advent of the Jewish Question in the emancipation, to its so called, "Final Solution" in the terrible literalizing of this image in the manufacture in the Shoah of the "living-dead"[the muselmaner], the image of the Uncannny Jew has, as it were, had a kind of "afterlife." The trope of the Jewish Uncanny and images of Jews as uncanny are evident in explicitly post-Holocaust fiction and memoirs as well as in contemporary novels about Jewish identity. But it has perhaps been most prevalent and influential in its appearance in contemporary French critical theory, from the writings of Maurice Blanchot and Jean-Francois Lyotard to those of Jacques Derrida, Edmond Jabes and Emmanuel Levinas. Most of these writers treat the figure of Jewish wandering, exile, and nomadism, a number of them doubling this figure with that of the writer.

But what I want to focus on here, in moving toward the conclusion of this essay, is how Judaism, Jewishness, and anti-semitism are treated as intertwined topics in some of these texts. For the questions I raised in relation to Rosenzweig's views of the Uncanniness of the Jews and Pinsker's pointing to Judaism and anti-Semitism as "inseparable companions" remain and must be further addressed, if not resolved.

In The Infinite Conversation, Blanchot writes, Anti-Semitism, in this sense, is in no way accidental; it gives a figure to the repulsion inspired by the Other, the uneasiness before what comes from afar and elsewhere: the need to kill the Other, that is, to submit to the all powerfulness of death what cannot be measured in terms of power. One could perhaps say that anti-Semitism has three characteristics: (1) it turns all the "positive" values of Judaism into negatives and, first of all, the primary affirmation of the distance that is "infinite," irreducible, impassable (even when it is passed over), with which Judaism confronts us; (2) it transforms into fault (into an ethically and socially condemnable reality) this being-negative to which it reduces the Jew; (3) it does not restrict itself to a theoretical judgment, but calls for the actual suppression of the Jews in order better to exercise against them the principle of denial with which it has invested their image.

A denial so absolute, it is true, that it does not cease to reaffirm the relation with the infinite that being-Jewish implies....The anti-Semite, at grips with the infinite, thus commits himself to a limitless movement of refusal. No, truly, excluding the Jews is not enough, exterminating them is not enough; they must also be struck from history, removed from the books through which they speak to us, just as the presence that inscribed speech is must finally be obliterated: the speech before and after every book and through which, from the farthest distance where all horizon is lacking, man has already turned toward man—in a word, destroy "autrui."

A number of questions haunt this text, only some of which I will raise in conclusion. Can the two questions of Judaism and anti-Semitism be separated or are they, as Blanchot suggests, rather one—not only political, but metaphysical—Jewish Question? I observe... that anti-Semites, too, seek fundamentally only to avoid the metaphysical exigency that Judaism poses to each of us by way of Jewish existence, and that is in order better to suppress this question that they want to suppress all Jews.... To neglect this aspect of anti-Semitism is to renounce coming to grips with its gravity, to renounce finding it in one of its roots, and therefore to refuse to see what is at stake when, in the world, in whatever form it may take, anti-Semitism affirms and strengthens itself.

Is this a "universal problem," or can Judaism and/or Jewishness separate itself from the metaphysics of Europe and its anti-Semitism? But is this not precisely the question at stake in all of this: the relation of Judaism, Jewishness, and the West? Can and must they be thought of separately or are they always together? What if we cannot separate these questions? Would, then, the discourse of anti-Semitism define Jewishness (in, for example, contemporary critical theory) the way for Jean-Paul Sartre the anti-Semite's gaze fixes and defines the Jew? Whether these discourses in principle can be separated or not, many Jewish thinkers have taken up, turned, and transformed anti-Semitic images such as the Jewish Uncanny as part of their representation of Judaism and Jewishness.

What are the responsibilities of these Jewish—and other non-Jewish—writers and what are the consequences of the images they employ? Some seem to treat these metaphors, images, and tropes with an, as it were, unbearable lightness. How, then, to account for their gravity? Can the instability and volatility of these images—in this case, that of the "Jewish Uncanny"—be directed and contained? Or do the images have a power that rules and persists beyond and despite authorial intent? It seems clear, however, whatever the response to these questions, that once having been raised in these terms and images, the "Jewish Question" cannot be put to rest but continues to haunt our discourses of self, of other, of nation, of religion, of identity and identification.

"Starting with modernity, we have entered an era of production of the Other. It is no longer a question of killing, of devouring or seducing the Other, of facing him, of competing with him, of loving or hating the Other. It is first of all a matter of producing the Other. The Other is no longer an object of passion but an object of production." Jean Baudrillard "The void which opens up in the realm of the Mothers is the emptiness of the abject. Kristeva describes it as that position in the psychogeography of the individual in which neither subject nor object exists but rather the pure movement of splitting, the very creation of positional itself." Helga Geyer-Ryan.

The uncanny moment of accounting (of bringing to terms, of "adding up") for all terms of a series, can never be reached—that is precisely the moment of the splitting of the uncanny from the sublime. The incalculabilities of the sublime must of necessity in any system change registers to another 'system' of accounting procedures (which must more properly be called a-counting, as in a-nomos, or an irregularity or exception in the law). The linear checks and balances (which the sublime always runs past the available margins) no longer seems to be a stable place-holding system ('system' always implying overt articulation, the possibility of the extension of that articulation to arenas not presently under consideration, and the concomitant necessity to convert everything into articulable elements; while over-articulation produces the sublime, so too does under-articulation—not the uncanny—both being moments along a register of accounting and, eventually, production.

The uncanny is not a telos for production, as is the sublime, but a Something Else which begins to manifest in modernist society, a component of which is unassimilable trauma, a wounding which cannot be 'accounted' for. However this is not to reduce the uncanny to a psychoanalytic moment, rather the reverse. As Mladen Dolar has it, "Psychoanalysis was the first to point out systematically the uncanny dimension pertaining to the very project of modernity, not in order to make it disappear, but in order to maintain it, to hold it open...what is currently called postmodernism is a new consciousness about the uncanny as a fundamental dimension of modernity. It doesn[1]t imply a going beyond the modern, but rather an awareness of its internal limit, its split, which was there from the outset."

More particularly, the arrival (and dominance) of the spectacular uncanny in modernism can be specifically attributed to the Œdiscovery[1] by western explorers of the various others that that have since come to haunt western discourse (if not technique). The "western world" has from the beginning been defined by its (largely unavowed) relations with its conquered/converted others, whether Moorish, Jewish, African, or tribal (any of the Americas). And more specific still, since all the above examples can be held at arms length by cultural considerations, the arrival of feminist discourse epitomizes the nature of the uncanny, arriving imminently, in the midst of.

The central placement of the feminine in the uncanny was of course not lost on Freud but who converted it into a species of vagina dentata, thereby confirming yet another western male attempt by an assimilated (Jewish) other to impound the uncanny and put it to work, to some productive use value, perhaps the number one marker for western ethics/aesthetics/economy etc. The psychoanalytic impounding is another attempt at creating technique for the production of labor intensive activity, a labor and fecundity crudely approximating that of the Original Female and working ever since to displace, delete, and virtual that Garden. A witch? A satanist? Possessed? Gifted? Used of God? Whatever you say, the evidence certainly suggests Mother Shipton was the closest thing to a prophetess that England had for unnumbered generations.

Of her life we know some, not much. Mother Shipton, sometimes called "the Yorkshire Sybil" was reputedly born Ursula Sontheil (or Southill) in 1488 in Norfolk, England (supposedly in the cave of Knaresborough), and died in 1561, burnt, we are told, at the stake. Her mother Agatha was well known for her exceptional powers. Ursula, too, exhibited prophetic and psychic abilities from an early age. At 24, married to one Toby Shipton, she eventually became known as Mother Shipton.

Many of her visions came true within her own lifetime and in subsequent centuries. I first learned of her through an old time Holy Roller preacher, Bishop Whitlock, in Lewiston, California. But with all the Y2K hoopla, her fame seems enigmatically to be spreading. These rare verses from Mother Shipton seem to have prophetic indications for our times, and while open to interpretation, they show this woman to have been uncannily prescient. "This was given to Laurent under the Tree in Athens, Georgia by Tim Mills in October, 1944. From an article in the Banner-Herald, Athens, and GA Monday, May 23, 1938:

We are in receipt of an alleged prophecy written five hundred years ago by Mother Shipton and vouched for by J.H. Phillips, of Ashdown, Arkansas.

Many of the prophecies have come true and on the suggestion of the owner of the copy of the prophecy, we are giving space to its publication." So timely it's almost spooky. Some people seem to believe the prophetic age passed with the Age of the Apostles (only to return with the Age of Aquarius?) Here is a prophecy written 500 years ago by a woman. Read and see if you can suggest how she could have improved it if she had written it this month. Before reading it, please undertake to transport yourself back across five centuries and live when there were no steamships, no steam railways, no sewing machines, no cook stoves, no radios, no automobiles, no flying machines, no submarines, and none of the many other inventions so common today.

Because of the uncanny manner in which the prophecies of Mother Shipton have been coming to pass during the century past, considerable attention has been attracted to this strange creature of five centuries ago, even those who have in the past scoffed at the weird predictions of this woman are now stirred by curiosity to wonder what will occur next in this direction. Historically, a note of warning might be offered. The newly "discovered" prophecies of Mother Shipton which appeared in 1862 are said to be clear forgeries. Not so these (above), which, so far as we can tell, are authentic – and probably original, except for spelling, punctuation and capitalization. We understand these were first published in England in 1641. The first biography of Mother Shipton came out in 1667, by Richard Head.

6

Circumcision, Abjection and the Uncanny Mother

In the Origin of the Idea of God, Father W. Schmidt and his colleagues have found it necessary to distinguish three basic types or stages of primitive society. The first is that of the simplest peoples knows to the science of ethnology: the little Yahgans (or Yamana) of the southernmost channels and coves of rugged Tierra del Fuago, an number of extremely primitive, scattered tribes of Patagonia and Central California, the Caribou Eskimo of northern Canada, the Pygmies of the Congo and of the Andaman Islands, and the Kurnai of South-eastern Australia. The ethnological circumstances of these humble hunting, fishing, and collecting peoples do not give rise to either a strong patriarchal or a strong matriarchal emphasis; rather, and essential equality prevails between the sexes, each performing its appropriate tasks without arrogating to itself any special privileges or peculiar rights to command.

The ceremonies of initiation at puberty are not confined to the boys and men, nor separated into male and female rites, but are nearly identical for the two sexes. Nor do the rites involve any physical deformation or the communication of mystical secrets. They are simply concentrated courses of education for adolescents, to the end of making good fathers and mothers of the initiates. Special tribal or group interests do not stand in the foreground of the teaching, since the tribal feeling in such groups is not greatly developed—the typical social unit being merely a cluster of twenty to forty parents and children, whose main social problem is hardly more than that of living harmoniously together, gathering food enough to eat during the day, and inventing pleasant games to play together after dark.

The second stage or type of primitive society recognized by this culture-historical school of ethnology is that of the large, totemistic hunting groups, with their elaborately developed clan systems, age classes, and tribal traditions of ritual and myth. Examples of such peoples are abundant on the plains of North America and the pampas of South America, as well as in the deserts of Australia. Their rites of initiation are secret. Women are excluded; physical mutilations and ordeals are carried sometimes to almost incredible extremes, and they culminate generally in circumcision.

Moreover, there is considerable emphasis placed on the role and authority of the men, both in the religious and in the political organization of the symbolically articulated community. Not infrequently, the circumcision of the boys is matched by comparable operations on the girls (artificial or ceremonial defloration, enlargement of the vagina, removal of the labia minora, partial or complete clitoridectomy, etc.), but in such cases the two systems of ceremonial—the male and the female—are kept separate, and the women do not gain through their rites any social advantage over the men. On the contrary, there is a distinct one-sidedness in favour of the male in these highly organized hunting societies, the influence of the women being confined—when it exists at all—to the domestic sphere.

The legend of the lodge (Hain) of the men's secret society: "In the days when all the forest was evergreen, before 'Kerrhprrh' the parakeet painted the autumn leaves red with the colour from his breast, before the giants 'Kwonyipe' and 'Chashkilchesh' wandered through the woods with their heads above the tree-tops; in the days when 'Krren' (the sun) and 'Kreeh' (the moon) walked the earth as man and wife, and many of the great sleeping mountains were human beings: in those far-off days witchcraft was known only to the women of Ona-land. They kept their own particular Lodge, which no man dared approach.

The girls, as they neared womanhood, were instructed in the magic arts, learning how to bring sickness and even death to all those who displeased them. "The men lived in abject fear and subjection. Certainly they had bows and arrows with which to supply the camp with meat, yet, they asked, what use were such weapons against witchcraft and sickness? This tyranny of the women grew from bad to worse until it occurred to the men that a dead witch was less dangerous than a live one. They conspired together to kill off all the women; and there ensued a great massacre, from which not one woman escaped in human form.

"Even the young girls only just beginning their studies in witchcraft were killed with the rest, so the men now found themselves without wives. For these they must wait until the little girls grew into women. Meanwhile the great question arose: How could men keep the upper hand now they had got it? One day, when these girl children reached maturity, they might band together and regain their old ascendancy. To forestall this, the men inaugurated a secret society of their own and banished for ever the women's Lodge in which so many wicked plots had been hatched against them.

No woman was allowed to come near the 'Hain,' under penalty of death. To make quite certain that this decree was respected by their womenfolk, the men invented a new branch of Ona demonology: a collection of strange beings—drawn partly from their own imaginations and partly from folk-lore and ancient legends—who would take visible shape by being impersonated by members of the Lodge and thus scare the women away from the secret councils of the 'Hain.' It was given out that these creatures hated women, but was well-disposed towards men, even supplying them with mysterious food during the often protracted proceedings of the Lodge. Sometimes, however, these beings were short-tempered and hasty.

Their irritability was manifested to the women of the encampment by the shouts and uncanny cries arising from the 'Hain,' and, it might be the scratched faces and bleeding noses with which the men returned home when some especially exciting session was over." [Descriptions of the various monsters deleted.] The mythological 'apologia' offered by the men of the Ona tribe for their outrageous lodge was marvellously close, as the reader may have noted, to that attributed to Adam by the patriarchal Hebrews in their Book of Genesis; namely, that if he had sinned, it was the woman who had done so first.

And the angry Lord of Israel—conceived in a purely masculine form—is supposed to have allowed a certain value to this excuse; for he then promptly made the whole race of woman subject to the male. "I will greatly multiply your pain in childbearing," the Lord God is declared to have announced; "in pain you shall bring forth children, yet your desire shall be for your husband, and he shall rule over you."

A very different course of development is to be traced, however, in the sphere of the tropical gardening cultures, where a third type or stage of social organization matured that was almost completely antithetical to that of the hunting peoples. For in these areas it was the women, not the men, who enjoyed the magico-religious and social advantage, they having been the ones to effect the transition from plant-collectors of roots, berries, grubs of various kinds, frogs, lizards, bugs, and other delicacies. Societies of the second type evolved in areas where an abundance of large game occasioned a Herculean development of the dangerous art of the hunt; while those of type three took form where the chief sources of nutriment were the plants.

Here it was the women who showed themselves supreme: they were not only the bearers of children but also the chief producers of food. By realizing that it was possible to cultivate, as well as to gather, vegetables, they had made the earth valuable and they became, consequently, its possessors. Thus they won both economic and social power and prestige, and the complex of the matriarchy took form said an Abyssinian woman: "How can a man know what a woman's life is? A woman's life is quite different from a man's. God has ordered it so. A man is the same from the time of his circumcision to the time of his withering. He is the same before he has sought out a woman for the first time, and afterwards. But the day when a woman enjoys her first love cuts her in two. She becomes another woman on that day. The man is the same after his first love as he was before.

The woman is from the day of her first love another. That continues so all through life. The man spends a night by a woman and goes away. His life and body are always the same. The woman conceives. As a mother she is another person than the woman without child. She carries the print of the night nine months long in her body. Something grows. Something grows into her life that never again departs from it. She is a mother. She is and remains a mother even though her child dies, though all her children die. For at one time she carried the child under her heart. And it does not go out of her heart ever again. Not even when it is dead. And this the man does not know; he knows nothing. He does not know the difference before love and after love, before motherhood and after motherhood. He can know nothing.

Only a woman can know that and speak of that. That is why we won't be told what to do by our husbands. A woman can only do one thing. She can respect herself. She can keep herself decent. She must always be as her nature is. She must always be maiden and always be mother. Before every love she is a maiden, after every love she is a mother. In this you can see whether she is a good woman or not." The men, in societies of this third type, were within one jot of being completely superfluous, and if, as some authorities claim, they can have had no knowledge of the relationship of the sexual act to pregnancy and birth, we may well imagine the utter abyss of their inferiority complex.

Small wonder, furthermore, if, in reaction, their revengeful imaginations ran amok and developed secret lodges and societies, the mysteries and terrors of which were directed primarily against the women! "The men's festivals not only were addressed to an ignoble, immoral aim, but strove for it through ignoble and immoral means.

The aim was to undo the harmonious state of equal privilege and mutual reliance of the two sexes that originally had prevailed in their simple society, supported by economic circumstance, and to establish through intimidation and the subjection of the women, a cruel ascendancy of the males." It is surely in the interplay and mutual spiritual fertilization of the sexes, no less than in the lessons learned of the animal, plant, and celestial kingdoms of the gods or in the profundities of the shamanistic trance experience that the motivations of the metamorphoses of myth are to be sought.

ABJECTION

The term Abjection literally means "the state of being cast off." In usage it has connotations of degradation, baseness and meanness of spirit.

ABJECTION IN CRITICAL THEORY

In contemporary critical theory, abjection is often used to describe the state of often-marginalized groups, such as people of color, prostitutes, convicts, poor people disabled people, and queer or LGBT people. In this context, the concept of abject exists in between the concept of an object and the concept of the subject, something alive yet not. This term originated in the works of Julia Kristeva. Often, the term space of abjection is also used, referring to a space that abjected things or beings inhabit.

According to Kristeva, since the abject is situated outside the symbolic order, being forced to face it is an inherently traumatic experience. For example, upon being faced with a corpse, a person would be most likely repulsed because he or she is forced to face an object which is violently cast out of the cultural world, having once been a subject. We encounter other beings daily, and more often than not they are alive. To confront a corpse of one that we recognize as human, something that should be alive but isn't, is to confront the reality that we are capable of existing in the same state, our own mortality. This repulsion from death, excrement and rot constitutes the subject as a living being in the symbolic order.

This act is done in the light of the parts of ourselves that we exclude: that is, the mother. We must abject the maternal, the object which has created us, in order to construct an identity. This is done on the micro level of the speaking being, through her subjective dynamics, as well as on the macro level of society, through "language as a common and universal law." We use rituals, specifically those of defilement, in order to maintain clear boundaries between nature and society, the semiotic and the symbolic. This line of thought begins with Mary Douglas' important book, *Purity and Danger*, as well as in Kristeva's own *Black Sun*.

The concept of abject is often coupled (and sometimes confused with) the idea of the uncanny, the concept of something being "un-home-like", or foreign, yet familiar. The abject can be uncanny in the sense that we can recognize aspects in it, despite its being "foreign". An example, continuing on the one used above, is that of a corpse, namely the corpse of a loved one. We will recognize that person as being close to us, but the fact that the person is dead, and "no longer" the familiar loved one, is what creates a sort of cognitive dissonance, leading to abjection of the corpse.

ABJECT ART

In the 1980s and 1990s many artists became aware of this theory and reflected it in their work. In 1993 the Whitney Museum, New York, staged an exhibition titled Abject Art: Repulsion and Desire in American Art, which gave the term a wider currency in art. Cindy Sherman is seen as a key contributor to the abject in art, as well as many others including Louise Bourgeois, Helen Chadwick, Paul McCarthy, Gilbert and George, Robert Gober, Carolee Schneemann, Kiki Smith and Jake and Dinos Chapman.

THE ABJECT OTHER WORKS

According to Barbara Creed in *Horror and the Monstrous Feminine* a male's relationship with the mother and other females is complicated by the use of the feminine in horror and science fiction as we are forced to confront it as horrific and abject. Through an analysis of the film Alien (1979) and the female roles and representations, Creed explains how females are often related to the object of horror, be they as the object of horror or the object of the actual horrors' desire/ hatred. The conclusion is that through monstrous representations of the female or the Mother, the audience is drawn into viewing them as abject rather than subject or object.

The aliens themselves from the film in question are often described as having phallus-like appendages in the shape of their head and tongue, while maintaining an almost female form. Their interaction with the human crew takes on very abject roles as one crew member, a male, is forcibly impregnated (clearly as a product of rape) with an alien that eventually rips itself from the male 'womb' in a horrific scene of blood and gore. The process of a male being impregnated through the mouth with a creature that gestates – in a being that has no womb – and rips itself free in a shower of blood is one way in which this film objectifies female roles.

Abjection is also a major theme of the 1949 work The Thief's Journal (Journal du Voleur) by French author Jean Genet. As a criminal outcast from society, during a fictionalized account of his wanderings through Europe in the 1930s, he claims to actively seek abjections as an existentialist form of 'sainthood. Freud's theory of the "uncanny" is a highly influential concept in the analysis of horrific films and literature. But more than helping us to understand the appeal and effect of the horror genre, the uncanny as Freud explains it reveals much about his understanding of human beings as being essentially determined by unconscious processes.

In this essay I examine the concept of the uncanny from the perspective of the debate concerning free will and determinism, building on Freud's original conception based on repression to an understanding (following Slavoj Zizek's interpretation) of the uncanny as the experience of awareness of the controlling force of the id, a lack of control, a determination. I raise challenges to this theory of the uncanny (and determinism) based on existentialist thinking, specifically Heidegger's description of the uncanny as the revelation that there is in fact no core to the self, no determining id, but rather openness, possibility and freedom. I also examine Julia Kristeva's notion of abjection and whether this might be a way to reconcile psychoanalytic and existentialist perspectives in the study of the effects of horror, despite the obvious differences in their approach to philosophical anthropology.

THE UNCANNY IN PSYCHOANALYSIS

Freud offers as his most basic definition of the uncanny, "that species of the frightening that goes back to what was once well known and had long been familiar" (1919: 124). This thing which was "once well known" can take the form of either "repressed" or "surmounted" beliefs or desires which are brought up from the unconscious into the conscious mind. This involves a compulsion to repeat: "the uncanny element in the recurrence of the same thing can be derived from infantile psychology....In the unconscious mind we can recognize the dominance of a compulsion to repeat, which proceeds from instinctual impulses.

This compulsion probably depends on the essential nature of the drives themselves...." (1919: 145). The drives, originating in the id, are "essential" in Freud's view (this will become particularly noteworthy in the discussion of "existence over essence" in existentialism). Being essential, and involving a compulsion to repeat (the impulses themselves, as well as the actions of the individual subject to them), the drives (the id) and the unconscious represent the determining feature of the psyche. Any individual is influenced by forces he is not aware of.

Looking at this more closely in terms of the uncanny, we see that for Freud the experience of uncanniness is linked to unconscious desires and beliefs that are repressed or surmounted, and yet through their repetitive nature, and through the prodding of the work of uncanny texts, find their way back into consciousness and produce that discomfort, that aspect of the frightening we term the uncanny. One form the uncanny can take is the return of the repressed: if psychoanalytic theory is right in asserting that every affect arising from an emotional impulse - of whatever kind - is converted into fear by being repressed, it follows that among those things that are felt to be frightening there must be one group in which it can be shown that the frightening element is something that has been repressed and now returns. This species of the frightening would then constitute the uncanny....this uncanny element is actually nothing new or strange, but something that was long familiar to the psyche and was estranged from it only through being repressed. The link with repression now illuminates Shelling's definition of the uncanny as 'something that should have remained hidden that has come into the open'. (1919: 147).

Whenever something is repressed, then, its reappearance is a source of fear - it should have remained hidden but now comes into the open and confronts the conscious mind, creating the uneasy feeling of uncanniness. The compulsion to repeat is a "manifestation of the power of the repressed", illustrating the strength of the influence of the repressed and the unconcsious. Andrew Tudor notes that in studies of the effects and functions of horror, this aspect of the uncanny has often been seen to serve as a "safety valve, where repressed affect threatens to surface and as a figurative reminder of the fearful consequences if the 'rules' of sexual behaviour are broken. In a real sense, then, such perspectives see human agents as unaware victims of their cultures".

For Tudor sexual repression is key, though the "safety valve" theory has been applied also to destructive impulses or Thanatos in Freud's terminology. Indeed, we see in Tudor's remarks a mode of thinking similar to Freud's in *Civilization and its Discontents*, where the "renunciation of instincts" is crucial to the survival of human culture and civilization. The experience of the uncanny, from Tudor's perspective, is a way of dealing with cultural restraints on the id and of reinforcing these restraints by associating the emergence of repressed instincts with the uncomfortable feeling of the uncanny.

As an example of the return of the repressed theory in relation to the understanding and interpretation of horror I take the film *Psycho,* which besides being generally considered one of the best and most effective horror/suspense films ever made, also lends itself to psychoanalytic interpretation for obvious reasons. Norman Bates is a grown man stuck in an Oedipus complex, and in the film we see Norman driven to an act of murder through the jealousy he perceives his mother to experience when he is sexually aroused by another woman. Of course at the end of the film we discover that the mother is actually also Norman, who "becomes" his mother whenever he experiences sexual desire for other women (such as Marion, the woman "mother" murders in the shower), illustrating his inability to resolve the Oedipus complex and achieve a mature sexuality.

In her classic study of horror cinema, Barbara Creed claims that "the ideological project of horror films such as *Psycho, Carrie, The Brood,* and *The Hunger,* all of which feature the monster as female, appears to be precisely this - constructing monstrosity's source as the failure of paternal order to ensure the break, the separation of mother and child" (1993: 38). Analysis of this film using the return of the repressed theory would involve the obvious observation that much of what makes *Psycho* unsettling, or uncanny, is the relationship that Norman has with his mother, and as Creed notes, the absence or failure of a paternal order to ensure resolution of the Oedipus complex, serving as a reminder of the Oedipus complex that we have all experienced, and the repression of the desire for the mother that was necessary to resolve the complex. As we are confronted with this repressed desire, we experience the uncanny.

Along with repression, the uncanny can also come from being confronted with surmounted desires or beliefs. This form of the uncanny comes when "primitive beliefs that have been surmounted appear to be once again confirmed" (1919: 154). For example, at some point children give up the belief that their dolls might someday come to life, yet as adults when confronted with such an event in a horror film the revival of this surmounted belief is experienced as uncanny. In the case of both repressed and surmounted beliefs and desires, we are speaking not of everyday fears, and this is why the uncanny is a particular aspect of the frightening.

We are instead dealing with something that was once familiar to the psyche but has become estranged to it, something that has been repressed or surmounted and which now reappears. In the case of repression, the uncanny is a response to being confronted with aspects of the psyche that have been forced into the unconscious; the fear comes in the revelation that these desires and beliefs are not in fact gone, but have been lurking in the unconscious all along. It is this understanding of the uncanny that has been the foundation of most psychoanalytic study and interpretation of the horror genre, its effects, and its appeal.

Curtis Bowman offers a description of surmounted beliefs in relation to the uncanny: "surmounted beliefs are outmoded ways of thinking that are reactivated and confirmed in the experience of the uncanny....repressed material is always accompanied by anxiety as it returns to consciousness. Surmounted beliefs do not seem to be subject to repression, and thus their confirmation is not accompanied by anxiety....Perhaps the reemergence of surmounted beliefs signifies a painful loss of intellectual mastery.

Such a dynamic - we might call it 'the confirmation of the disavowed' - could account for any disturbance that might be found in the case of surmounted beliefs" (2003: 67). This 'loss of intellectual mastery' Bowman describes forms the basis of Slavoj Zizek's understanding of the uncanny.

In a brief passage in *The Plague of Fantasies,* Slavoj Zizek offers an interpretation of the uncanny which highlights some crucial aspects of Freudian psychoanalysis and philosophical anthropology:

The Freudian point regarding fundamental fantasy would be that each subject, female or male, possesses such a 'factor' which regulates his or her desire: 'a woman, viewed from behind, on her hand and knees' was the Wolf Man's factor...There is nothing uplifting about our awareness of this 'factor': such awareness can never be subjectivized; it is uncanny - even horrifying - since it somehow 'depossesses' the subject, reducing her or him to a puppet-like level 'beyond dignity and freedom' (1997: 8).

The implications of this passage are vast in scope. The "factors" Zizek speaks of here are things that awaken sexual desire - in layman terms, such a factor is something that "turns you on"; he gives the example of the sight of a woman viewed from behind on her hands and knees as awakening some deep and primitive desire. The awareness of such a factor is not uplifting, according to Zizek, because it depossesses the subject; that is, this factor exerts a control over the individual by provoking a response, a desire that has nothing to do with the conscious subject. The subject becomes a "puppet", mastered by the drives and desires embedded in his unconscious that spring up from the id.

The subject is "beyond dignity and freedom" because he is *determined* by his unconscious, a force that is outside of his control (in Bowman's terms, the subject experiences a loss of intellectual mastery). This view is in line with Freud's deterministic model of human nature: the psyche can be boiled down to its essential elements, the drives originating from the unconscious, exerting an influence on a subject who ultimately does not possess what we might term a free will. In this view, the id is the core of the psyche and is a determining force.

For Zizek, then, the uncanny is not brought about by the specific desires or beliefs that are awakened, but more fundamentally the realization that there are desires and beliefs that lie outside the realm of consciousness, buried deep within the id, which nonetheless have control of dispossessed subjects who are like slaves to their own desires. In relation to the horror genre specifically, Jonathan Lake Crane claims that

"Horror films are primers for the primitive....Returning to the horrible allows us to keep sight of the fundamental desires that rule the species.

Through any particular work, as horror films are nearly all identically constructed, an individual audience member can come to know not only the entire history of horror but also his or her biological/psychic destiny" (1994: 28).

Thus, the experience of watching horror is like a reminder of the rule of the id, and the determining influence of unconscious drives. In *Psycho,* the uncanny in Zizek's sense might be aroused by the shocking revelation at the end of the film that it is actually Norman who has committed the murders, and has been compelled to do so by an inability to escape the psycho-sexual complexes that have haunted him since his childhood.

In a scene leading up to the famous shower scene, Norman has a conversation with his unsuspecting victim in the motel's parlour where he reveals a desire to flee from his "mother's" tyrannical grip, but ultimately cannot summon the will to do so. This is Norman's failure to achieve the self-mastery that Freud claimed psychoanalysis might be able to provide. This is an understanding of the uncanny that is at a more primitive level than Freud's analysis, since he was concerned with the details of repression, while this is concerned only with the *fact* of the unconscious.

However, the elements of Zizek's interpretation of the uncanny can be seen in Freud's discussion of automata, or the "automatic - mechanical - processes that may lie hidden behind the familiar image of a living person" (1919: 135). Freud is referring explicitly to instances in horrific literature when we are confronted with persons whom we are not certain are living or dead; implicitly, however, we can see Zizek's version of the uncanny in the notion of automata, or people who are driven by forces outside of their control, not true subjects but slaves determined by their unconscious. Both Freud and Zizek's theories of the uncanny are based on a deterministic model of human nature that posits a "core" of the self in the form of the id.

THE UNCANNY IN EXISTENTIALISM

William Barrett offers a Sartrean definition of existentialism in the notion that existence precedes essence: "Man exists and makes himself to be what he is; his individual essence or nature comes to be out of his existence; and in this sense it is proper to say that existence precedes essence. Man does not have a fixed essence that is handed to him ready-made; rather, he makes his own nature out of his freedom and the historical conditions in which he is placed" (1958: 102). This is in direct contrast to Freud's (and Zizek's) determinism, which sees humans as being slaves to unconscious drives and processes. The existential view is that there is in fact no "essence" (for Freud, the id), or at least no essence that is prior to existence: what we are comes through our place in space and time and the choices we make, based on the infinite possibility of existence.

However, this ultimate freedom carries a price in the form of existential dread or angst, and it is this to which I turn now in relation to the question of how we might apply existentialist thought to an understanding of the uncanny, specifically through Curtis Bowman's (2003) reading of Heidegger in relation to horror. While Heidegger's version of existentialism differs in crucial respects from the "existence precedes essence" definition given by Barrett (for Heidegger man does not 'make himself' exactly, but rather there is a possibility for man to break from habit and experience moments of authenticity), it retains the principle that we are essentially free to make choices and thus presents a challenge to Freud's determinism.

In *Being and Time* Heidegger argues that angst is not the same thing as fear (much like Freud says that the uncanny is not the same thing as fear), but rather it is a mode of insight into Dasein's nature, which is one of an open possibility of being, an absence of permanence. Uncanniness, like angst, comes with the realization of the possibility of being, and that there is nothing to turn to for guidance, no inner force or core, but only infinitude of choice. In a reading of Heidegger in relation to the uncanny and the study of horror, Curtis

Bowman claims that the threat from the uncanny "lies in the fact that Dasein is a scene of possibility that burdens it with responsibility and uncertainty" (2003: 72).

When there is nothing determining us, we are responsible for our own choices, whereas some have interpreted Freud as saying that individuals are ultimately not responsible for what they do since they are subject to forces beyond their conscious control. This argument does not recognize that Freud claims we are not all id, but also ego and superego (the id exerts an influence, but doesn't absolutely determine since it is only one part of the psyche), and that we make unconscious *choices*, so it is not a hard determinism and we still hold responsibility for our actions. Bowman's application of Heidegger's understanding of the uncanny to horror texts is novel, and though somewhat vague it presents some interesting challenges and options to the Freudian version of the concept and opens a space for dialogue in this area of horror film interpretation.

The uncertainty that is Dasein's burden is key in Bowman's reading: "Heidegger's concept of the uncanny essentially relies on the overthrow of our ontology, even if it lasts only for a moment. This loss of intellectual mastery is almost certain to disturb us - hence the uneasiness that we usually feel in uncanny circumstances" (2003: 73). This is "ontological uncanniness", and it comes about when an established ontology in disrupted. This uncanniness reveals the arbitrary understanding we have of the self, and that there is in fact an infinite possibility of being. Uncanny horror films, then, are aids to self-understanding, thus accounting for their appeal - they reveal to us a truth about ourselves, even if it's one that might cause anguish, such as the fact that we are burdened with responsibility for our actions.

Again, this is a somewhat vague notion, and the application of the Heideggerian uncanny to horror films is a difficult project beyond the usually unexplained term "existential dread" that film critics often employ in reviews of horror films. What might we say about an ontological disruption in *Psycho*? In a Freudian reading, the uncanniness is based on repressed desires. From Zizek's perspective, it would come from Norman's helplessness against the force of his own unconscious. Finally, in Bowman's reading of Heidegger, we might have to say that the horror in *Psycho* stems not from the causes of Norman's actions, but rather from the fact that they have no cause in the sense of a determining force and are instead the outcome the choices Norman has made to cope with the world he lives in, his loneliness and isolation in the secluded Bates Motel (which often, Norman explains to his unsuspecting victim Marion Crane, has twelve cabins and twelve vacancies).

Further, Hitchcock establishes a characterization of Norman throughout the film, and at the end disrupts this ontological foundation through the revelation that Norman and his mother are not who we think they are, and that they in fact inhabit the same body. Finally, Hitchcock skillfully makes use of his own reputation and film history by setting the film up as a typical "Hitchcock film", with an elaborate set-up involving a woman who has committed a crime on the run from the law, with the audience expecting the story to play out in a certain way based on their experience of previous Hitchcock films.

The film takes a major left turn, of course, when the major character for the first forty minutes of the film is suddenly murdered and Norman becomes the main character, and a story of a woman on the run from the law becomes the story of a peculiar young man and his deranged, homicidal mother. The film's established ontology is disrupted through a sudden act of violence, leaving the viewer disoriented and not knowing what to expect - after the shower scene anything seems possible and narrative formulas must be forgotten.

Through this interpretation we see at least that the seeds are there for an existentialist understanding of the uncanny in the horror genre, presenting a challenge to traditional psychoanalytic views. Along with this existentialist critique of the uncanny there also comes a critique of psychoanalytic determinism, positing the individual as being characterized by his existence (for Heidegger, the social and historical conditions of such) rather than by any determining essence (or core of the self) that might be prior to it - nothing is fixed, any ontology can be disrupted.

While a Heideggarian version of the uncanny is not quite as aptly applied to Psycho as Freud's version, if we look at a very different kind of horror film such as Dario Argento's Suspiria, we suddenly find the Freudian version of the concept less aptly applied than the existentialist one. Argento as a director is the antithesis of Hitchcock: while the master of suspense guided his films with great precision and with intentions of producing certain effects in the audience (Hitchcock famously boasted of his power to manipulate audiences), the Italian director is noted for his fractures narratives, logical loopholes and inconsistencies that produce a sense of confusion and disorientation, which are Argento's methods of achieving suspense and a pervasive sense of dread. Suspiria's narrative is a convoluted mess, involving a coven of witches at a boarding school and series murders that happen for no apparent reason and to characters who sometimes appear out of nowhere and have little to nothing to do with any kind of plot.

The film is essentially a series of elaborate murder set-pieces loosely knitted together by the "plot" involving the witches; still, it is a classic in the genre and for many represents the pinnacle of Italian 'Giallo' horror cinema, and is noted for its use of colour and music in creating an eerie atmosphere. An attempt to apply a Freudian version of the uncanny to Suspiria would be more difficult than applying the Heideggerian version to Psycho - there would seem to be nothing that one could point to as an illustration of the return of the repressed or being confronted with surmounted desires or beliefs.

Rather, the randomness of the acts of violence, and the main character's inability to make sense of her surroundings and the events transpiring, contribute to what might more aptly be described as a sense of existential dread or uncanniness: Suspiria shows us a world where anyone at any time can be the victim of a gruesome murder for no apparent reason. In Psycho the uncanny helps us to explain the mechanisms behind the character's behaviour and our response to it, while in Suspiria there is little explaining to do, as the horror comes partly from the fact that there is no determining cause to look to for an explanation? It has been noted by many that the uncanny is not intended to explain all of horror cinema, but this seems to be an excuse for the concept's shortcomings.

It may be that we simply need a more dynamic understanding of the uncanny that incorporates both the psychoanalytic and existentialist perspectives (and thus permits an understanding of human beings as being essentially free but also subject to determining forces). I propose that Kristeva's notion of abjection provides a way into a middle ground and a more dynamic understanding of the effects of horror.

In *Powers of Horror* Julia Kristeva offers a theory of the experience of horror based on the concept of abjection, a psychoanalytic alternative to Freud's uncanny that, like Zizek's version, focuses on the notion of the subject. She uses the term uncanny in her initial description of the abject: "There looms, within abjection, one of those violent, dark revolts of being... opposed to 'I'...A massive and sudden emergence of uncanniness, which... now harries me as radically separate, loathsome" (1982: 1-2). While Kristeva does not deal with horror as a genre specifically, the notion of abjection has been taken up by many studying the genre and it has become an influential concept in the field. Jonathan Lake Crane, in applying Kristeva's ideas to horror film, begins by defining the abject as "those objects....

That desecrates our narcissistic mirage of self by effacing the boundary between me and that which is not 'I'. The object provides proof that our idealized portraits of pristine flesh and whole egos are unfortunately nothing more than brittle fantasies" (1994: 30). Kristeva's analysis of the subject demonstrates that there is no one identifiable subject, no "core" of the subject as there is in Freud, but a fractured subject that experiences the abject when faced with the blurring of the distinction of I and Other. This blurring of the subject's boundaries disrupts the integrity of our understanding of self. Abject objects reveal the true constitution of the subject as empty and incomplete - abjection is a means of separating the human from the non-human and the fully-constituted from the partially-formed subject.

Like the uncanny, the abject is unconscious, but according to Crane, can return to consciousness in the horror film, where "we are forced to restyle the unsullied self-images we manufacture for ourselves. The screams we let loose in the theater as the horror film plays on do not signify the release of tension or the expulsion of pent-up libidinal energy. They are the shrieks uttered whenever cherished fancies about the self are shattered". The "fancies about the self" in question are related to the self or subject as a whole, a distinct 'I'.

Horror texts involve a negation, according to Kristeva, which shows us to be empty. Donald Carveth (2004) summarizes Kristeva's view of the subject: "our experience is pervaded by difference, absence, nothingness, gap and lack." The cause of abjection is recognition of this lack, or "what disturbs identity, system, order. What does not respect borders, positions, rules? The revelation of the nature of the subject that abjection brings makes it a kind of narcissistic crisis, as we are horrified when confronted with the notion that we are incomplete, with permeable and shifting boundaries.

Applying the notion of abjection to the study of horror, Crane notes that from Kristeva's perspective "Whatever blurs the human frame, whatever disturbs the line between human and nonhuman, every unclear delineation between the not-us and the subject with constitutional integrity is horrific" (1994: 35). That is, anything that challenges the borders of "I" as the subject perceives them, anything that reveals an incompleteness or lack in the self is an object that provokes abjection and is horrifying.

Returning to Psycho, we would have a different perspective on the horrific aspects of the film using Kristeva's abjection as the basis of analysis. We are horrified at Norman's inability to detach himself from his mother, but not in the sense of the uncanny as described by Freud and Zizek. The horror in this case lies in the blurring of the lines of the "I", seen in Norman's inability to conceive of himself as a subject, a whole, separate from his mother, going to such lengths to preserve the illusion of an ongoing relationship with his mother that he goes beyond preserving her corpse to ultimately wearing her clothes and allowing a space for her within his own psyche. The abject in this film comes through the character of Norman, who represents that which we are horrified to acknowledge: that we are fractured subjects, that I is an illusion and that we are bound to the Other.

Norman "becomes" his mother when he is sexually aroused or when he is faced with a threatening situation (as in the murder of Arbogast, the private investigator who gets a little too close to the truth). The latter illustrates Norman's longing for the comfort and security the mother offers to her child, and his explicit inability to be independent and escape this link to his mother. Kristeva's articulation of the maternal element in abjection can be applied directly to Psycho: "The abject confronts us... with our earliest attempts to release the hold of maternal entity even before existing outside of her... It is a violent, clumsy breaking away, with the constant risk of falling back under the sway of power as securing as it is stifling".

Norman falls back under the sway of his mother's power, which he finds comforting and, at the same time (as he confesses to Marion in the parlour shortly before murdering her), he strongly desires to escape her domineering and stifling influence but cannot. In terms of abjection this is not exactly a result of an inability to resolve an Oedipus complex, but rather the subject's (Norman's) inability to escape an essential incompleteness.

In abjection the borders of the subject are broken down, stability is disrupted, and the emptiness of the self is exposed, which is precisely what we see in Norman and is what makes *Psycho* unsettling (the final scene, where Norman thinks to himself in his mother's voice while sitting alone in a room in the police station, is particularly creepy, as he has finally and utterly failed to mark a boundary between himself and his mother). In this respect of the essential emptiness and incompleteness of the self, Kristeva may represent a version of psychoanalysis that is more compatible with existentialism, at least in respect to how we understand the uncanny and our experience of horror texts in relation to the question of free will vs. determinism.

WILL, DETERMINISM, AND THE UNCANNY

We are finally left with the question of whether an existentialist understanding of the uncanny negates the applicability of Freud's version to film and literature, and particularly the horror genre. This involves the question of free will and determinism, and whether this distinction in fact needs to be reconciled to have a workable theory in either case. Donald Carveth (2004) brings up the point that free will and responsibility (in other words, an existentialist understanding of human nature) are not incompatible with psychoanalytic practice:

"One need not subscribe to a complete causal determinism in mental life to ground the psychoanalytic practice of bringing to light the conscious, preconscious and unconscious connections between mental events—that is, to interpret their multiple meanings or significations. Since to reproach someone for acting in a certain way necessarily implies they could have chosen to act otherwise, a belief in free will and responsibility is necessary for moral judgment to make any rational sense whatsoever. But while such a belief is certainly incompatible with complete psychic determinism, it in no way contradicts the principle of psychic signification and the practice of decoding encoded meanings. In other words, belief in free will and responsibility is in no way incompatible with actual clinical psychoanalytic practice, however much it contradicts the determinism of Freudian metapsychology."

Carveth argues that free will is not incompatible with psychoanalysis, only with Freud's metapsychology. This seems to be a valid point, since for Freud the project of psychoanalysis is to help patients achieve self-mastery by helping them deal with things that are happening in their unconscious. If this is the case, free will must be possible. As Carveth notes, "Psychic reality is characterized by both determinism and freedom" (2004). Following this, it would seem that there is not necessarily an absolute tension between psychoanalysis and existentialism regarding how we should understand the experience of the uncanny. It may be that both positions can offer something to the interpretation of horror and the relationship the viewer has with it in terms of its effects and its appeal.

It has been admitted already by many that the Freudian uncanny is not intended as a universal explanation of the effects of horror; supplementing this version with the existentialist one might provide the opportunity for a more dynamic approach to the study of horror. Further, Kristeva's theory of abjection might provide a version of psychoanalysis that is more compatible with existentialism, working as a bridge between what have often been seen as incompatible fields, at least regarding this particular aspect of experience. In any case, it seems clear that an examination of the experience of horror provides a unique entry into the question of determinism, and vice versa, the question of determinism provides a unique entry, and presents interesting challenges, to the concept of the uncanny and the study of horror.

THE ABJECTION OF THE FEMALE BODY

Hell as a Metaphor for Birth Paola Bono A new-born baby, really just born, the umbilical cord not yet cut; naked and crying, its face screwed up in the effort. Still dirty with blood and mucus, marks of its passage through the physical, corporeal threshold it has crossed to come to life. Carnal threshold, vagina of the mother's body, whence it comes, in whose womb it has grown - living matter on its way to being; so that the traces of that body still show on its little body. Some of you might remember this image: one of Benetton's "scandalous" ads, which some years ago did in fact provoke, scandalized reactions, at least in Italy. Because it was being used for commercial ends because it exploited childhood - nay, babyhood, for mercenary purposes.

Or so the argument went. While childhood and exploitation would seem to have nothing to do with those babies who appear in numberless ads for diapers and baby-food; there has never been such an outcry in those cases. But then those babies are so pretty, so smiling and, most important, so clean! A further criticism (perhaps not spelled out exactly in these terms, but certainly this was its meaning) maintained that the ad violated - again, for those reproachable commercial ends - a most important and sacred moment, the moment of birth. And here I think is a crucial point, a truth at the core of those scandalized reactions: in the concept of the sacred, and in the focus on birth. The reasons given for it may strike one as hypocritical, but the spontaneous recoiling in disgust was sincere.

What that image signified was birth in its "improper" physical reality, showing its traces on the baby's body dirty of the confusion with the mother's body. Mucus, blood, the wet stickiness of the carnal threshold, confusion: elements which, in Kristeva's term, we could recognize as belonging to the category of the abject. Because they are secretions, because they are inscribed in a borderline area: between the outside and the inside of the body, between the undefined self and other of the pre-natal dyad. It was an indecent image which exposed a secret everybody knows, the secret of an event everybody has experienced. It was unheimlich, uncanny in its familiarity and in its bringing to conscious attention what was and should have remained buried in the unconscious.

Building upon Freud's notion of the uncanny as taboo, and referring to anthropological research, especially Mary Douglas' on purity and contamination, Kristeva in Powers of Horror identifies abjection - "one of those violent, dark revolts of being" - as the horror of not knowing the borders of the self, a primary uncanny originated in the fertility and generative power of the mother's body. Like abjection, pregnancy and the pre-natal period are borderline phenomena, they are a space-time of confusion, bodily co-existence (coincidence) of identities which it links in a vital and deadly relation, at the same time preparing their separation and distinction. Space-time which both confuses and produces one and another, identity questioning that subject/object demarcation on which the delusive stability of the self is founded.

Forever threatened by the frailty of a boundary built on the originary void of loss and on the impossible refusal of corporeality, the subject experiences in the feeling of abjection the uncertainty of its identity; the risk - fear and desire - of falling back into that space-time where it grew, which it left in order to be. Rejected, repressed, expelled, yet inevitably present and forever to be kept at bay, the abject physically inhabits those areas of the body which will become erotogenic zones, in that tension and coincidence between attraction and revulsion which also - especially - marks the female/maternal body. Borderline, marginal areas; and, Mary Douglas reminds us, "all margins are dangerous. So that we should expect the orifices of the body to symbolyse its especially vulnerable points".

Eyes, mouth, nose, anus, genitals and their secretions which "by simply issuing forth have traversed the boundary of the body". Tears, saliva, vomit, mucus, faeces, urina, sperm, menstrual blood. As though in "horrendous excremental drains", in counter- Reformation Catholic culture these bodily secretions characterize the post-Tridentine hell, obscene site of a promiscuous and chaotic carnality; a vision which lasts until the 19th century, as Pietro Camporesi shows in The Fear of Hell. Images of Damnation and Salvation in Early Modern Europe where he explores and analyzes the figurations of hell in art and literature.

Thus, in the "oafish underworld" of Belli's sonnets - he argues - this vision becomes "almost a Tartarean version of birth ex-putri" (Camporesi 1991: 12, 13), where the phantasma of the great collective body of humanity, the archaic belief in a fertile death, a pregnant death, the nursemaid of new life, the sense of continuity in death-life re-emerged. The hidden shadow of the one belonging to the many reappeared, as did the sense of a fatal, cyclical rotation, an uninterrupted pendulum between life and death, between decomposition and rebirth (Camporesi 1991: 13-14).

Continuity is not a reason for hope, in the awareness of belonging to the cycle of being; on the contrary, it engenders horror for the corrupting, destructive confusion of the self, a condition of imperfect and improper not-being-anymore. Imperfect and improper like the not-yet-being of the pre-natal period, spent in the closed, red, pulsating space of the mother's womb: suffocation and protection, dreaded hell and longed for Nirvana which in this longing is inhabited by the death drive. The womb is a liminal space, which must necessarily be crossed to come into the world; as in a rite of passage, this limen is ambiguously connoted, it is not-life and not-death.

Analysing the liminal phase of rites of passage, Victor Turner remarks that its symbolism draws upon both "the biology of death, decomposition, catabolism" and "processes of gestation and parturition"; thus the same symbols - huts and tunnels, for instance - signify both the maternal womb and the tomb. While stressing the positive value attributed by Turner to the transitional liminal phase as a field of open potentialities, Paola Cabibbo underlines this "coincidence of opposing processes and notions [which] characterizes the peculiar unity of liminality; it is neither this nor that, and yet it is both this and that".

Or, to use Turner's own words again, the subjects of a rite of passage "are neither living nor dead from one aspect and both living and dead from another. Their condition is one of ambiguity and paradox, a confusion of all the customary categories". Ambiguity, confusion: abjection. But in a socially and culturally created rite of passage there is no return to the limen between the before and after of initiation, once the subject has been re-defined and redemarcated in a new social and subjective space. Abjection, on the contrary, is the recurring, threatening sensation of an incurable instability of the self; it is the radical and repeated questioning of the integrity of the subject. It finds expression in the body, in the secretions which crossing its boundaries exceed it, in its hollows, crevices, orifices.

Sites of expulsion and - for example in the case of food of incorporation; borderline sites of horror and pleasure, of abjection. Kristeva writes: We may call it a border: abjection is above all ambiguity. Because, while releasing a hold, it does not radically cut off the subject from what threatens it - on the contrary, abjection acknowledges it to be in perpetual danger. But also, abjection itself is a compromise of judgment and affect, of condemnation and yearning, of signs and drives. Abjection preserves what existed in the archaism of pre-objected relationship, in the immemorial violence with which the body becomes separated from another body in order to be - maintaining that night in which the outline of the signified vanishes and where only the imponderable affect is carried out.

And she goes on to argue that the abject is the violence of mourning for an 'object' that has always already been lost. It takes the ego back to its source on the abominable limits from which, in order to be, the ego has broken away - it assigns it a source in the non-ego, drive, and death. In the fear and desire of being overwhelmed by that lost body is a form of the feeling of abjection, which in many cultures is expressed and contained through rituals of purification. Rituals: because the abject borders upon - coincides with, says Kristeva - the sacred.

With the interdictions against the danger of its contamination, the abject lays at the roots of the sacred. "As abjection - so the sacred" is the title of a passage where she briefly looks at the modes of purification in religion, from so called primitive religions to Jewish monotheism to Christianity: exclusion and taboo, transgression, sin - then to suggest that in our culture the abject finds expression and containment in writing. "Outside of the sacred, the abject is written" - she maintains, talking of "the aesthetic task - a descent into the foundations of the symbolic construct - which amounts to retracing the fragile limits of the speaking being, closest to its dawn, to the bottomless 'primacy' constituted by primal repression".

Literature can thus be seen as an exploration of the abject; metaphorization of lack and fear so that the self can come to life again in signs. In a century marked by the process of secularization, but also traversed by a renewed need of the sacred, writing becomes "a cache for suffering"; in the unbearable instability of the boundary between subject and object, "the narrative is what is challenged first"; its linearity is shattered up to the scream of a language which resembles violence and obscenity. The descents into hell of Céline's and Lispector's writing are the collapsing of narration into that crying-out theme which, coinciding "with the incandescent states of a boundary-subjectivity called abjection", is according to Kristeva "the crying-out theme of suffering-horror".

In the journey towards the origins, where life and death meet, where the danger and pleasure of the loss of self are intertwined, in literature as well the feeling of abjection often becomes embodied in the female/maternal body. Already signified in religions and myths, revisited by psychoanalysis, the mother and the maternal are the privileged figure of the inextricable proximity of life and death at the centre of the symbolic construction. In the temples of Çatal Hüyük, in today's Turkey, the great mother goddess is often represented in the physical posture of childbirth, in the moment when life begins, emerging from her body; and it is said that in one of her shrines - the walls and floor all painted red, like the inside of a womb - women would go to give birth.

But there is also a temple, sacred to her, where seven huge vultures painted in blood-red on a pink background hover with wings outspread over stylized human figures, their arms raised to greet the goddess as she appears in this form. It is a gesture of acceptance and worship, expressing trust in her powers of regeneration as well as fear for her proximity to death. For the vulture, feeding on carrion, does not so much 'bring' death as transform what is already dead back into life, beginning a new cycle by assimilating the end of the old one. In this way the goddess of death and the goddess of birth are inseparable.

All the great mother goddesses of the ancient oriental religions are characterized by this double power, at times thoroughly controlling it, at times becoming articulated in various figures in order to signify it through a multifaceted unity. Travelling and changing, their cult lives on, recognizable in full or only in some elements, among the Jewish tribes and then in the Greek and Roman worlds. According to some interpretations, its influence is also visible in the central female figure of Christianity, Mary the bride and mother of god. Many of these goddesses descend to the underworld, often - in later versions, such as those about Ishtar and Isis - in order to find and bring back to life their son-lover.

It is not so in "The Descent of Inanna", the oldest of all; she seems rather motivated by a wish for knowledge, willing to risk her divine powers in order to achieve this aim. Inanna travels into the black realm of her sister Ereshkigal leaving behind the symbols of her power, as she undresses step by step at the seven gates of the underworld. She will be kept a prisoner there for three days, plunged in the sleep of death, until her faithful companion Ninshubur convinces Enki, god of wisdom, to send two messengers to ask Ereshkigal to free her. Inanna ascends back to heaven, where she reigns as morning and evening star, mistress of fertility and of destruction; but she must send down in her stead her spouse Dummuzi, who is here sacrificed and not saved. I do not propose to go into this myth at length, thoroughly exploring its connections with other religious narratives - the already mentioned stories of Ishtar and Isis, those of Demeter and Cybele - also in their possible links with the story of Christ's passion.

Indeed it would take us too far; here I will only highlight briefly some of their features relevant to this reflection on the widespread "cultural convention that the mother's gift of birth is also the gift of death", so that woman "functions as privileged trope for the uncanniness of unity and loss, of independent identity and self-dissolution, of the pleasure of the body and its decay" (Bronfen 1992: 56). In doing this, and just as briefly, I will look at some stories of descent into hell - from different times and places and contexts - as stories which somehow are always also stories of birth, metaphors of its beauty and its horror. Celebrated around the Spring Equinox, the festival of the Phrygian goddess Cybele remembered the self-castration; death and resurrection of her son-lover Attis; and Easter - Jesus's willing death, descent into Hell and resurrection - can be seen as a version of the sacrificial mating theme.

"Hell", in the vision of patriarchal collective unconscious, would be the dreaded feminine aspect: the mother - the goddess - within whose body birth is prepared, and into whom the sacrificed god is plunged as the necessary prelude to rebirth. Truly hellish - and maternal - is the sacrificial scene which in Angela Carter's The Passion of New Eve - precedes the rebirth in a woman's body of Evelyn, prisoner in the underground realm of the great Mother. "A sacred monster", "personified and self-fulfilling fertility", Mother is one of the figures of sexuality and excess around which Carter builds the itinerary of the Passion.

Her apparently monumental body is disrupted by the double tier of nipples, the irruption of the animal, "breasted like a sow", in the human body. The grotesque asserts itself in this image of "self-fulfilling fertility"; it brings to mind Bakhtin's comment about the Kerch figurines of old pregnant women, which in its turn makes one think of the post-tridentine hell as described by Camporesi. This is typical and very strongly expressed grotesque. It is ambivalent. It is pregnant death, a death that gives birth. There is nothing completed, nothing calm and stable in the bodies of these old hags. They combine senile, decaying and deformed flesh with the flesh of new life, conceived but as yet unformed. They are monstrous, de-formed by pregnancy and by the decay of aging.

Inscribed in their bodies is the fatality of human life and death, the inevitable process of degeneration of the flesh which "demonstrates the way death gains presence in life in the realms of the real"; and within it the growth of an yet unformed living matter. Impregnated with the anguish and repugnance which are often evoked by the biological processes of reproduction, Carter's Mother easily fits into that "rhetoric of abjection" retraced by Kristeva in her analysis of Celine's texts. Disconnected, violent, obscene narration, a descent into hell which in the trilogy on the II World War becomes an apocalyptic vision; Céline's writing is filled with abjection, it explodes in images of putrefaction, evacuation, vomit, it finds in birth and in the maternal the final revelation - desire and repulsion.

Talking specifically about Rigadoon, as she continues and heightens her reflection on the "powers of horror", Kristeva writes in an incandescent passage which seems to partake of Céline's language: When Celine locates the ultimate of abjection in the birth-giving scene, he makes amply clear which fantasy is involved: something horrible to see at the impossible doors of the invisible: the mother's body. The scene of scenes is here not the so-called primal scene but the one of giving birth, incest turned inside out, flayed identity. Giving birth: the height of bloodshed and life, scorching moment of hesitation (between inside and outside, ego and other, life and death), horror and beauty, sexuality and the blunt negation of the sexual. At the doors of the feminine at the doors of abjection.

Blood colours the scene, and the feminine is the ultimate secret, annihilation and conquest. The same is true in Carter's Passion, when in the underworld of Beulah (the Pilgrim's land of peace and joy turned into a station of the passion), in a room of closed, red walls, Evelyn is terrified by the booming refrain growing louder and louder in his ears:... other women's voices took up the refrain: Now You Are At The Place Of Birth, Now You Are At The Place Of Birth I realised the warm, red place in which I lay was a simulacrum of the womb. For in this room lies the focus of darkness. She is the destination of all men, the inaccessible silence, the darkness that glides, at the last moment, always out of reach; the door called orgasm slams in his face, closes fast on the Nirvana of non-being which is gone as soon as it is glimpsed. She, this darkest one, this fleshly extinction, beyond time, beyond imagination, always just beyond, a little way beyond the fingertips of the spirit, the eternally elusive quietus who will free me from being, transform my I into the other and, in doing so, annihilate it.

Bringing it to the extreme of the uncertainty and crossing of the boundary between the sexes, this scene of rebirth (and death) gives voice to the painful feeling which accompanies the loss of self. Evelyn will become Eve, and experiencing the Other will free himself of the abjection of the maternal, readying herself to become in her turn a mother, in a world which can now be imagined as no longer dominated by the One. Playing with excess, Mother's abjection in The Passion of New Eve is at the same time a critique and an overcoming of the situation it also represents. Mother is the negative figure of a feminine reduced to the reproductive function, she is a phrase in a mystifying discourse which defines and labels: a discourse of power imprisoned in the narrowness of a partial representation which aspires to universality.

Yet it is only passing through her hellish uterine realm that the new Eve can be born, to meet in her own body knowledge capable of surpassing those mean and arrogant partialities. Carter disliked myths - she called them "consolatory nonsense" - and in The Passion Mother is reserved an inglorious end, hidden in a cave with a nervous breakdown. She disliked the way in which myths - in the case of women especially the myth of the mother goddess - have been used "to dull the pain" of an unsatisfactory present with the comfort of a past greatness.

Obviously, this is not why these myths are mentioned here; what interests me is to retrace and question, and re-interpret, some elements which have been taken up and modified in the patriarchal symbolic construction, where the life-and-death motive certainly plays an important role. Let us then go back to Inanna's voyage in the netherworld, to notice the imagery of regeneration which runs through the poem. Ereshkigal, sister and alter-ego of the goddess, is giving birth when she receives Enki's messengers. It is to Inanna that she gives (gives back) life, after the goddess - who is herself a goddess of life - has accepted the experience of death, descending into "her own depths in order to be reunited with her underworld aspects".

The goddess's experience of the unknown and fearful reality of hell dramatizes the initiation to the awareness - at once terrible and reassuring - that death is an essential part of life; that both are inscribed in the maternal power of generation, which guarantees a continuity surpassing single lives as well as single deaths. In the interpretation of Adriana Cavarero in *In Spite of Plato*, the same awareness - at once terrible and reassuring - can be read in the myth of Demeter. In the strength of Demeter's relationship with her daughter Kore, whom the infernal god Hades abducted into his reign, this myth has as its central theme the power of the mother, which is inscribed in all of nature as the power both to generate and not to generate.

This is an absolute power that presides over the place from which humans come into the world and over nothingness, as birth-no-more, the endpoint of the maternal continuum which also marks symbolically the end of the world. It is the nothingness of birth-no-more, different from the no-more or not-yet of single lives, which makes this power absolute: the core of being beyond all single beings. In the same book, re-reading the figure of Diotima, Cavarero again takes up the concept of a maternal life continuum when discussing Clarice Lispector's A Paixão segundo G.H. (The Passion according to G.H.) Narrative of experience and transcendence, the Passion - of G.H., of Lispector, of each and of all - can certainly be called a descent into hell. The text itself repeatedly signals the possibility of such a reading, also pointing to the close connection with birth and the female/maternal body. G.H. enters "the hell of living matter", "a hell of raw life [...] specimen of quiet living horror".

She leads us towards nothingness, in the "room which was empty and therefore primarily alive. I had reached nothingness, and nothingness was alive and moist". In her passion for/of knowledge, which drives her towards and beyond annihilation, life and horror are revealed to her together. And like the cockroach G.H. meets and kills, whose "only differentiation in life is that it has to be either male or female", nothingness is female, as it is disclosed to her "alive and moist" in the maid's room which is "the womb of [the] building". Or, once again using Kristeva's terms, we can see the Passion According to G. H. as a crying-out theme of suffering, an example of literature of abjection.

Written after an abortion, it is marked by this experience - life and death, death in life - and according to Rosi Braidotti it can be interpreted as a ritual purging the memory from the traces of the meeting with the organic matter which is or can be within a female body. It is also the confrontation with the maternal as the abject but inevitable site of female identity. The Passion is a text many women have loved and interrogated, and among them several feminist thinkers who have written about it, offering reflections relevant to the issue under discussion here. It is indeed a text of and about passion - suffering and ecstasy; it has been for many the discovery, as Hélène Cixous says, of a voice "come from far away", who "wrote to none and to all, to writing itself", teaching us "to be the contemporaries of a living rose, and of a concentration camp".

Teaching us to accept life and death together, as part of human experience - and of the female experience of maternity; to accept them positively. With reference to the abjection of the maternal in Céline, and also to the theorizing of abjection put forward by Kristeva, there is in Lispector a clearly different outcome. A fascinating in-depth analysis of the "state of the question", Kristeva's discourse is firmly positioned within the given symbolic order; she highlights, but does not question, the horrifying centrality in this symbolic order of the maternal figure, of woman as (potentially) maternal body.

As moments of abjection - in experience and in memory - pregnancy, the pre-natal period, and birth are analyzed in Powers of Horror as threateningly uncanny - unheimlich; they are fraught with danger, inhabited by death and the death drive. This sensation is also present, but with totally different effects, in the painful itinerary of G.H., sacrificial ritual of a journey beyond the self and into the origins, into the feminine; we're reminded of Inanna, Attis, Demeter, of Evelyn as well... and of Christ's passion. For Luisa Muraro, the experience G.H. narrates could indeed be called a "religious itinerary", the opening up of a divine horizon - although "there is no religion for it, nor is one necessary".

The figure of this itinerary, a vertical movement accompanied by a horizontal widening, is the cross; and the text, Muraro remarks, is organized in 33 sections, besides presenting a great number of identifiable references to Christ's passion - right from the title, which is an obvious signal, as it was also true for Carter's novel. Towards the end, when she is well into the process of depersonalization, well beyond the limits of subjectivity, approaching silence through the effort of language, G.H. will say:...then my nature will be accepted with its bewildered torment where suffering is not something that happens to us, but what we are. And our condition will be accepted as the only possible one, because this is what is, and not something else. And because living it is our passion. The human condition is Christ's passion.

The acceptance of death, of nothingness - which was "alive and moist" (and one is inevitably reminded of Irigaray's discourse on fluids in Ce sexe qui n'est pas un) - does not lead G. H. to despair, but to a renewed awareness of the pervasiveness of life, to the adoration of the life in her that does not have her name. It is an acknowledgement of the finite and yet infinite nature of being, already signified when "the first cry, at birth, frees a life"; because, Muraro comments (1987: 68), "in its ups and downs, the spontaneous undulating rhythm of life does not belong to us".

Undergoing a progressive dissolution of the boundaries, as though divesting herself of definitions, defences, powers - and does she not resemble Inanna, in this "process of immersion in the depth of her self"? - G.H. celebrates the "sacrament" of difference, for in renouncing humanity she discovers the inevitability of her being-sexed, and truly becomes "the woman of all women".

As Muraro puts it, in "her search for the 'unexpressing', the 'neutral', the being which is left when all is lost is a sexed being. Sexual difference is not something a woman can lose" (Muraro 1987: 78). G.H. finds the living matter of this sacrament in a cockroach - its white secretion oozing out of its crushed body: the cockroach, "borderline being, between the animal and the mineral: a configuration of eternity. It is also, by definition, an abject being, object of disgust and rejection". G. H. physically incorporates it, thus signifying a full acceptance of the abject as the site of transcendence and of life. Céline on the contrary is drunk with death - "the truth of this world is to die", he writes in Journay to the End of the Night - and in his passionate curiosity for birth he shivers with horror.

The mother, caring and nourishing figure, source of language and beauty, is for him also guilty at the same time as she gives life; for in the very moment of its beginning, there also begins the journey towards nothingness - "She did all she could to keep me alive, I just shouldn't have been born", he muses and moans in Death on an Instalment Plan. The anguish a finite life, a life dominated by death, is embodied in the female body, oxymoron of generation and annihilation; "... those females can wreck the infinite..." is Céline's tormented cry, again in Death on an Instalment Plan. The relationship to death, to one's individual "singular" death, is quite different in Lispector's text, for here life is acknowledged as both zoe and bios. In Kerényi's words, "Zoe is the thread upon which every individual bios is strung like a bead, and which, in contrast to bios, can be conceived of only as endless", as "infinite life".

In the itinerary of her passion, process of depersonalization towards the "forbidden weft of life", G.H. comes "to face within [herself] the degree of living so originary that it bordered on the inanimate". As Cavarero points out, from this dehumanized perspective, death is but an event experienced by the living individual in his or her passage toward infinite, impersonal life. There is a sort of contrasting perspective between the singularity of the living individual, who experiences his or her own death as a definitive threshold to the irreparable, and therefore as his or her nothingness, and the infinite life that lives on from this individual death and from a thousand deaths in 'tranquil rawness'.

G.H.'s journey - paraphrasing Céline we might call it a journey to the beginning of the day, and of the night - is an immersion into zoe, at a time the acceptance and overcoming of both finitude and ambiguity, the crossing of a series of thresholds of the self whereupon the subject meets the abject, and in meeting it is reborn even in death. The "hell" of the maternal, its fascination and its horror, do not disappear, they are re- interpreted as a transcendence rooted in the female body; arduous truth of being which in the singularity of each man and each woman can - differently - still be experienced as uncanny. But when death is the measure of a life which is only bios, it becomes impossible to read the traces on the new-born body as signs of that infinite thread - zoe, a life which is in us but does not have our name.

On the contrary, it is a reason for fear and scandal, that little creature exhibiting in its "alive and moist" body, marked by the mother's womb, that origin of female power where death changes - or perhaps gains - sense. So that, looking back to the endless chain of generation, to "her fifteen million of daughters", G.H. can say: "I had always been in life, it mattered little that it was not I properly speaking, not the thing that I customarily call 'I'. I have always been in life".

CONTEMPORARY CRITICAL THEORY

In the humanities and social sciences, critical theory is the examination and critique of society and literature, drawing from knowledge across social sciences and humanities disciplines...., abjection is often used to describe the state of often-marginalized groups, such as people of colour, prostitutes, and convicts.

POVERTY

Poverty is the shortage of common things such as food, clothing, shelter and safe drinking water, all of which determine our quality of life. It may also include the lack of access to opportunities such as education and employment which aid the escape from poverty and/or allow one to enjoy the respect of fellow citizens.

DISABILITY

Disability is a lack of ability relative to a personal or group standard or norm. In reality there is often simply a spectrum of ability. Disability may involve physical impairment such as sense impairment, cognitive impairment or intellectual impairment, mental disorder or various types of chronic diseases.

QUEER

Queer has traditionally meant odd or unusual, but its use in reference to LGBT communities as well as those perceived to be members of those communities has largely replaced the traditional definition and application in modern usage.

LGBT

LGBT is an acronym and initialism referring collectively to Lesbian, Gay, Bisexuality, and Transgender people. In use since the 1990s, the term LGBT is an adaptation of the initialism? LGBT which itself started replacing the phrase gay community which many within LGBT communities felt did not represent accurately all those to which it people. In this context, the concept of abject exists in between the concept of an object.

OBJECT (PHILOSOPHY)

In philosophy, an object is a thing, an entity, or a being. This may be taken in several senses. In its weakest sense, the word object is the most all-purpose of nouns, and can replace a noun in any sentence at all and the concept of the subject.

SUBJECT (PHILOSOPHY)

In philosophy, a subject is a being which has subjective experiences, subjective consciousness or a relationship with another entity. A *subject* is an observer and an *object* is a thing observed, something alive yet not. This term originated in the works of Julia Kristeva.

JULIA KRISTEVA

Julia Kristeva is a Bulgarians-France philosopher, literary critic, psychoanalysis, French feminist, and, most recently, novelist, who has lived in France since the mid-1960s. Often, the term space of abjection is also used, referring to a space that abjected things or beings inhabit.

According to Kristeva, since the abject is situated outside the symbolic order, being forced to face it is an inherently traumatic experience. For example, upon being faced with a corpse, a person would be most likely repulsed because he or she is forced to face an object which is violently cast out of the cultural world, having once been a subject.

We encounter other beings daily, and more often than not they are alive. To confront a corpse of one that we recognize as human, something that should be alive but isn't, is to confront the reality that we are capable of existing in the same state, our own mortality. This repulsion from death, excrement and rot constitutes the subject as a living being in the symbolic order. This act is done in the light of the parts of ourselves that we exclude: that is, the mother.

We must abject the maternal, the object which has created us, in order to construct an identity. This is done on the micro level of the speaking being, through her subjective dynamics, as well as on the macro level of society, through "language as a common and universal law." We use rituals, specifically those of defilement, in order to maintain clear boundaries between nature and society, the semiotic and the symbolic. This line of thought begins with Mary Douglas.

MARY DOUGLAS

Dame Mary Douglas, Order of the British Empire, Fellow of the British Academy was a British anthropologist, known for her writings on human culture and symbolism' important book, *Purity and Danger*.

PURITY AND DANGER

Purity and danger: an analysis of the concepts of impurity and taboo is an influential study by British anthropologist Mary Douglas published in 1966, as well as in Kristeva's own Black Sun.

The concept of abject is often coupled (and sometimes confused with) the idea of the uncanny, the concept of something being "un-home-like", or foreign, yet familiar. The abject can be uncanny in the sense that we can recognize aspects in it, despite its being "foreign". An example, continuing on the one used above, is that of a corpse, namely the corpse of a loved one. We will recognize that person as being close to us, but the fact that the person is dead, and "no longer" the familiar loved one, is what creates a sort of cognitive dissonance.

COGNITIVE DISSONANCE

Cognitive dissonance is an uncomfortable feeling caused by holding two contradictory ideas simultaneously. The "ideas" or "cognitions" in question may include attitude and beliefs, and also the awareness of one's behaviour, leading to abjection of the corpse.

In Powers of Horror, Julia Kristeva describes the abject as that which "disturbs identity, system and order... [and] does not respect borders, positions, rules." It is "that which defines what is fully human from what is not." By this, Kristeva is referring to that which threatens us by transgressing the bodily boundaries between self and other, challenging our bodily identity. Most of what is abject centres around the body - shit, piss, vomit, blood, saliva, filth, waste, pus, bodily fluids, and open wounds - those substances which are disturbing because they turn our insides out, dissolving the acceptable perimeters between inner/outer, living/dead, human/animal, male/female, clean/defiled, natural/supernatural.

The films of Canadian director, David Cronenberg, challenge us by incorporating the abject (body horror) by displaying the body as disfigured, deformed, diseased, infiltrated, mutated and transformed. Kristeva says we feel repulsion and horror when confronted by images of the abject because of their ambiguity, whether the other is external or internal, a part of ourselves. We define ourselves in opposition to that repulsive body that disgusts us, and it is that slippage between us and them that threatens to dehumanize us because it is so close to ourselves. In Cronenberg's films, it is the human animal that becomes the monster by transgressing taboos of the flesh.

In Shivers (1976), Cronenberg embarks on his first journey into his obsession with 'body horror' by infecting the inhabitants of a remote island with disease: a parasitic virus that is injected into a young girl by a deranged doctor. Soon, the virus spreads through sexual encounters (this before the advent of AIDS) and the whole island becomes infected. The theme of an infectious virus colonizing a living body and transforming it into the abject is a recurring one in many of Cronenberg's films. In many ways the director identifies more with the virus than the humans in his stories.

In an interview with David Cronenberg in Mondo (2000), he states, "A virus is only doing its job... The fact that it's destroying you by doing so is not its fault. It's about trying to understand interrelationships among organisms, even those we perceive as disease... of what goes on physically, psychologically and biologically to us... I identify with [the characters in Shivers] after they're infected. I identify with the parasites..."

Although Shivers is one of the first of Cronenberg's films to tap into our fear of the diseased or deformed body, the director takes this idea to a whole new level in The Brood, The Fly, Naked Lunch and Videodrome. The parasites in both

The Fly (1986) and Naked Lunch (1991) are insects – those vile creatures that trigger reactions of disgust and fear, because they remind us of our body's decay and eventual death. These creatures are the most loathsome; the fly because it colonizes and feeds from our dead flesh and excrement, and the cockroach because it invades our homes feeding off our food waste.

In Naked Lunch and Videodrome (1983), the parasite takes on a psychological manifestation as well, by metaphorically linking the addiction to drugs and sadomasochistic porn (snuff videos) to the main characters' neurosis. Here, it is the mind that becomes diseased, through the deterioration and defilement of the body. In Videodrome the body rebels against the mind by transforming into a killing machine, its physical manifestation, the abject open wound that appears on Max Renn's (James Woods) stomach that both swallows and vomits objects like a mouth. The body's orifices, including the mouth, are objects of the abject – the anus and vagina, both reminding us of our visceral nature and the boundaries of the flesh.

"The most accessible version of the 'New Flesh' in Videodrome would be that you can actually change what it means to be a human being in a physical way... mutate... [T]he flesh is necessarily treacherous, evil, bad. It is cantankerous, and it is independent... It really is like colonialism. The colonies suddenly decide that they... should detach from the control of the mother country. At first the colony is perceived as being treacherous. It's a betrayal... I think that the flesh in my films is like that... That's what it is: the independence of the body, relative to the mind, and the difficulty of the mind accepting what that revolution might entail."

In The Brood (1979), the main character's rage is manifested physically with the abject in the form of sores and open wounds. Nola Carveth (Samantha Eggar), a psychiatric patient, undergoes a new treatment called 'psychoplasmics' which gives a tangible shape to her anger in the form of mutant children. This 'brood', birthed from a gruesome sac growth on her ribs, are neither dead nor alive. They are deformed monstrosities who exist in a liminal state, an abject state on the boundaries of the sacred and profane. The open wounds and birthing sac are similar to the body's orifices, and produce in us the same kind of horror and revulsion.

THE MONSTROUS-FEMININE

"The female is as it were a deformed male." - Aristotle

Kristeva further categorizes the abject as food, bodily wastes, the mutated or mutilated body, the female body and the sexual body. Barbara Creed, in her essay "Horror and the Monstrous-Feminine: An Imaginary Abjection", uses Kristeva's concept of the abject and traces it to representations of the mother (the monstrous-feminine) in her analysis of gender and the horror film.

According to Creed, the uncanny nature of the feminine is characterized by abjection in her body through her sexuality and reproductive functions whose transgressions and deviations undermines the social order. Both sexually alluring and physically disgusting, the female body is most threatening because it represents man's desire, disgust and fears, as well as reminding him both of his birth and death. In The Brood, Nola is the 'monstrous womb' giving birth to these terrible creatures. In one scene, she is shown licking the birthing fluid from one of her newborn monsters like a feral animal.

This image disgusts the viewer because she is crossing a boundary - she is not quite human, but nor is she animal. She is a monstrous creature somewhere in-between. And, her children, who are of the same flesh, "in a sense... the double of the mother... horrify because they testify to the power of the mother, through her uncanny womb, to give birth to a diminutive double of herself." In Crash (1996), both the abject and the monstrous-feminine are manifested and fetishized in the wounds of a car crash victim, Gabrielle, played by actress Rosanna Arquette.

Transformed by modern technology and prosthetic limbs, Gabrielle is a modern embodiment of the Frankenstein monster. Although horribly disfigured by the car crash, Gabrielle's wounds and scarred body become objects of fetishistic desire, as do the wounds of other victims throughout the film. Fuelled by their perverse obsession with bodies deformed by motor-vehicle accidents, the characters' transgress into a territory that both repels and attracts, simultaneously. Just as we cannot look away from a real-life car crash, we cannot unglue our eyes from the deviant sexuality portrayed onscreen. In Dead Ringers (1988), the concept of the 'monstrous womb' is taken to the ultimate extreme when gynecologist Beverly Mantle (Jeremy Irons) – the feminine half of the Mantle twins – examines his patient's womb, Claire Niveau (Geneviève Bujold).

He discovers that her womb is severely deformed, containing three cervixes. Claire, like other stereotypical women portrayed in horror film, leads Beverly into a path of self-destruction which ultimately results in his death. As Beverly becomes increasingly dependant on drugs and delusional, he designs specialized gynecological tools, which look more like torture devices, to cure all of his patients' reproductive deformities. These 'tools', which he later claims are used for separating Siamese twins, eventually become the weapons that he uses to kill his identical twin, Elliott.

CARTESIAN DUALISM

In Dead Ringers, Cronenberg also explores the Cartesian concept of the mind/body schism, a recurring theme that has preoccupied him throughout his career. In each of his films, the characters must deal with their rebellious body that confronts the autonomy of the mind – a battle in which the intellect eventually looses as it surrenders to madness. "Gynaecologic is such a beautiful metaphor for the mind/body split. Here it is: the mind of men – or women – trying to understand sexual organs. I make my twins as kids extremely cerebral and analytical. They want to understand femaleness in a clinical way by dissection and analysis, not by experience, emotion or intuition. 'Can we dissect out the essence of femaleness? We're afraid of the emotional immediacy of woman ness, but we're drawn to it. How can we come to terms with it? Let's dissect it.'"

Cronenberg's films invade the space of the viewer by forcing us explore the both physical and mental manifestations of our existence as human animals. Although, at times his plots seem surreal, there is an element of truth in each that horrifies us, because it shows how we are vulnerable to outer and inner forces that we cannot control the forces that threaten the boundaries of the self and transgress social boundaries. Forces that portray us fallible, temporal and corporeal and we are not immune to disease or death.

In Mary Shelley's original *Frankenstein; or The Modern Prometheus* (1818)—unlike nearly all of its many adaptations—there are at least two levels of "dream" for Victor Frankenstein, the title character. The first, which is given a dream-like quality by his insistence that it is not "the vision of a madman", is his hopeful daydream of what the creation of a human life through science might ultimately mean:

Life and death appeared to me ideal bounds, which I should first break through, and pour a torrent of light into our dark world. A new species would bless me as its creator and source; many happy and excellent natures would owe their being to me. No father could claim the gratitude of his child as completely as I should deserve theirs. Pursuing these reflections, I thought, if I could bestow animation on lifeless matter, I might in the process of time (although I now found it impossible) renew life where death had apparently devoted the body to corruption.

To be sure, it is this vision to which Victor refers, along with his hope that his creation might be "beautiful," when he later laments, on actually seeing his creature come to life, that "the *beauty of the dream* vanished" to be replaced by "horror and disgust" at a "wretch" more "hideous" than a "mummy again endued with animation". Even so, this daydream raises far-reaching questions on its own that persist in the Western world to this day, among the many reasons for the long survival of Shelley's arresting story. To what degree, as the biological sciences have developed (now quite rapidly in our age of biotechnology), is Victor's aspiration a valuable one, even within the long-standing middle-class ideology of men whereby the self-made individual achieves his potential in products of his ingenuity that can change the world?

Exactly when does this dream, appealing as it was in 1818 and remaining in 2002, "cross a line" (and where *is* that line?) that separates worthwhile ambition from socially destructive obsession? Is there so much ego in Victor's *hubris*, with all the "I"s and "me"s in the above passage, that *Frankenstein* is primarily an attack on scientific aspiration as too often self-serving, as exploitative of manipulated "others" mainly for the sake of how they will reflect back on the scientist or discoverer? Indeed, is such ego separable from the aspiration?

Are we looking at science "going too far," assuming a more moderate and sociable version of itself, or is Mary Shelley exposing a dynamic of selfish dominance that is endemic to such quests from their very inception? After all, Victor tells his story using these words, among others, to Robert Walton, the arctic explorer who "frames" Frankenstein's and his creature's stories within a packet of letters sent from the ice-floes of the far North to his sister back in England. Victor's stated purpose for his narrative is to offer warnings to others who "seek for knowledge and wisdom," as Walton is doing, as though Frankenstein's desires and errors could be universalized to apply to many individuals who have, as Walton has, dreamed of an ultimate discovery (such as the North Pole) that "presents [itself first] to the imagination as a region of beauty and delight".

Are the features of Frankenstein's daydream, then, too much those of Shelley's contemporaries and too persistent even for many of us today? Is Mary Shelley, as some have suggested, writing a critique of male or Romantic aspiration as she knew it, particularly in such poets and dabblers in science as Lord Byron and Percy Bysshe Shelley (whom she married in December of 1816)? Or are such longings bound up, at their time and since, with our best ambitions for making the world a better place and human life longer? Are the darkest and brightest sides of this dream inseparably mixed together? Have they been so for almost two hundred years in Western culture? And if so, why?

The problems that Victor's conscious dream presents, however, are greatly complicated when we recall that there is a second, more *pre*conscious dream (really a *nightmare*) into which Victor falls in Mary Shelley's novel. Right after he recoils from the first sight of his finished, and now breathing, creation, at least as he remembers in his narration to Walton, Frankenstein "rushes" in frightened disgust from his makeshift laboratory and, finally giving way to exhaustion after long "depriv[ing him]self of rest and health", throws himself on his bed, with his most conscious thoughts of escape from his problems being focussed on his fiancée, Elizabeth Lavenza: I slept indeed, but I was disturbed by the wildest dreams. I thought I saw Elizabeth, in the bloom of health, walking in the streets of Ingolstadt [his present location].

Delighted and surprised, I embraced her; but as I imprinted the first kiss on her lips, they became livid with the hue of death; her features appeared to change, and I thought I beheld the corpse of my dead mother in my arms; a shroud enveloped her form, and I saw the grave-worms crawling in the folds of the flannel. I started from my sleep with horror; a cold dew covered my forehead, my teeth chattered, and every limb became convulsed; when, by the dim and yellow light of the moon, as it forced its way through the window-shutters, I beheld the wretch—the miserable monster whom I had created.

This stunning moment, virtually unique to the novel in the many versions of *Frankenstein*, has understandably provoked numerous and varied interpretations, several which I will review shortly. Its immediate effect, though, is to undermine Victor's lofty daydream by revealing a preconscious disposition towards a sort of necrophilia with his mother as what is more truly symbolized in the sewn-together features of the being he has created. Is this the real dream—the actual dark urges—at the foundation of

Frankestein's project, a deeper motivation that is covered over and obscured by his conscious ambitions?

Especially in juxtaposition to its hopeful counterpart, what does this dream tell us about the larger meanings and cultural resonance of *Frankenstein* the novel, about the wider Romantic quest for "brave new worlds" to which it clearly responds, and about the development of this story after the novel appeared in versions that are clearly based on this nightmare, even if (or perhaps because) they refuse to repeat it? In other words, what *is* "Frankenstein's dream" at bottom? What lies most fundamentally behind this tale's ongoing importance to us as a persistent Western myth? The essays in this collection all strive to answer these questions and to do so from very different perspectives that have rarely been applied to *Frankenstein* before now.

Most of the answers so far, of course, given the contents of Victor's second dream, have been psychoanalytic ones. *Frankenstein* unquestionably joins with other early nineteenth-century texts in beginning to craft the ingredients of the unconscious and the interpretation of dreams that Sigmund Freud proposed as scientific truth by the 1890s. For most Freudian critics, Victor's pursuit of life's deepest secret by digging up body-parts in Mother Earth therefore stems, like his inconsistent pursuit of Elizabeth, from an unconscious desire for *and* a resistance to a reunion with the body of his deceased mother—the very feminine origin he has tried to avoid by producing a "child" without a woman or sexual intercourse.

Indeed, Victor's mother in Shelley's novel, Caroline, dies shortly before he leaves for Ingolstadt because she catches scarlet fever from Elizabeth (the initial object of Victor's embrace in his dream), whom the older woman lovingly nurses in the Frankenstein household until her own "fever was very malignant".

Her death, as Victor recalls to Walton by stopping his narrative cold at this point, is the most devastating event in the young scientist's life:

I need not describe the feelings of those whose dearest ties are rent by that most irreparable evil, the void that presents itself to the soul, and the despair that is exhibited on the countenance. It is so long before the mind can persuade itself that she, whom we saw every day, and whose very existence appeared a part of our own, can have departed for ever—that the brightness of a beloved eye can have been extinguished, and the sound of a voice so familiar, and dear to the ear, can be hushed, never more to be heard. These are the reflections of the first days; but when the lapse of time proves the reality of the evil, then the actual bitterness of the grief commences.

Still shattered by such an enormous loss for him, even when he speaks to Walton, Victor not surprisingly covers up his extreme longing in his supposedly very different process of creation. But the repressed manifestly returns the more his efforts come to fruition. Victor's finished product is revealed by his dream at the moment of "birth" to be a cover for his drive to return to his mother—to rejoin himself to her body, for which Elizabeth is but a displacement—and to do so by entering, Orpheus-like, into the world of buried dissolution (the charnel houses and graveyards from which he steals pieces of bodies) where his mother, like Eurydice, has been taken by Death itself and from which he longs to recover her (though with no more success than Orpheus had).

Such impulses turn out to be the most fundamental of the infantile drives that Freud finds sequestered in the human unconscious and describes as disguising themselves in half-conscious displacements, especially in dreams. By these lights, Victor is continuing the universal childish longing to return to the body of the mother from which the infant has been thrust (one basis of all the longings of *eros* in life) and pursuing that goal, more than most do consciously, by manifesting a death-wish to re-enter his and everyone's intrauterine state prior to birth (the drive of *thanatos* in Freud's *Beyond the Pleasure Principle* [1920]).

Since such drives have to be radically obscured in any manifestations of the unconscious for Freud, even in dreams, it is no surprise for the psychoanalytic reader that they appear most overtly throughout *Frankenstein* in figures that seem their opposite, in this case the fabrication of a male body by a man that seems to avoid women and motherhood altogether while supposedly making life out of death and not vice-versa. The hero's nightmare in *Frankenstein*, it seems, is at least the Freudian displacement where we are all shown to be concealing, in fact to be *reversing*, infantile longings of both *eros* and *thanatos* (loving procreation and death-seeking destruction) so that they are sublimated within our most "adult" pursuits.

Within this theory, the longings and violence in both these deep drives, which Freud sees in some of his works as the drives of the *id*, come out in Victor's creature as they do not in the creator who has projected, even othered them, onto his creation as though they all belonged "over there" and not in himself. Such a combination of life-creating and life-destroying impulses in the "monster" is part of what makes him enact the killings of little brother William, the servant Justine, Elizabeth, and even Victor's best friend, Henry Clerval, that Victor subconsciously wishes to bring about, both to dominate his world and to return it all to death, the inclinations he is most unwilling to face as basic aspects of his fundamental being.

It is in this way; after all, that Frankenstein's creature is a form of "the uncanny" as Freud defines that feeling of profound revulsion and déjà vu in his 1919 essay of that name. What Victor comes to call his "daemon" is so abhorrent in its grotesque unfamiliarity, according to "The Uncanny," because what it harbours is the deeply familiar, his creator's own repressed and most infantile drives. For several insightful feminist critics, however, this Freudian scenario about Frankenstein's dream is a cover for another hidden—and more widely cultural and political—unconscious.

While seeming to long for a reunion of himself with both his mother and death, Victor in his usurpation of "making a baby" may be striving to "kill" the feminine powers, from Elizabeth's to Caroline's, that threaten male supremacy in ways quite apparent to Mary Shelley, the daughter and namesake of Mary Wollstonecraft (best known then and now for *A Vindication of the Rights of Woman* [1792]). After all, Victor's "researches into [the] secrets [of the mother], to usurp her powers," be she Mother Earth, his own, or *any* mother able to conceive a child, as Margaret Homans shows, really "require that she be dead," that her literal body recede behind and beneath Frankenstein's male metaphor (or substitute) for the process of birth.

Since well before Frankenstein's and Mary Shelley's time, "woman" in the West has come to be associated with earthy "nature" (as opposed to "culture"), "death" just as much as life (with Euridyce, like Persephone, staying in the underworld as long as Death commands her, while Orpheus ascends back to the earth), uncontrolled "emotion" or "sensibility" (in contrast to masculine "reason"), and the "body" more than "the mind" (especially as the birth-source of all human beings in their bodily forms). All of that means that woman is too often "the literal," the possibly chaotic and uncontainable "Real" or "Thing in itself," Kant's imperceptible and irrational *Ding an Sich* of which only mental (and masculine) Reason and Understanding can supposedly make some sense.

The standard male quest, taken to a revealing extreme in *Frankenstein*, is to contain and distance that amorphous feminine Real by fabricating rationalized constructs and symbols that seem to contain it, or even transcend it, by way of distinctly male frames of reference (such as his male "demonstration" of fabricated life) through which we glimpse the deep and primordial Feminine only "through a glass darkly," preferably as though she were dead and the male constructs that repress her were alive.

It is this process that is the real monstrosity, according to this important feminist view. The horror he faces there is that the mother whose birth-powers he has sought to usurp, now joined with death, is also the object of desire that he most wants and does not want simultaneously. With this kind of unconscious as its real foundation, then, "the novel is about the collision between androcentric [male-centered] and gynocentric [woman-centered] theories of creation, a collision that results in the denigration of maternal childbearing through its circumvention by male creation".

There is even a further dimension in Victor's creature *and* his dream if we consider both from the perspective of a pro-feminist psychoanalytic approach that is more recent—and far reaching—than these others we have noted. According to the view of "monstrosity" advanced by Julia Kristeva (herself a psychotherapist as well as cultural theorist) in her *Powers of Horror* (1980, trans. 1982), grotesque "others" in Western culture are really forms of the "abject" created by the psychological process of "abjection." Literally abject means both "to throw off " and "to throw under," so Kristeva defines "abjection" as a process of ejecting or displacing preconscious multiplicities in the self into an externalized alter ego through which what is preconscious, already quite disguised, is "thrown under" the eventual dominance of sanctioned cultural discourses and other forms of social control.

For Kristeva, moreover, the multiplicities most abjected by us—the anomalies we most want to "throw off" from the deepest roots of our being—are the state of being half-inside/half-outside the mother at the moment of birth (and thus self and other all at once) and the concomitant state of being half-dead and half-alive at the same moment (thus intermingling in our very foundations what are later thought to be total opposites). Such primordial conditions of the self as "in-between... ambiguous... composite" are for all of us an "immemorial violence" out of which any child strives to become "separated from another body in order to be" and hence to be able to construct a distinct public identity.

The thrown-off abject, the product of abjection, is thus the symbolic and disguised repository of that violence and basic otherness-of-the-self-within-itself, the means for staking out a supposed identity over against it. The monstrous "other" that uncannily seems to harbour all this ultimately exposes and conceals it by being both highly compelling and highly repugnant at the same time. According to this view, Frankenstein's creature is a quintessential example of the abject in being a highly differentiated and horrifying double of his creator.

The strongest evidence of that in Mary Shelley's novel is Frankenstein's "monstrous" dream of being re-enveloped by his mother and death simultaneously, since there the creature's revolting visage is shown to be ultimately based on the two deepest anomalies that Kristeva sees as the most abjected of all: the visceral sense of being both separate from and absorbed into the mother and the sense, both fearful and seductive, of being embraced by death right at what seems the birth of a new form of life. In addition to being a return of the primarily repressed and the "uncanny," then, Victor's non-waking dream is also the exposure of an abjection and the abject, in which the irreconcilable deep differences in the self are made to seem outside it in a pasting-together of bodies as manifestly different from each other as the abjection subject really is at its most underlying levels.

Victor's creature and dream as containing the abject, in fact, allow both of them to harbor numerous thrown-down anomalies basic to Frankenstein, Walton, and their readers well beyond those that Powers of Horror emphasizes. The creature, as the many studies on him have shown, is a throwing off social and cultural intermixtures that are just as repugnant as the anomalies in Victor's dream—and consequently as fully abjected — because they are just as basic to the sources of Victor's (and any middle-class Anglo male's) construction of a self, even as it wants to leave those very sources behind more than most others.

That is why the creature is as racially mixed as Victor claims not to be, pointing to the interdependency of white and other races in a colonial economy; as working class (indeed, as like the "wandering beggars" of Shelley's time) as Victor tries to avoid being in his aspirations to scientific supremacy, thereby showing how the managerial middle classes are creating the "monstrosity" of the industrial working class they claim to rise above; as partly self-educated in his accidental reading of older books, as Victor works to be formally educated, indicative of Victor's own early process of learning that he falsely claims he transcends at the time he makes his creature; as artificial and industrial as well as organic while Victor claims to be only organic and able to keep these domains entirely distinct; and as rebelliously uncontrollable in his insistent and increasingly independent multiplicity, while Victor, without admitting as much, consequently denies the vision in his lofty daydream.

The mix of supposed opposites in the creature is the mix in Victor that the young scientist, again and again, tries to deny but can only "abject" onto an other who is pointedly not him and very much him (or at least the many anomalies on which he is really grounded) at the same time. Frankenstein's preconscious dream, though it reveals less of these mixtures than the creature does, at least shows the abjection of deep Kristevan levels of somatic memory as the fundamental throwing-off-and-under that makes all of the other abjections possible in one terrifying and sympathetic creation.

The dream even includes its own dimension of socio-cultural abjection in that it throws off Frankenstein's (and many men's) extremely mixed attitudes towards women as objects of desire and domination, mixed with fears of and longings for reabsorption by the mother, in a scene of symbolic shifting where attraction changes into the repulsion connected to it and sexual longing becomes a death-wish both for the self and for the fundamental Femininity that is so basic to male existence that men often believe they must throw it off to be really masculine beings.

These mixtures repeat themselves, we should remember, in Victor's later waking nightmare when he attempts the creation of a female mate for his monster and feels he must finally destroy her instead, killing the potential of her life both for increased female independence and for the reproduction of a different race that could challenge white, as much as male, supremacy. The dream behind Frankenstein's conscious hopes, it turns out, underwrites his aspirations with several repressed—and abjected—levels of personal and cultural contradictions, many of which remain as basic to us today, fortunately or sadly, as they were coming to be in 1818.

One reason that *Frankenstein* and the creature in it have become such lasting and important cultural touchstones since the novel appeared is that Victor's creation, with its foundations in the conflicts animating his dream, has become a symbolic focal point for the abjection of a great many cultural, as well as psychological, inconsistencies and quandaries basic to us all since the Enlightenment, if only so that these anomalies can be both addressed and disguised in a way that allows us to face them or avoid them, as we choose.

Frankenstein, from the novel through all its adaptations, may well be our modern world's most lasting dark dream, the one that most consistently haunts the industrial and post-industrial West with the many consequences of our fear (or is it sometimes our desire?) that mechanical reproductions of various kinds may replace or threaten the forms of human reproduction in many different ways. After all, we might say, it all began as a dream, one that occurred right at the juncture where the rising industrial world and the science connected to it were now clearly replacing, while many were still upholding older economies and the social orders that they sustained.

If we can believe Mary Shelley in her Preface to the 1831 revised edition of *Frankenstein*, her title character's visions, both conscious and preconscious, look back to one dream she claims to have had herself in 1816 near Geneva, Switzerland. There, while staying near and often with Lord Byron at the Villa Diodati, she agreed, as many of her readers know, to join a ghost-story writing contest between herself, P.B. Shelley, Byron, and the latter's live-in physician and occasional lover, Dr. John Polidori.

At first she says she made no connection between this group's nocturnal readings in Gothic tales of reanimated portraits or specters—such as those in Jean Baptiste Eryiès's

Fantasmagoriana (1812), which is heavily indebted to Horace Walpole's *The Castle of Otranto*—and the many other conversations she recalls overhearing between Byron and Percy Shelley on "the nature of the principle of life" and on whether it was possible, based on the surmises and experiments of Dr. Erasmus Darwin, Charles's grandfather, that "a corpse would be re-animated" by "galvanism" or some other method.

She states that she heard Byron and Shelley, themselves rebellious descendants of a fading aristocracy, say that it was possible that the component parts of a creature might be manufactured, brought together, and endued with vital warmth" (Ibid., my emphasis). She then goes on:

> Night waned upon this talk, and even the witching hour had gone by, before we retired to rest. When I placed my head upon my pillow, I did not sleep, nor could I be said to think. My imagination, unbidden, possessed and guided me, gifting the successive images that arose to my mind with vividness far beyond the usual bounds of reverie. I saw—with shut eyes but acute mental vision,—I saw the pale student of unhallowed arts kneeling beside the thing he had put together. I saw the hideous phantasm of a man stretched out, and then, on the working of some powerful engine, show signs of life, and stir with an uneasy, half vital motion.
>
> Frightful it must be; for supremely frightful would be the effect of any human endeavour to mock the stupendous mechanism of the creator of the world. His success would terrify the artist; he would rush away from his odious handiwork, horror-stricken. He would hope that, left to itself, the slight spark of life which he had communicated would fade; that this thing, which had received such imperfect animation, would subside into dead matter; that he might sleep in the belief that the silence of the grave would quench for ever the transient existence of the hideous corpse which he had looked upon as the cradle of life. He sleeps; but he is awakened; he opens his eyes; behold the horrid thing stands at his bedside, opening his curtains, and looking on him with

yellow, watery, but speculative eyes. I opened mine in terror.... On the morrow I announced that I had thought of a story.

To be sure, we should not simply take this account to be absolutely true, since it is hardly immediate or objective. Given its "witching hour" and "possession" by the "imagination" – quite conventional literary figures by 1831 – it is quite clearly heightened for its new readers fifteen years after the events recalled. It is also quite selective in its memories – and repressive in being so. The dream that arises when Frankenstein sleeps, our principal focus here, is completely absent from Shelley's initial dream.

Was something like Victor's embrace of his dead mother, and thus the immediate connection of birth with death, too painful to be admitted to consciousness then, considering that Mary Shelley still blamed herself somewhat for the death of her mother just a few days after Mary Wollstonecraft gave birth to her in 1797 and was still in great pain from the death of her own first infant shortly after it was born to herself and Percy Shelley in 1815? Did the disguising of these dimensions in Victor's dream come after this story was much more developed, or was such nightmarish dream-work already behind the initial conception of the idea and therefore repressed beneath its remembered surface?

We will never know for sure, but we can say, given the above passage's oscillation between age-old Christian images of the "unhallowed" and the far more recent "mechanism" of the "spark of life," that it does mark, as a dream, the psychological and symbolic effects of a major transition in Western history as many of its elements became "galvanized" together in a well-focussed fictional image. While it may "throw off" what is most abject for Mary Shelley herself by 1831, this remembered or reconstructed or constructed dream at least abject the irresolution in Western culture around 1818 (and since) between hearkening back towards old Christian prohibitions about human presumption that might claim the life-giving powers of God and aspiring towards scientific advancement and early industrial technology that could allow human beings to improve their lives themselves. It even abjects the indecision of the eighteen-teens between the source of life as an infused and infusing principle outside any single body, advocated in England by Dr. John Abernathy, and the opposing materialist view that life is generated by the structural interrelation of organic and circulating elements within bodies, argued by Sir William Lawrence, all of which was debated quite publicly from 1816 on. Which of these is the "powerful engine" in the stretched-out "phantasm": a "spark of life" which might just be left to go out or a "vital motion" stirring from within the body dreamt of as coming to life? Moreover, is the use of "engine" here a suggestion of organic vitality or of the ultimately mechanical and industrial possibly taking control of the biological, especially since woman, even here, is pointedly left out of the birth process?

If Mary Shelley's inaugural dream contains the wish-fulfillment of at least giving artificial birth to a story in the face of the deaths of both her mother and her child, it also registers the cultural nightmare of being caught at a crossroads of historical tendencies pulling at each other in the early nineteenth century—and still drawing us into a tug of war today. Whether or not we accept this authorial dream as the "source" of the dreams—and especially Victor's dream—in *Frankenstein* the novel, it joins these others in showing that all these dreams have profound psychological and cultural dimensions, layer upon layer, ones that still need more of the further exploration attempted by the essays in this collection for the Romantic Circles *Praxis* series.

What I have tried to provide here, with occasional intrusions of my own perspective, is a coalescence of the dominant existing interpretations of Victor Frankenstein's dream as Mary Shelley renders it. After all, it is this previous range of responses to that rich symbolic tangle, along with the novel and its many adaptations, to which the scholars in the accompanying essays react by pointing to several possibilities that remain unexplored in Victor's dream and the others connected to it. All of these expert contributors, like myself, are not so much out to undermine the interpretations I have summarized or interfaced here as to expose what is so abjected in Frankenstein's dream that it has not yet been accommodated by analytical criticism. Though we have not worked towards any uniformity in this collection, the general argument advanced by the included essays is that Victor Frankenstein's dream, despite all that has been said about it, still reveals to us some as-yet-unexamined relationships—ones that go to the heart of both Romanticism and Gothic writing, it turns out – between literary forms, conflicting cultural agendas, psychological anomalies, and functions of language and images. The need to study Frankenstein's dream remains as ongoing and pressing as it has been for decades because it still causes us to confront what Victor Frankenstein's and the reader will not face steadily: the unaccommodated tugs-of-war between cultural tendencies that have been and remain "cathected" onto *Frankenstein* and the endless adaptations of it.

If I could recommend an order of reading these all-new interpretations, I would urge proceeding from my overview of the interpretive tradition here to the provocative piece by Anne Williams, author of the important *Art of Darkness* (1995) on the roots of Gothic fiction and their reappearance in Romanticism. In the key dream in Mary Shelley's novel and much that surrounds it, Williams recovers the interplay so many of us have forgotten—or repressed?—between the established eighteenth-century tradition of sentimental fiction in England and France, well known to, and often used by, Mary Shelley in ways that very few have discussed, and the dimensions of *Frankenstein* that are genuinely sadistic in the quite literal sense that they recall the fictions (and even the life) of the Marquis de Sade (1740-1814).

These seemingly opposite registers of emotion, vision, and writing, Williams's shows, surprisingly interpenetrate each other throughout Shelley's novel and especially in Victor's dream. That established, this essay goes on to reveal what is repressed behind and within this combination. Why, Williams asks us, would these symbolic strains be so interrelated, despite their apparent rejection of each other? For her, we discover, their interaction, itself long repressed, serves to both cover and articulate an even deeper abjection enacted by them both: the "throwing off" and "under" of a broadly Feminine set of biological, social, and linguistic levels on which Western culture, like Frankenstein and Sade, is far more dependent than almost anyone wants to admit.

The next essay I would recommend is Matthew VanWinkle's, since it builds so well on his established expertise with the parodic side of Romantic literature in England. This piece joins Williams' in explaining the intertextuality of Shelley's original novel—very extensive in the book and thus a rich subject for interpreters already—by focusing, not only on its parodies of several texts prior to it, but how it also imports parody into the very core of its story and thereby foregrounds a deep parodic strain in a "second generation" Romantic literature that has long been separated from such impulses except in analyses of Byron.

Lest we take "parody" in too simple a sense by emphasizing only its satirical dimension, which is also there in *Frankenstein* in its jibes at solipsistic Romantic aspiration, VanWinkle grounds his discussion helpfully by showing us a fuller range of what parody can embody in writing prior to and in Frankenstein itself. He then demonstrates that Victor *Frankenstein,* as much as the novel about him, is driven by parodic "demons" against his conscious intentions, enough that the creature he makes is itself/himself a parody both of contemporary biological debates and of the several texts it/he reads and half-imitates in order to, among other things, come into discourse—a process VanWinkle therefore finds parodic of standard human discourse in the end.

Parody even extends to Frankenstein's dream, VanWinkle argues, in the way it persistently echoes and plays off of Coleridge's "Christabel" (first published in 1816) and in that fashion intensifies what is already parodic in Coleridge's most openly Gothic poem. Though many have explored *Frankenstein*'s allusions to *The Rime of the Ancient Mariner* as the main key to the novel's extensive conversation with Coleridge, VanWinkle reminds us of a quite different interchange between two Gothic renditions of a deeply parodic dreamscape. He thereby reveals that this kind of nightmare, albeit in several different forms, is one that troubles and underlies much of Romanticism in general far more than most of us have realized.

In the next essay I would recommend in this itinerary, the remarkable piece by John Rieder, author of *Wordsworth's Counter revolutionary Turn* (1997), we return to the perspectives of psychoanalysis, but in a strikingly different way from any of the readings I have recounted above. This analysis probes the most "disgusting" aspects of the creature and Victor's dream in Shelley's novel and then shows how these are altered and/or avoided in later adaptations ranging from R.B. Peake's play *Presumption* (1823) to George Romero's film *Dawn of the Dead* (1978). Rieder thereby exposes the basic story's links to what Freud in 1916 saw as the child's frequent impulse to duplicate the powers of the mother by imaginatively "giving birth" through the bowels, thus producing the abhorrent but fascinating "fecal child."

We are then shown, not surprisingly, how Victor's original creature and his dream embody many more dimensions than any other adaption has suggested of what the 'fecal child' abjects, in part because of a strong cultural resistance since 1818 to facing those very dimensions. With this point made, however, Rieder then follows its implications out to expose the as-yet-unseen social critique that Mary Shelley is unleashing through her novel's use of the fecal child. Such a figure, as Freud saw, defies traditional male-female distinctions and the patriarchal order that sustains them. Some possibilities of this defiance are thus embedded in *Frankenstein's* positive dream, as well as in his nightmare and Mary Shelley's novel. It is above all this set of potentials, Rieder shows that adaptations of Frankenstein have tried to occlude by effacing, while still dimly recalling, the fecal child of the original book.

The concluding essay in this recommended succession, the highly arresting contribution by Marc Redfield, shifts the focus quite radically by working backwards from a major adaptation—James Whale's *Frankenstein* film for Universal Studios in 1931—to the movements of phrases and images in Mary Shelley's text, particularly the progression of dissolves in Victor's maternal nightmare. Building on modes of analysis already used suggestively in his prize-winning *Phantom Formations* (1996) and his forthcoming *Politics of Aesthetics*, Redfield exposes how self-reflexive Whale's film really is and thus how it foregrounds the fundamental process of mechanically reproducible image-production and the sheer positioning of manufactured motion pictures prior to any narrative or meaning, though the audience is admittedly most conscious of these latter levels in viewing the film.

Despite all the differences between the 1931 film and the Shelley novel in plot-elements and characterizations, this essay argues that the strongest resemblance between the two, not much noted until now, may appear in those dimensions—most revealed in Frankenstein's dream, the many artificial composing of the creature (including his learning of language), and the movement of doublings across characters and descriptions in the book—where the "work in the age of mechanical reproduction" (echoing Walter Benjamin) announces its emergent and relentless process of self-duplicating manufacture.

It is *this* "monstrosity," given the rise of industrialism and its post-industrial successors that may be the most feared and resisted of all the horrors that appear in the novel and its film adaptations. If there is a repressed level in Victor's aspirations of both desire and death-wish associated culturally and psychologically with the deeply Feminine (as Redfield suggests), that level is made possible, as well as partially concealed, this final essay shows, by the moving "technics" of images becoming other images that not-so-subliminally enable and threaten our modern and postmodern lives. As much as abjections of feminine foundations appear in the creature and his creator's dream, so do the most basic modes of image-production that we fear, but in *Frankenstein* we are forced to recognize them as the means by which we construct ourselves and our extensions of our manufactured beings in our post-"Enlightenment" world.

These arguments, to be sure, are not the end of the debate over Frankenstein's multiple dreams and therefore make no pretense of being "last words" on a subject that still bedevils us, as it should. Indeed, by highlighting levels in Mary Shelley's novel and its progeny that have not yet been clearly exposed amid the barrage of readings that have interpreted this cultural phenomenon, this collection shows the wide range and still-burning urgency of the issues that *Frankenstein* has raised and continues to raise for us as the most reproduced and studied Romantic and Gothic story in the history of published literature and Western film production.

Because of the questions raised here, as in *Frankenstein*, these essays are pleased to claim that we are thrown back on the most basic kinds of reflection on Western self-representation, on how "we" have come to be and remain what "we" think we are in the Anglo-European-American West. To be sure, like many readers and viewers, we can ignore these unsettling revelations and let them recede behind the words and images that have vividly articulated them since 1818 in version after version of *Frankenstein*.

The collective hope of these pieces, however, is that Western minds will not continue to "throw off" these several anomalous tangles that ground and disturb our modern lives. In our view, we should face them and their consequences, if only to refuse their most destructive possibilities, so that they will not finally be "lost in darkness and distance," as Shelley's famous creature threatens to be (Shelley 221) but in fact has never been, we are happy to say, since *Frankenstein* began haunting us at the height of English Romanticism.

7

Hatred of Women in Religions

MISOGYNY IN GENERAL

Misogyny, the hatred of women, is present in all of the five major world religions. They all use sinister means in cooperation with others to implement and maintain this practice. This unfavourable prejudice against women violates the United Nation's Universal Declaration of Human Rights that affirms the principle of the inadmissibility of discrimination and proclaims that all human beings are born free and equal in dignity and rights and that everyone is entitled to all the rights and freedoms set forth therein, without distinction of any kind, including distinction based on sex. It is explicitly stated in an UN document: Go to Convention on the Elimination of All Forms of Discrimination against Women.

Misogyny is very similar to racism and it is as pernicious. The perpetrator's mindset is close to those who hate the victims of their actions because the victims give them a bad conscience. The "sacred" scriptures and guiding interpretations of these religions describe women as dangerous temptresses, ignorant, subhuman, even sub-animal, and the root and cause of all suffering in this world. This extreme prejudice has harmed the whole of humanity. It diverted from identifying the real causes of misery. Moreover, it excluded women from obtaining an education and opportunities outside the home. Hence, it prevented them from making contributions to the humanities and in particular religion, the sciences, and progress in general.

To invoke the male sex organ as a proof of superiority is laughable, irrelevant, ugly and pernicious. Its only religious "value" is to attract male followers whose self-esteem is easily raised because they have little to begin with. But it is idiotic and obscene to make every male brute superior to even the most accomplished female. In reality, there is no measurable difference in intelligence between the sexes (and the races). Moreover, brute force aside, women are physically stronger as indicated by an average seven-year-longer life expectancy. Also, the morality or sociability of women's actions in society are superior as the overwhelmingly 85% male prison population demonstrates.

An antidote for counteracting the poison of misogyny is the separation of church and state. It allows a nation to liberate itself from the worst consequences of this irrationality. Democracies that practice a separation of church and state have largely succeeded in neutralizing this prejudice. However, the hierarchy of their religions is still strictly patriarchal. It is an orthodox force that resists change and wants to turn the clock back to return women to their "divinely ordained" place. For instance, the Roman Catholic Church is obsessed with depriving a woman's right to control her body when it fights birth control and the termination of even early pregnancies. In short, while refusing to participate in child raising themselves, for them nothing but mandatory pregnancy for women will do.

But it was not always this way. Several thousand years ago, in the early cultures of Egypt, Mesopotamia, and India, female deities were the main object of reverence. These goddesses included the Mother Goddess Earth, the fertility goddesses of prehistoric times, and the goddesses of the later Roman, Greek, and Egyptian cultures.

MISOGYNY IN HINDUISM

The Hindu laws of Manu describe women as demonic, morally unrestrained in sexual activity, generally immoral and dangerous. In agreement with this law, women are completely dependent on their husbands. It is written that husbands, though destitute of virtue, or seeking pleasure elsewhere, must be constantly worshipped as a god by a faithful wife. Moreover, according to Manu, sons should be the sole inheritors, because a son delivers (trayate) his father from the hell called Put. Here are five quotes from the law of Manu:

"By a girl, by a young woman, or even by an aged one, nothing must be done independently, even in her own house." (Manusmriti V.147) Her father protects (her) in childhood, her husband protects (her) in youth, and her sons protect (her) in old age; a woman is never fit for independence." (IX.3)

"For women no (sacramental) rite (is performed) with sacred texts, thus the law is settled; women (who are) destitute of strength and destitute of (the knowledge of) Vedic texts, (are as impure as) falsehood (itself), that is a fixed rule." (IX: 18)

Women have no right to study the Vedas [sacred scriptures]. That is why their Sanskaras are performed without Veda Mantras. Women have no knowledge of religion because they have no right to know the Vedas. The uttering of the Veda Mantras is useful for removing sin. As women cannot utter the Veda Mantras, they are as unclean as the untruth." (IX.18)

"A man, aged thirty years, shall marry a maiden of twelve who pleases him or a man of twenty-four a girl of eight years of age. If (the performance of) his duties would otherwise be impeded, he must marry sooner." (IX.94)

And according to the Manu (IX: 17) "women love their beds, seats, ornaments; impure desires, wrath, dishonesty, malice and bad conduct from parts of their nature."

In the great religious epic, the *Mahabharata,* there is an entire chapter that explains how women are the root of all evil. Women are considered as much more dangerous and harmful than poison, snake, the angel of death or the god presiding over the underworld (*Yama*). Abortion of female fetuses and female infanticide is rampant in India. As stated in the "unerring truth" of the Hindu scriptures "Let a female child be born somewhere else; here, let a male child be born (Atharva

Veda.6.3.4). Moreover, bride-burning, witch-burning, wife-burning, and rape still occurs and not infrequently.

Bride-burning is frequent in India. Women are first tortured to extract more dowries from their parents. Frequently, if this is not forthcoming, she is burned completely by pouring kerosene over her and setting her on fire. This is then reported as an unfortunate kitchen fire.

Witch-burning for it is easy to accuse women of being witches. The grounds may be as harmless as talking back to men or priests or simply a man wants a new wife. "Witches" are hunted down and killed in a most gruesome manner such as being eaten alive by wild dogs, having boiling oil poured over them. Others are being nakedly paraded through town and have subsequently their genitals mutilated.

Wife-burning a wife suspected of infidelity may be tried by ordeal. That is, she must walk through a fire, and any signs of burns are taken as proof of guilt. Then, as prescribed by the law of Manu.VIII.371, the guilty wife is to be devoured publicly by dogs. Lower caste women are expected to submit to rape by upper caste men. For this reason the laws prohibiting such action are not enforced by the police.

MISOGYNY IN BUDDHISM

Present day Buddhism is as misogynist as Hinduism, Judaism, and Islam. Also, it is as patriarchal as the other four major world religions which include Christianity. But unlike the others, this is only in part due to the basic teachings of its founder, the Buddha. It appears that sexist vices originally present were exacerbated with adaptations from the cultures in which Buddhism spread. As one researcher points out: Buddhism became a patriarchal power structure that viewed women as lustful temptresses immersed in sensuality and not in [the virtues of] dharma. A famous passage from "The Tale of King Udayana of Valsa" in the collection of Jewels states unequivocally the monks' attitude towards nuns and women in general:

"Women can be the cause of great suffering.
If desire is destroyed, there will be everlasting happiness.
The dead snake and dog are detestable,
But women are even more detestable than they are."

According to Buddhist monks, because a female body is associated with evil, lust and greed, it is not possible for a woman to become spiritually realized. However, if she desires to become a man and mentally becomes a man, she can get realization. Buddha himself said, "The female's defects - greed, hate, and delusion and other defilements - are greater than the male's... You (women) should have such an intention...Because I wish to be freed from the impurities of the woman's body, I will acquire the beautiful and fresh body of a man."

MISOGYNY IN JUDAISM

The Hebrew Scriptures (The "Old" Testament) are foundational to the Judeo-Christian-Islamic religions. Hence, the condemnation of women in Genesis 3.16 is a doctrine for all of them. There, God (Yahweh) curses the first woman, Eve, for the sin of offering Adam the forbidden fruit from the tree of knowledge of good and evil:

"Unto the woman he said, I will greatly multiply thy sorrow and thy conception; in sorrow thou shalt bring forth children; and thy desire shall be they husband, and he shall rule over thee."

By this "original sin," all women are punished with the pains of childbirth and subservience to men. But it is also claimed that this transgression by Eve brought endless suffering to all of humanity while on earth. This, supposedly, explains why there is so much suffering and who is responsible for it. Furthermore, the Hebrew scripture treat women as the property of men (chattel, cattle), thus, promoting blatant misogyny. The wretched status of women in Judaism is acknowledged by the male prayer: "Blessed art thou, O Lord our God, King of the universe, who has not made me a woman."

MISOGYNY IN CHRISTIANITY

This religion and the Bible require of woman everything, and give her nothing. They ask her support and her love, and repay her with contempt and oppression.

Although women, and the underprivileged, were initially among the early converts and received equal treatment by its founder, this egalitarianism withered away with the self-appointed Apostle Paul and disappeared completely when Judaic Christianity was replaced with Imperial Christianity in the fourth century. The trinity of Christianity, the Father, the Son, and the Holy Spirit are all male, and so is the hierarchy of almost all Christian Churches. The condemnation of women starts in the Hebrew Scriptures with Genesis and this "rule over thee" is reinforced and demanded on the same grounds in the Christian Scriptures, known as The New Testament (quotes are from the King James Version).

The Apostle Paul demands:

In I Cor 14: 34, 35, "Let your women keep silence in the churches: for it is not permitted unto them to speak; but they are commanded to be under obedience, as also saith the law. And if they will learn any thing, let them ask their husbands at home: for it is a shame for women to speak in the church"

In Timothy 2.11-12, "Let the woman learn in silence with all subjection. But I suffer not a woman to teach, nor to usurp authority over the man, but to be in silence."

In Timothy 2.13-14 Paul attempts to give a justification: "Adam was first formed, then Eve. And Adam was not deceived, but the woman being deceived was in the transgression."

In Ephesian 5.22-24, Paul orders "Wives, submit yourselves unto your own husbands, as unto the Lord. For the husband is the head of the wife, even as Christ is the head of the church: and he is the savior of the body. Therefore as the church is subject unto Christ, so let the wives are to their own husband in everything."

Questions to Paul:

1. "Why did you not choose the other version of Genesis where Adam and Eve are created at the same time?"
2. "Why did God, since He created both, give Satan a superior power of persuasion and Eve an inferior power to resist?"
3. "Was God on the site of Satan or did He make a mistake?"
4. "Why must even the completely innocent, children and animals, suffer for God's or Eve's error?"

MARTIN LUTHER ON THE QUALITY OF WOMEN

It is evident that woman is a different animal to man, not only having different members, but also being far weaker in intellect. But although Eve was a most noble creation, like Adam, as regards the image of God, that is, in justice, wisdom and salvation, she was none the less a woman. For the sun is more splendid than the moon... so also woman, although the most beautiful handiwork of God does not equal the dignity and glory of the male (Luther in his lectures on Genesis 1535-36).

MISOGYNY IN ISLAM

Women were among the earliest who converted to Islam perhaps on promises for equal treatment as stated in the religion's most sacred text, the Koran. This religion was founded by Mohammad around 622 CE. The text, it is claimed, was the original word, or speech, of God delivered to Muhammad by the angel Gabriel. However, this has not been the only guiding text. Over generations after the founder's death, a traditional account of things said or done by Muhammad or his companions was consolidated in a literary work named the Hadith collections. This text is full of misogynic stories rules and regulations.

The alleged sayings by the prophet Mohammad include:

- "I have left behind no temptation more harmful to my community than that which women represent for men."
- "Three things bring bad luck: house, woman, and horse."

- "I took a look at paradise, and I noted that the majority of people were poor people. I took a look at hell, and I noted that there women were the majority."

Moreover, the Hadith texts explain:

- How God created Hawwa (Eve) from a rib bone of Adam.
- Why wives should prostrate before their husbands
- That dogs, donkeys, horses and women belong to the same category.
- It is a noble sacrifice for a man to share his life with the woman... she being deficient in mind, religion and gratitude.
- If a woman offered one of her breasts to be cooked and the other to be roasted, she still will fall short of fulfilling her obligations to her husband.

And Al-Ghazzali (1058-1111), one of the most celebrated scholars in the history of Islamic thought, has said: "... Their [the women's] deception is awesome and their wickedness is contagious; bad character and feeble mind are their predominant traits..."

Shariah, a system for devising laws, evolved out of:

- Interpretations of the Koran that were often eisegetical, that is, they expressed the interpreter's own ideas, bias, or the like, rather than the meaning of the text.
- The Hadith sayings which are not necessarily authentic.
- The tradition of Islam and apparently the cultures in which it found itself.
- Centuries of debate, interpretation, and precedent.

It is the shariah laws that determining the Muslim way of life by all traditional schools of jurisprudence. In the case of women, they legitimize the oppression, humiliation and persecution of Muslim women almost everywhere in the Muslim countries and elsewhere.

In sum, with regards to women, traditional Islam as practiced by Muslims asserts:

- Women are inferior to men; therefore, they have lesser rights and privileges than men.

- The testimony of one man is equivalent to that of two women.
- Women have been created for the well-being and gratification of men.
- Men are at liberty to keep and enjoy multiple wives and mistresses in special circumstances.
- Men may divorce their wives at will while women may only separate themselves from their husbands, whether abused or not, by returning the dower to them with the permission of the court the wife's property received from the groom as part of the marriage contract.
- Women must not come out in public without covering their body, hair, and face (in some Islamic nations).
- Women are deficient, not intelligent enough to operate governments or be head of state.
- Women do not need higher education – it is actually detrimental to them.
- Women should inherit half of what men inherit.

In case of rape, complains by women are taken as proof that they have committed adultery or fornication. They are then charged accordingly and arrested. Obviously, as this religion promulgates, women are innately evil; hence, they must have irresistibly tempted the innocent perpetrator. In police custody, 72% of these women are physically and sexually abused according to Woman's Action Forum, a women's rights organization. The rapists, who are considered victims, usually get off free under this system. The women in Islamic nations are not much better treated than women in Hindu India.

As many Christians tend to claim that all social progress can be traced back to their particular religion (even while resisting such progress as far as contemporary issues are concerned), I thought it prudent to provide a short introduction to the history of Christian misogyny:

Judging by the content of the New Testament, it is quite possible that Christianity was a rather egalitarian movement during the first few decades of its existence: it shows Jesus defending an adulteress, Jesus speaking to foreign women, Jesus reprimanding his audience for discarding their wives like pieces of furniture, and so on and so forth. Note also how the first to see the empty grave and the risen saviour happens to be a woman, rather than one of the male disciples.

Further proof of these egalitarian tendencies can be found in the Epistles of Paul (of all places), where he addresses specific eminent female figures among the Christian communities he writes to. However, things changed drastically shortly thereafter. The pseudepigraphia attributed to Paul already speak a different language, and so do the writings of virtually every "church father". We might muse that this radical change was brought about by the rivalry with gnostic sects (in which women featured prominently), or by some other outside influences (Aristotle served as a source of misogyny, after all).

But the fact remains that for almost two millennia; Christianity actively suppressed, denigrated, and in some instances even demonized women. Here's what the greatest theologians of Christianity had to say about the topic:

St. Clement of Alexandria (c150-c215), the Greek Father of the Church, had such contempt for women that he believed such a feeling must be universal. He wrote, in his book Paedagogus that in women, "the consciousness of their own nature must evoke feelings of shame." That women is clearly inferior to men, Clement has no doubt. As a form of exercise for this "weaker sex", he suggested that, "Women should also fetch from the pantry things that we need."

Tertullian (c160-c225), the African Father of the Church, called women "the devil's gateway." His reasoning, based on the story of The Fall in Genesis, is theologically impeccable: "Do you not realize that Eve is you? The curse God pronounced on your sex weighs still on the world. Guilty, you must bear its hardships. You are the devil's gateway, you desecrated that fatal tree, and you first betrayed the law of God, you who softened up with your cajoling words the man against who the devil could not prevail by force. The image of God, the man Adam, you broke him, it was child's play to you. You deserved death, and it was the son of God that had to die!"

The famous and influential theologian, Origen (c185-254) is well known for his hatred of sex and women. At the tender age of eighteen, he castrated himself in his quest to achieve Christian perfection. Origen's teaching weaved together the Christian hatred for women and abhorrence for the sexual act into one system. According to him, women are worse than animals because they are continuously full of lust. [Eerily reminiscent of how men are often viewed these days, isn't it?] Origen does not approve of the sexual act even in marriage and taught that although widowers can remarry, they are by no means crowned for this.

St. Gregory of Nazianzum (329-389), the Bishop of Constantinople had this to say about women, "Fierce is the dragon and cunning the asp; But woman have the malice of both." The other St. Gregory (330-395), Bishop of Nyassa, taught that the sexual act was an outcome of the fall and that marriage is the outcome of sin. St. Ambrose (c339-397), a Doctor of the Church, and Bishop of Milan reminded believers that the way women were originally created confirms her second class status: "Remember that God took the rib out of Adam's body, not a part of his soul, to make her. She was not made in the image of God, like man."

Like all Christian misogynists, Ambrose glorified virginity. To him virginity was the Christian virtue. He advised that marriage was to be avoided like a burden. For those who do marry, he forbade intercourse for any other reason except the procreation of children. Naturally, Ambrose taught that old couples, in which the woman can no longer conceive, should not have sex at all.

St. Jerome (c342-420), the well known Biblical scholar and translator of the Bible into Latin (the Vulgate) have a simple view of women. To him "woman is the root of all evil." Like all the early Christian theologians, Jerome glorified virginity and looked down on marriage. He reasoning was also rooted in Genesis: "Eve in paradise was a virgin... understand that virginity is natural and that marriage comes after the Fall. The marital act to Jerome cannot be good because it only acts as a relief valve: "Thus it must be bad to touch a woman. If indulgences are nonetheless granted to the marital act, this is only to avoid something worse. But what value can be recognized in a good that is allowed only with a view of preventing something worse?" Jerome wrote that the only good thing about marriage is that "it produces virgins." St. John Chrysostom (c347-407), Doctor of the Church and Bishop of Constantinople, said that women are, in general, "weak and flighty." He neatly put together the twin theological ideas of anti-women and anti-sex in this passage: "It does not profit a man to marry.

For what is a woman but an enemy of friendship, an inescapable punishment, a necessary evil, a natural temptation, a domestic danger, delectable mischief, a fault in nature, painted with beautiful colours?" To help believers overcome the temptation of women, Chrysostom devised the following description: "The whole of her body is nothing less than phlegm, blood, bile, rheum and the fluid of digested food... If you consider what is stored up behind those lovely eyes, the angle of the nose, the mouth and the cheeks you will agree that the well-proportioned body is only a whitened sepulchre."

Religion has both revered and reviled women, exalting their fertility and fearing their sexuality. While religions throughout history have mutated, gone extinct, and propagated — the position of women within their ever expanding reach has usually fared poorly. Yet, women are far more likely to be religious, attend religious services, and inculcate their children with their beliefs. Why are women so willing to give in to religious dogma and subject themselves to the degradations often inflicted upon them? This is a fascinating question, and is especially perplexing when you consider the great strides toward equality women have gained in the West. Yet, without women passing on faith, belief, and dogma, religion could not survive through the generations.

The answers we seek shall neither come easily nor be all-encompassing. As with all things psychological, we must account for individual differences, culture, family, friends, media and politics. However, we can begin to unravel the mystery of why women willingly submit to male domination through religious hierarchies by examining our most evolved psychological adaptations. While it is not possible to cover all the details necessary to treat such a vast and complicated subject, I hope to tease you into considering ideas that challenge long-held assumptions.

SEXUAL SELECTION

In case it has escaped your notice (or fallen foul of your political sensibilities), men and women differ. In terms of our physical differences, women on average are smaller, weaker, more gracile, and distribute fat differently. There are a number of physical secondary sexual characteristics, that is, characteristics that are not necessary for reproduction but differ between the sexes, some of which are obvious such as more muscular development in men and exaggerated breast development in women. Other characteristics are more subtle; For example, women have fuller lips, larger eyes, and smaller chins on average than men. These characteristics are mediated by hormones, largely testosterone, estrogens, and progesterone.

But the physical characteristics we can see are not the only differences that come about because of hormones. Our brains are awash in hormones throughout our fetal development, during our childhood, and then the familiar (some might say ominous) surge during adolescence. As adults, our hormones still continue to affect us and as we age, the waning of hormones affects us as well. It is because of hormones that male and female brains differ. While there is no evidence for differences in intelligence (as was believed in the nineteenth century and on into the twentieth - women were not even allowed to vote until 1920!), to deny that differences exist is simply wishful thinking. Evolution cares nothing for either misogyny or feminism; it cares not for what is moral or immoral, just or unjust: without caring at all, it builds survival machines to carry genes into the next generation.

But what has this to do with religious beliefs among women? Quite a bit actually. When we look at some of the behavioural and psychological differences between women and men, we can glimpse some of the adaptations necessary for our ancestors' survival. What make humans human is our large brains, and in order for our brains to develop, evolution had to 'intervene'; Ancestral women had to develop a wider pelvis to allow the large head of a newborn through the birth canal. Another way to facilitate and accommodate big brains was to give birth to premature infants. This is why human neonates are so helpless compared to all other primates. As hominid brains grew in size and complexity, so too did the need for extended childhood, late-onset reproduction, and extended life-span.

The vulnerability of infants and children would have led our ancestral females to select mates who were more likely to stay around, as well as to rely heavily on support from the group. Women would have relied on close female relatives to provide both emotional and practical support. Males within the group would have provided protein and defence against invading males. It was not only a woman's individual survival that was dependent on the group, but more importantly it was essential to the survival of her offspring and in other words the future of her genes. With this in mind, we can begin to understand why it is so essential for women to fit into their social group.

Exclusion would have meant extinction since those women who could not live in accord with the other members of their group would have had fewer or no descendants. Thus, the evolutionary pressures that shaped the need to live in harmony with the group pressed more strongly on women than on men. This is not to suggest that there were not strong evolutionary pressure for males, too, to conform, indeed there were. However, males who risked upsetting the status quo and did so successfully would have gained an advantage in their own reproductive success. Females who tried the same would not.

Before going on, I need to go touch on a rather obvious but extremely important element of male/female differences:

unequal reproductive success. This simply means that men are capable of producing a far greater range of offspring than women. Reproductive success of the average male equals that of the average female. But the most successful male is far more successful than the least successful male, and than any female. Males can hold harems (which mean that some males never reproduce at all). Females cannot hold harems - or at least there would be no point in their doing so. Sperm is cheap, wombs are costly and gestation time consuming.

Women are limited in the number of offspring they can produce, while men, feasibly, could sire thousands of infants if only they could find willing partners. Thus, where women tend to range between 0 and 5 offspring, men can range from 0 to double digits (and beyond!). This very simple fact makes it far more advantageous for men to risk everything, including social exclusion and death, if there is a chance they can gain sexual access to a substantial number of women. However, women gain very little by risking it all, since they cannot increase their ability to have more offspring by increasing their number of sexual partners. Women therefore would have been under much stronger evolutionary pressures to 'play it safe' and remain with the status quo. Let the man take the risks, and if he succeeds choose him as a sexual partner.

RELIGION AND CULTURAL NORMS

It is not my purpose here to discuss the relationship between religion and culture, but I will suggest that, for as long as written history has existed, cities, states, and empires have enlisted the help of religious leaders, and religious leaders have relied on the protection of the state. This is true of all the major religions of today, with no exception. Religion is a human invention, the gods and goddesses that have come and gone during our short history have all displayed the best and (more often) worst human traits. They fell in love, jealousy was common, revenge, anger and trickery prevailed, the struggle for power was universal, and all could be brought to folly and woe due to excessive hubris, greed, and lust. Soap operas pale in comparison! What concerns me, though, is that religion reflected the culture of the times - and, for better or worse, the religions most prominent today are all rather ancient beasts that grew out of a time when women were subservient to men, and often considered as property to be bartered, battered, and controlled.

So we are back to our original question: Why do women today continue to fall victim to an archaic system of beliefs that foster misogynistic behaviour? Why are women even more likely to be religious than men? The simple answer is that it is safe. Please don't take this as a slight against women – it isn't. Male/female differences exist, but I'm certainly not suggesting that risk taking is a better option than playing it safe. After all, women are less likely than men to die doing incredibly stupid things (check out the Darwin Awards it is nearly exclusively male 'winners'). But the fact that women are less likely to push the status quo for fear of social exclusion and even retribution makes a lot of evolutionary sense.

RELIGION AND KINSHIP

Religion creates the illusion of kinship, and kinship is crucial to a woman's reproductive success. Even today, single mothers (and fathers) who receive support from family often avoid many of the pitfalls that single parents without support endure. Family support reduces stress through emotional support as well as practical support, and throughout the last 100,000 years would have been a critical factor in raising an infant to reach reproductive age. The instant support group that religious institutions offer remains today. Churches, synagogues, temples, mosques offer immediate female fictive kin (assumed family).

Raising a child, with or without a partner, is a difficult and daunting task. Women, especially new mothers, seek out other women for advice, encouragement, and support. Certainly, women who were raised with a religious upbringing would be more likely to become dependent on these intimate social relationships with other women. This inter-dependency taps into deep psychological needs, and being excluded from it would trigger a very primal fear response. In order for women to abandon religion and its securities, there needs to be something tangible to replace the support that it offers. This is especially true in small and/or insular communities where one could face being shunned by family and friends.

And in some parts of the world, abandonment of belief would bring a death sentence to be carried out by family members. Women traditionally have had the strongest ties to family compared to men: thus breaking those ties will be more difficult and more psychologically painful. While nobody has done a specific study of atheism and women, it is easy to guess that those women, who have been raised in more traditional religious homes, with family and religion closely tied together, are most likely to fear of rejection and isolation if they announce their lack of faith. Some manage to break through, but not without significant loss. Ayaan Hirsi Ali's book, *Infidel*, shows the strength and courage it takes to leave one's faith and family. The psychologist Jill Myton also reveals not only her own struggles against religious indoctrination, but also documents the struggles of others who left one of the most secretive and exclusive religious cults in the West.

Humans have the capacity to show great strength, courage and integrity. Sometimes we need just a little push, to encourage us to question those ideas and long-held beliefs we hold most dearly. It is threatening to question not only our own beliefs, but those of our family and friends. We feel safe, even in falsehoods, as long as others believe the same. In order for women to move on from the archaic falsehoods of religion, dialogs need to be opened and our most intimate fears revealed. Women can abandon the tyranny of religion, but it will take courage - the same sort of courage that won women the right to vote, the right to work, and the right to steer their own destiny.

HATRED FOR WOMEN AND ISLAMIC TERROR

During the last three years we have been witnesses to the atrocities perpetrated in Afghanistan by the Taliban regime on their own women. Women hatred is nothing new; however, the extent of the abuse and its ferocity has no precedent in the history of mankind. It is in act a real genocide which, since it is being committed on their own women, must be interpreted also as an act of collective suicide. The Taliban's do not limit them to controlling and humiliating their women, which is quite common in many primitive societies, but their aim seems to be the actual destruction of the other sex.

Women in Afghanistan are not only excluded from public life and deprived from every civil and human right. They are even prevented from receiving basic medical care. Preventing women from going to school and from having an education points to the intention of holding them in a state of submission and humiliation, but preventing from them even medical care, points to the intention of extermination.

Phenomenologically speaking, the drive of destroying the object of lust is peculiar to the oral sadistic stage of evolution, and we must understand what happened in Islamic society, and particularly in Afghanistan, that induced such a self destructing regression in an entire people. Hatred for women is so absolute that the Talibans don't want any contact with them, and their society became a basically homosexual one.

Men live only among themselves, and their common endeavor and cement is Jihad, the Holy War, which, as a Taliban cleric expressed himself, became not only an aim, but a way of life. As he said: "it will never end". Jihad is filling the void left by their own renunciation to women, and so there will always be some infidels left, in order to fill that void. They seem a re-enactment of the primal Freudian Horde of the Brothers, who wandered outside the main camp, hindered by the tyrannical father from the female body. Now they are imposing on themselves this inhibition, and the tyrannical castrating father has become their own Super-Ego, to whom they blindly obey.

According to deMause's theory, hatred for women is the consequence of the abuse suffered during childhood by the hand of mothers. As he says, quoting St. Augustine: "give me other mothers and I shall give you another world". According to this theory it is a question of simple and natural retaliation: the sons do to women what their mothers had done to them. As the French say: "Chérchez la femme", the culprit is there. However, even if we admit that in primitive societies children are routinely abused, there is no reason to believe that Moslem women abuse their own sons more than Japanese, Indian, Balkan, Slavs or German women.

German women severely abused their children, and doing so they raised generations of anal sadists who eventually masterminded concentration camps, but they have never been targeted themselves by such a ferocious and exclusive hatred, neither had they been imposed veils, chadors and other sexual austerity measures, nor had they been secluded and excluded from society to the point of oblivion.

In my opinion, in order to understand the real reason for such ferocious hatred for women and such extreme zeal in repressing every sexual connotation, we must compare Islamic society to other groups, and find the peculiarity that causes such particularity. In what Moslem society is different from others? Child abuse is not peculiar to Moslems. Even if we pinpoint to a trait that may be considered peculiar, like clitorectomy, this unfortunate custom is acted out by women on their own daughters. Circumcision is a male affair. Men do it to their sons. Mothers have no part in it. So, are Muslim mothers more abusive than others towards their own sons, to the point of triggering such resentment? We don't think so. What can therefore be the peculiar reason for this peculiar hatred?

If we check attentively, the main difference between Moslem society and others is the structure of the family. Only Moslems are actively and structurally polygamist, while all the others are monogamist, or bigamist, at most, and in quite rare cases. Now that we have found these two peculiarities: ferocious hatred for women and for sexuality on one hand, and polygamy on the other hand, we must also find the correlation between those two phenomena. In the monogamist family there is one wife and a limited number of children.

Fathers are there, and are usually in control. They are a presence. In Hitler's family abuse was perpetrated by both parents, so the little Adolph became an anal sadist and went out to act on others what he had suffered by the hand of his parents.

Let's take the instance of Stalin's family. The father was a drunk, and we should probably never define him as a "strong" person. But he was there, abused his child and wife, and the little Joseph Stalin for sure perceived him as a strong presence. We must understand how the little child perceives his father. He cannot gauge him with the same parameters as we do. The little Joseph identified with him, and became an abusing person and a drunk himself. However, Hitler's and Stalin's hatred for mankind never translated in sexual abstinence, hatred for women in particular, and into deep horror for sexuality. Distorted as could be, nevertheless their sexuality was there. German and Russian women had never been imposed veils and chadors.

In a polygamist society, in contrast, there is not a centralized family nucleus. There are many children. Every group of children rotates not around the father but around the mother. When an Arab man takes another woman, she doesn't live with the former wife and her husband, but in another house, or tent, and there she raises her children. The husband may go there once a week or once a month. If she is not the preferred one, her children will never meet or play with their father. As in the monogamist society the even abusive father is a presence, and sometime the more he is abusive, the more he is perceived as present by the child, so in the polygamist society the father is perceived as an absence.

Now, take Bin Laden, one of fifteen children by one of ten wives, and another 35 siblings from his father's other wives: he probably never met his father, or only occasionally. He never had the occasion of even being abused by him. Instead of a father figure, he has a void.

"Terror overlord Osama bin Laden called his adoptive mother two days before the Sept. 11 attacks against America to tell her he was going underground. While bin Laden's family has publicly disowned him, step-mom Al-Kalifa bin Laden has reportedly remained in close contact with him [she] raised Osama after his birth mother died [and] keeps an apartment in Paris..." In "Bin Laden: The Man Who Declared War on America" is said that his mother was the 10th wife and the least liked or should we say, the most hated, and that he had 15 siblings.

As Joan Lachkar pointed out in her article: "Folie a deux in Marital and Political Relationships" (The Journal of Psychohistory 22 (2) Fall 1994), many Moslem leaders were orphans or abandoned children themselves: Saddam Hussein, Khoumani, Arafat, and I shall add: abandoned by their fathers. Even those children, who had not been physically abandoned by their fathers, feel that way, because, in a polygamist society, they perceive their father as absent.

The entire Muslim saga is that of the child abandoned by his father, from Ishmael to the Prophet Muhammad himself. A Talibani leader, two days ago (November 2001) had a very interesting slip of the tongue. Speaking of Muhammed he said: "Even the Prophet was an orphan". And this was in direct association with their acts of terror. Why "Even"? Who else is an orphan if not the Talibans themselves?

Interestingly enough, Muhammed himself was very fond and respectful of his wife Hadija, but she was an elder widowed woman, who probably did not arise his sexuality very much. And, as we have seen, Bin Laden, two days before the attack, called his step-mom, to whom he is very attached. Being she a step-mom, he is able to disassociate her from his own lust and sexuality. As we see, we have no reason to believe that Muslims hate women because they had been abused by their mothers, and wherever (very rare cases) they can dissociate between a woman and sexuality they may be even dedicated step-sons and husbands.

My conclusion is that they do not hate women per se, but they hate them as symbols of their own lust and repressed sexuality. Now, how can we find a correlation between a perceived absent father, a condition of orphan, and this extreme horror for women and sexuality? Why the former drives to the latter? In the last decades, particularly in America, Freud's work has been misunderstood, disregarded and, even worse, outright repressed. The founder of psychoanalysis has already told us what happens to a child, who reaches the oedipal level, at the age of three to five, while he is over flooded by genital energies, and he is abused: he feels guilty. And he interprets the abuse as a punishment for his own genital arousement and sexuality. He will regress to a previous stage of erotic evolution.

He has no other choice. A four year old child is not a philosopher, and he cannot understand that what happens to him, by the hand of his caretakers, is independent of what is happening inside his own body. Even if, at the same time, there is a major calamity, an earthquake or a death in the family, he will interpret those events as dependent on what he is feeling inside his body. So, if we speak of abuse, as the major cause for psychogenic regression, we must understand this definition in a much broader sense than just spanking and beating. Parents who are not mentally and affectively present are, in an unintended way, inflicting the worst form of abuse of all, even if they have never spanked their child, nor abused him in any other way.

Let's take a four year child, who feels all his energies channeled in his little genitals and directed towards his mother. This child needs first of all a father to identify with. Whoever has raised a child could not to have noticed how, particularly at this age, the male imitates his father in the most pathetic ways: the same expressions, the same gestures. And how he speaks of him: "My father is stronger than yours; my father will win yours....and so on". His father's identity is his own; his father's virility is his own. If he has no father to identify with, he will have a void, instead of an identity. And he will interpret this void as a consequence of his own sexual arousement. Lacan, who was French, understood very well that the name of the game is the Name of the Father, the Ego, and the Identity. He underlined this point even more than

Freud, who had discovered that without identification with the idea of the Father there is no society, no moral standards, no Super-Ego, but only drives and wild instincts. If an Oedipal child is abused or rejected by his mother, he will unconsciously hate women too, but this hatred will find expression in a premature ejaculation, or other forms of sexual incompetence, in order to self-punish and get even with his mother, at the same time. If he regresses to the anal stage he will find gratification only controlling women may be even beating them, but the suffered abuse will never translate into the extreme form of horror and hatred for every form of sexuality, as we are actually seeing happening in the Islamic world.

The moral stance against sexuality must have its source in the psychic instance where every morality and ethical value are created, meaning in the Super -Ego and in the presence of the father. Only a child, who had no father and no identity, at the critical oedipal stage, will cast the blame for this most important form of abuse on his own sexual arousment and on the target of his lust: the woman. Even the most loving and dedicated mother will not be able to compensate for this void, and she will be unconsciously hated in the most extreme form because, by punishing her, the man will punish his own sexuality, which he had interpreted as the cause for the abandonment by his so needed father.

Now the equation: sexual arousment - woman - punishment becomes clear. Blaming women for the sin is nothing new. As is written: "...The woman whom thou didst give me, she gave me of the tree and I did eat". In a healthy family the oedipal sense of guilt is mediated by the presence of the father through the process of identification. A sediment may well remain, but a compromise is eventually reached. But if there is no father, there can be no compromise too. The missing father will translate into a hallucinated one, and therefore also the Super Ego will be hallucinated in an uncompromising and threatening imago, whose demands are impossible to fulfill. It is not casual that both St. Augustine and Lloyd deMause put the major blame on women. Christianity exacerbated the sense of guilt for man's own sexuality, which was almost non-existent in the ancient world. DeMause's Psychohistory is the byproduct of American society where, on one hand they have relaxed standards, complete sexual freedom and equality, to the point that they are moving in the direction of an unisex society, which, by itself, to some may well be a blessed phenomenon, but, on the other hand, has very detrimental consequences too. They have diminished the central figure of the father as a reference point of identification. The result is a malaise as for their own roots and identity. This malaise is producing a disturbing unconscious guilt, which is been cast, as usual, on women. In a very subtle way, the message is the same: women are guilty.

If fathers are non-present, the culprit is the woman. We may very well enlist our Platonic logic, and tell to ourselves that women are equal to men (indeed they are), and that fathers and mothers must have the same importance in the family, but the human psyche, particularly that of a four years child, doesn't work with Platonic logic. If a child at the critical stage does not perceive his father as THE must important, he will find difficult to overcome the oedipal threshold, and will be tempted into evolutional regression. As the say goes: opposites do touch at the extremities. Paradoxically, the Islamic terrorists have targeted America because of their sexual freedom. They hate free people because they hate their own sexuality. America is the perfect alter ego to the Islamic culture of repression. If they punish America they will punish their own sinful drives.

However, there are some hints that they also unconsciously perceive America's Achilles heel. It is as they were saying: "You see, we, like you, are also lacking a Father and an identity, but we are punishing the cause of our loss, our sinful drives. You, on the contrary, are indulging in your sins, and therefore you deserve your punishment manifolds". As the Talibans' slip of the tongue disclosed: "The Prophet was an orphan too", meaning: like me and you. If this was not his intention, why to tell this sentence in American media. He was explaining to Americans why they deserve to be punished.

Bin Laden father not only was necessarily absent, having 10th wives and 15 sons from Bin Laden mother alone, but he also died in a plane crash outside of San Antonio. He had no father - his father died in a plan crash- he has masterminded 4 planes full of people crashing into the TWC and other targets. My guess is that he identifies with his own victims, who crashed in the planes. Identify not in the sense that he empathizes, but in the sense that he introjected the lost object (the father), who died in a plan crash, and now he is himself the passengers of the planes.

He is hallucinating to die in the same way in order to reunite with the hallucinated father. In the meantime he is sending others to the same death and he identifies with them. There is here an interesting condensation:

1. He himself is dying through his victims, and in this way he recovers the lost object.
2. He is punishing his father for not having been there, restaging the scene of his death. It is as if he is killing him again.

So, he is hallucinating a father (Allah). He cannot identify with him in the oedipal sense, but only through the introjections of the hallucinated lost object. Haven't you seen how the Arabs pray? The Muezzin closes with his left hand his left ear. He brings the right hand to his mouth, as a megaphone, and shouts loudly into the sky: "Allah". He is shouting for the absent father. He is calling him to come down from his hiding place. Now, compare with the Jews. They sit or stand, toss with their head and body, speaking among them. They talk with their Father, they converse, they discuss with him. They ask him questions, and respond by themselves. A real Jew never rotates his eyes into the sky, because his Father is there with him.

A real Synagogue looks like a market, and everybody tosses in another direction, murmuring between themselves, and sometimes uttering some sentences loudly, as if they had been asked a question and now they are responding. If Judaism, as Freud stated, is the religion of the Father, it is the religion of the present father, as in Jewish families. Islam, in contrast, is the religion of the absent father, as in Islamic families. The worst riots in the Moslem world happen when they exit the Mosque, at the end of Friday's prayer. Even the leaders of Islamic states, like Mubarak, king Hassan of Jordan and Musharraf, are very afraid of this moment.

They are erotically aroused by the hallucination of the lost object, the Father, and they are in a collective trance. They are eager to re-unite with him in the Paradise of the Martyrs. This is the Placenta. In the Placenta they will be reunited, not with the Mother, but with the Father. Like Pinocchio who re-unites with his father in the belly of the whale. The Prophet Jonah too, ends into the belly of the whale because he was regressing from the presence of the Father (escaping from him).

What the tale of Pinocchio and the Biblical story tell us is that a regression from the oedipal level, because of a refusal of the paternal presence, leads all the way back into the placenta. I have sustained, so far, that every regression into a borderline condition is caused by the absence of the father, real or just perceived, or, even only in relative terms, versus the mother. Being a condition of total withdrawal from the Ego, it may or may not cause paranoid hallucinations, as it seems to be at the moment the situation in the Islamic world. They exploded two jets into the WTC, but they feel completely justified because they are the persecuted ones. THEY demand empathy and sympathy. They are threatening America with retaliation, if she does anything.

Who did what to who is being completely disregarded? To the best of my understanding, retaliation is something that the offended side does, not the offending perpetrator. So, no matter what they do, they feel the victims: the abused ones. As it happens in every paranoia An Iranian Ayatollah has even said on television that it is all a Zionist plot. It is in act here a complete withdrawal from the Reality Principle, like in psychotic hallucinations. Moreover, I have sustained that every ulterior pathology in a Borderline personality is only a defense against the primary cause.

In order to better understand this point I'll give an example. Let's assume that a baby, who at the oral stage has all his erotic energies concentrated in the need to suck, will be deprived at this stage of the so much needed breast. He will hallucinate a breast. Depriving a baby of this vital erotic need is a very serious form of abuse. Then, at the next stage, he will be gravely abused while he is sitting on the pot. Spanking, violence, enemas, and so on, like in 19th century German society. At the genital stage, rejected by his mother, not loved, insulted, and soon and so on. At the Oedipal level he has no father to identify with. Then there will be a regression through all this stages into the oral sadistic stage, and may be even straight into the placenta. However, having been abused all his way up, he will bring with him, on his way down, various symptoms from the conflicts he had been exposed to.

Let's assume that he settles at the sadistic oral stage. Now, if he goes into psychoanalysis, for many years nothing will emerge of the primary cause which is responsible for his fall. For many years, on the couch, will emerge only contents associated with the level, the stage, where he actually is now. Only after many years he will be penetrated by the consciousness not of what happened and why but of his actual condition. If he is an oral sadist, he will be induced into thinking that the cause of all his troubles is that he had been abused as a baby, and deprived of the much needed breast. This may well be true, but it has nothing to do with the causes of his regression into that stage. The same as for an anal personality and so on. This is what Lloyd is saying in his book: after seven years of personal psychoanalysis he concluded that he is in the placenta. So, he could so well describe what the conditions are in that place. There, he stopped his analysis, and therefore he still is in the placenta, he thinks that everybody else is there too, and never occurred to him that his condition is a consequence of a regression from the Oedipal stage, through all the other stages, because his lack of an identity, a father figure.

When I mentioned the Father and the primal murder, he reacted with a paranoid hallucination, very similar to Bin

Laden, and accused me of intriguing for his assassination. Now he identifies with all the fetuses of the world, because fetuses have no father and no identity. But what is he doing? He describes all the possible abuses suffered by children, as a defense against the real cause of his fall, which is the same in every borderline. I want to emphasize that I would never enter personal details, had it not been for the simple reason that he himself rendered them public through his book. If anybody publics personal details, he should also expect others to relate to them, to the best of their understanding. He suggested himself as a model, and this is the point which is totally unacceptable.

When de Mause says that childhood abuse is the real cause of wars, aggressiveness and all the evils that happen to us, he is right, of course but only because child abuse induces a regression into previous stages of evolution and into anal, oral, or placental sadism with the endogenous aggressiveness peculiar to those stages. It is not by denying endogenous aggressiveness that truth is well served, but by understanding that childhood abuse triggers in children a sense of guilt, and doing so it induces them into evolutional regression, and re-enacts a natural aggressiveness that, in normal conditions, would have been overcome, channeled, and sublimated into social constructive endeavours.

Let's assume that a child has been severely abused, while he was a fetus, by particularly hard conditions, and even during the first two year of life, and then, by some miracle, he changed parents, and the new ones are very considering, loving and understanding, particularly in his Oedipal stage. This child will never suffer a regression into placental or oral sadistic contents. He will never need to. His archaic suffering will be successfully repressed and removed. After all, the human being is the king of all creatures, and he became such because of his extraordinary resilience. It doesn't matter if birth took place in the best or the worst of conditions. Philo, Maimonides, Spinoza, Freud, Einstein, Oppenheimer, Yitzhak Stern, Rubinstein, Leonard Bernstein on one hand, and Torquemada, Hitler, Stalin, Bin Laden, Arafat and Saddam

Hussein probably had the same placental conditions. The first group has been even circumcised, which, according to deMause, it is one of the worst forms of abuse.

The difference is that the first group had caring families and present father figures. So, they could successfully repress forms of very early abuse. The second group, in contrast, had been abused along all the stages of their development. And, as we have seen as for the Moslems, the worst form of abuse was the absence of the father at the oedipal stage. And it is not casual, if the oedipal stage is the pivotal one. In the first five years of life the human being is repeating in a concentrated way millions of years of evolution. The Oedipal stage is the climax of this evolution. As Freud exposited, the ambivalence of hatred and love at this stage, the guilt, the compromise and the identification, are the point were the first humans diverged from the pack of wolves and the horde of primates, and became homo politicus. Animals don't organize themselves in articulated societies. They have no guilt and no conscience, and therefore also no society, and not mental illness either.

So, every mental illness must have as its primary cause the relationship with the father. Of course, mothers are very important, but other mammals have mothers too. They don't have fathers. After a very short span, of days at best, the father is not there anymore. To a seal and a calf it is irrelevant who its father is. Therefore they have no society, no morality, no Ego and not Super-Ego. Every mental illness is the consequence of an internal conflict between the Id (the natural drives) and the Ego and Super-Ego, the conscience, the moral instance, represented by the father. Only humans have mental illness, because only humans need fathers to guide and to educate them. And if they don't have them they become perverts, the likes of Bin Laden, or sick people. All this intensive dealing, in America, with placental conditions and early abuse, and therefore with the "responsibility" of mothers, is ridiculous, at best. It is the direct consequence of the repression of the IDEA of the father, and therefore of the anchor and the identity, that makes human society so unique. A man who had a caring and loving mother will always feel secure and successful, on one condition: that he had a strong father presence to identify with. Otherwise he will be a borderline floating creature, with no self identity and strong self, no matter how much a good mother he had. Now we can understand also why Freud's teachings are so disregarded and misunderstood in modern Western society. If a therapist encounters borderlines who have suffered much kind of injuries, on their way up into the oedipal bottleneck, he may well be induced to believe that those injuries are real, and perhaps they are, but they are not the cause, they are the rationalization for their condition.

Those injuries, suffered on the way up, are for sure making their situation worse on their way down. A borderline, who has suffered an injury at the Oedipal stage, from his mother, will hate women too, and not only men. If he had been abused at the anal stage, he may also suffer from a very serious compulsive obsessive neurosis. And if he had been deprived of the breast, now, on his analyst's couch, he will hallucinate biting breasts. However, all this will be enlisted as a defense against the primary cause, which will become clear in his analysis only after many years, if he can climb back all his way up into the top of the hill, the oedipal threshold, and beyond. If he is a borderline, it will never happen because, having lost the Reality Principle, and having withdrawn from the Ego, he has no more lever to colonize and to submit the Id.

Freud understood very well this point, and suggested never to take into analysis psychotics. In the same way you will never be able to treat borderlines. They will tell you again and again of all their injuries, but they have no motivation for changing their situation. A borderline will complain about his suffering, but he will really never do anything to cease it. Only lips service. Psychologists are very fond of their borderlines patients, because the latter are very skillful into manipulating them into believing that they are doing a lot of progress.

Don't forget that borderlines are very manipulative, and will easily make lever on the narcissistic side of the psychologist. A therapist feels in control, his anal-narcissistic side has his best satisfaction treating borderlines. He will give them a lot of sympathy and support and empathy, but it will remain some sort of masturbation. They will be able to advise their patient on every step he has or has not to do, they will receive a lot of gratefulness, and even letters of thanks and appreciation, but after one hundred years the patient will still be there, at square one. He will only manipulate the therapist into thinking that he has made a lot of progress.

It is the same with the Palestinians: After years of progress talking peace, after Israel almost totals withdrawal from every land inhabited by Palestinians (95%), after they have their own autonomy and institutions, when offered full independence and statehood, they blew it up, and now they are back at square one. They retreated into the hallucination of being persecuted, and reacted with anger, bloodshed, and suicide missions. However, they have manipulated the world into thinking what they feel themselves, that they are the victims.

Actually, much worse than square one I had never seen such hatred, until now. Suicide missions are a new affair. Until a few years ago, we had never had such a thing. Offered a real cure to their situation, they reacted with panic. Independence and democracy are the achievement of a mature Ego, which, as we have seen, may only exist where there is a present supportive father. The deprivation of this essential presence has left them only with the envy for their sibling, Yitzhak, who had a Father, and therefore could do it. Therefore, their hatred for him.

Their aim is not to be independent, free, having open borders and interaction with Israel, because Israeli society example and closeness will trigger demands of sexual and political freedom by their women and children. So, the only way, which is open to them, is an ulterior internal repression by the gang of assassins that is in power, and manipulating Israel into closing her borders.

The instrument is suicidal terror, and escalating violence every time there are talks of peace. In the four years since they achieved autonomy, more Palestinians have died, under torture, in Palestinian prisons than in thirty years of Israeli occupation. However, while the sporadic cases which occurred in Israeli jails had been brought to Court and to public attention, because Israel is a free society with free press and Courts of Law, what is happening in the Palestinian Authority is concealed under a veil of silence. No free speech, no Courts of Law, no civil tribunals, no rights to anybody, no free elections: only a struggle of power among the gangs that are trying to prevail on each other. Israel's biggest mistake has been assuming that the Palestinians have her same agenda. Israel wanted to put and end to the conflict, and therefore wrongly assumed that this is the other side agenda, too. However, the other side agenda, because of the reasons we have exposited above, it is not peace, but repression and a close society, where they could act out their regressive psychological needs.

'Where we are standing in Kentish Town does not look much like a Judaean hillside, and the other church to which we are walking does not look much like Jerusalem. But as we go, holding our palms, let us try to imagine the first Palm Sunday.' And so we set off, singing All Glory, Laud and Honour! and holding up our palm crosses, to the faint bemusement of passersby, who looked out of their windows at us, tooted their horns as we blocked the traffic or smiled from sunny pavements. We were walking, as it were, in the footsteps of Jesus as he entered Jerusalem on a donkey while crowds threw palms before him.

Except our journey was along the pavements strewn with the usual North London discarded syringes, chewing gum and Kentucky Fried Chicken boxes. When we had reached our destination, a small choir and two priests sang the whole of St Mark's account of the last week of Jesus' life - that part of the Gospel that is called The Passion. It is said the chant used for this recitation dates back to the music used in the Jewish Temple in Jesus' day.

We heard of his triumphal, palm-strewn procession into Jerusalem, his clash with the Temple authorities, his agonized prayer in the garden of Gethsemane, his arrest by the Roman guards, his torture, his trial before Pontius Pilate, his Crucifixion and his death. So there we were, all believers, and a disparate group of people, of various ages, races and classes, re-enacting once more this extraordinary story. A story of a Jewish prophet falling foul of the authorities in an eastern province of the Roman Empire, and being punished, as were thousands of Jews during the governorship of Pontius Pilate, by the gruesome torture of crucifixion.

This Easter weekend we revisit the extraordinary ending of that story - the discovery by some women friends of Jesus that his tomb was empty. And we read of the reactions of the disciples - fearful, incredulous, but eventually believing that, as millions of Christians will proclaim tomorrow morning: 'The Lord is risen indeed!' But how many in Britain today actually believe the story? Most recent polls have shown that considerably less than half of us do - yet that won't, of course, stop us tucking into Easter eggs (symbolizing new life) and simnel cake (decorated with 11 marzipan balls representing the 11 true disciples, with Judas missing).

For much of my life, I, too, have been one of those who did not believe. It was in my young manhood that I began to wonder how much of the Easter story I accepted, and in my 30s I lost any religious belief whatsoever. Like many people who lost faith, I felt anger with myself for having been 'conned' by such a story. I began to rail against Christianity, and wrote a book, entitled Jesus, which endeavoured to establish that he had been no more than a messianic prophet who had well and truly failed, and died. Why did I, along with so many others, become so dismissive of Christianity? Like most educated people in Britain and Northern Europe (I was born in 1950), I have grown up in a culture that is overwhelmingly secular and anti-religious. The universities, broadcasters and media generally are not merely non-religious, they are positively anti.

To my shame, I believe it was this that made me lose faith and heart in my youth. It felt so uncool to be religious. With the mentality of a child in the playground, I felt at some visceral level that being religious was unsexy, like having spots or wearing specs. This playground attitude accounts for much of the attitude towards Christianity that you pick up, say, from the alternative comedians, and the casual light blasphemy of jokes on TV or radio. It also lends weight to the fervour of the anti-God fanatics, such as the writer Christopher Hitchens and the geneticist Richard Dawkins, who think all the evil in the world is actually caused by religion.

The vast majority of media pundits and intelligentsia in Britain are unbelievers, many of them quite fervent in their hatred of religion itself. The Guardian's fanatical feminist-in-chief, Polly Toynbee, is one of the most dismissive of religion and Christianity in particular. She is president of the British Humanist Association, an associate of the National Secular Society and openly scornful of the millions of Britons who will quietly proclaim their faith in Church tomorrow. Of all the elements of Christianity, the most repugnant is the notion of the Christ who took our sins upon himself and sacrificed his body in agony to save our souls. Did we ask him to?' she asked in a puerile article decrying the wickedness of C.S. Lewis's Narnia stories, which have bewitched children for more than 50 years. Or, to take another of her utterances: 'When absolute God-given righteousness beckons, blood flows and women are in chains.'

The sneering Ms Toynbee, like Richard Dawkins, believes in rational explanations for our existence and behaviour. She is deeply committed to the Rationalist Association, but her approach to religion is too fanatical to be described as rational. Perhaps it goes back to her relationship with her nice old dad, Philip Toynbee, a Thirties public school Marxist who, before he died, made the hesitant journey from unbelief to a questing Christianity. The Polly Toynbees of this world ignore all the benign aspects of religion and see it purely as a sinister agent of control, especially over women.

One suspects this is how it is viewed in most liberal circles, in university common rooms, at the BBC and, perhaps above all, sadly, by the bishops of the Church of England, who despite their Episcopal regalia nourish few discernible beliefs that could be distinguished from the liberalism of the age. For ten or 15 of my middle years, I, too, was one of the mockers. But, as time passed, I found myself going back to church, although at first only as a fellow traveller with the believers, not as one who shared the faith that Jesus had truly risen from the grave. Some time over the past five or six years - I could not tell you exactly when - I found that I had changed.

When I took part in the procession last Sunday and heard the Gospel being chanted, I assented to it with complete simplicity. My own return to faith has surprised no one more than myself. Why did I return to it? Partially, perhaps it is no more than the confidence I have gained with age. Rather than being cowed by them, I relish the notion that, by asserting a belief in the risen Christ, I am defying all the liberal clever-clogs on the block: cutting-edge novelists such as Martin Amis; foul-mouthed, self-satisfied TV presenters such as Jonathan Ross and Jo Brand; and the smug, tieless architects of so much television output.

But there is more to it than that. My belief has come about in large measure because of the lives and examples of people I have known - not the famous, not saints, but friends and relations who have lived, and faced death, in the light of the Resurrection story, or in the quiet acceptance that they have a future after they die. The Easter story answers their questions about the spiritual aspects of humanity. It changes people's lives because it helps us understand that we, like Jesus, are born as spiritual beings. Every inner prompting of conscience, every glimmering sense of beauty, every response we make to music, every experience we have of love - whether of physical love, sexual love, family love or the love of friends - and every experience of bereavement, reminds us of this fact about ourselves.

Ah, say the rationalists. But no one can possibly rise again after death, for that is beyond the realm of scientific possibility. And it is true to say that no one can ever prove - nor, indeed, disprove - the existence of an after-life or God, or answer the conundrums of honest doubters (how does a loving God allow an earthquake in Italy?) Easter does not answer such questions by clever-clever logic. Nor is it irrational. On the contrary, it meets our reason and our hearts together, for it addresses the whole person. In the past, I have questioned its veracity and suggested that it should not be taken literally. But the more I read the Easter story, the better it seems to fit and apply to the human condition. That, too, is why I now believe in it.

Easter confronts us with a historical event set in time. We are faced with a story of an empty tomb, of a small group of men and women who were at one stage hiding for their lives and at the next were brave enough to face the full judicial persecution of the Roman Empire and proclaim their belief in a risen Christ. Historians of Roman and Jewish law have argued at length about the details of Jesus' trial - and just how historical the Gospel accounts are. Anyone who believes in the truth must heed the fine points that such scholars unearth. But at this distance of time, there is never going to be historical evidence one way or the other that could dissolve or sustain faith.

Of course, only hard evidence will satisfy the secularists, but over time and after repeated readings of the story, I've been convinced without it. And in contrast to those ephemeral pundits of today, I have as my companions in belief such Christians as Dostoevsky, T. S. Eliot, Samuel Johnson and all the saints, known and unknown, throughout the ages. When that great saint Thomas More, Chancellor of England, was on trial for his life for daring to defy Henry VIII, one of his prosecutors asked him if it did not worry him that he was standing out against all the bishops of England. He replied: 'My lord, for one bishop of your opinion, I have a hundred saints of mine.' Now, I think of that exchange and of his bravery in proclaiming his faith. Our bishops and theologians, frightened as they have been by the pounding of secularist guns, need that kind of bravery more than ever. Sadly, they have all but accepted that only stupid people actually believe in Christianity, and that the few intelligent people left in the churches are there only for the music or believe it all in some symbolic or contorted way which, when examined, turns out not to be belief after all.

As a matter of fact, I am sure the opposite is the case and that materialist atheism is not merely an arid creed, but totally irrational. Materialist atheism says we are just a collection of chemicals. It has no answer whatsoever to the question of how we should be capable of love or heroism or poetry if we are simply animated pieces of meat. The Resurrection, which proclaims that matter and spirit are mysteriously conjoined, is the ultimate key to who we are. It confronts us with an extraordinarily haunting story.

J. S. Bach believed the story, and set it to music. Most of the greatest writers and thinkers of the past 1,500 years have believed it. But an even stronger argument is the way that Christian faith transforms individual lives - the lives of the men and women with whom you mingle on a daily basis, the man, woman or child next to you in church tomorrow morning.

THE IMPLICATIONS OF MYTHOLOGY

Most religions portray women as a source of evil, inferior and in need of a man to lead and direct them. There are many early myths and religions about the creation of man and woman and about the evil, destructiveness, and mysteries of women. Williams and Best (1990) showed that here was consistency on a number of gender stereotypes in the western religions: Pandora (Greek Myth), first mortal woman. She opened the cover of a forbidden jar containing Hope together with evils of mortals. Hope remained in the jar, evils flew out scattered throughout the world and "for mortals devised sorrowful troubles." Pandora is seen as the origin of all the world's evils. Adam and Eve portray women as evil. Most Western religions Eve is considered the source of original sin, on which many theological principles are based.

This conception stresses the patriarchy system. Two traditions about Eve: first before her fall (before beguiled by serpent and eats fruit) she is equal to man; Second - after fall depicted as subject to man. Goddesses: Women in mythology have been worshiped for their power to give life; they have also been feared and resented for their power to take it away.

Some said that magic and fear were also associated with women because the special ness of menstruation may have caused envy among men who were "denied" this power, no cultural rite could endow males with the power to menstruate and bear children Even in primitive societies today women are physical isolated in huts during menstrual period. Recurring theme about women and menstruation is taboo, unclean and magical. Women are seen as unclean, unstable and primitive. Energy modes acting together: Yang: masculine, active warm dry bright procreative positive; the sun, anything brilliant, south side of a hill, north side of a river, fire. Yin: fertile and breeding, dark, cold, wet, mysterious, secret; the female or negative principle in nature.

INDIA – BUDDHISM, HINDUISM AND JAINISM

Not only did Hindu thought and scriptures relegate females to lowly status, but they were assigned the low caste - The caste system - became more rigid, its impact on women soon probed to be severe. Doubly damned as women and banned by decree...from contact with the scriptures, deities and Brahmins (the highest most powerful caste). (This is an excellent example that demonstrates how, in places with racial and ethnic discrimination we also find discrimination and oppression of women.) These two religions Jainism and Buddhism, and the development within Hinduism, emerged as the three major Eastern religions, each of which involved concepts of reincarnation and salvation. In each, we find many examples of the domination of the male over the female.

Buddhism – charged its followers to love all humans with a mother's love. This involved only sons but says nothing about daughters. Buddhism generally bias toward women and went along with Indian tendency to subject women to men's control. Women did have other option not available: many female Buddhist teachers who lectured on the responsibilities of wives and husbands and household management. Now most of the schools have become fully egalitarian, offering greater opportunities within the teachings to women. Later Hinduism – polygamy actively encourages, especially for upper castes. Wives eat separately from husbands, last to bed. Later - Hinduism became more flexible and liberal. Childhood marriage, infanticide and suttee outlawed. Modern legislation in India now permits divorce and legislates women have same political rights as men. Western religion and science have had impact on Hinduism in its approach to education, social welfare and women. Now - although changes have been positive for women, force of tradition still impedes progress. Even in current times, tradition keeps wives subservient to their husbands. Education one of most important changes necessary for the improvement of conditions for women - religion historically been and continues to be one of the main inhibitors of the education of females. Which religion practices dowries? Indian Summary of Religions in India - gender stereotypes formulated years ago, continued to be maintained in one form or another to present. Although modified attitudes toward women, these religions are still plagues with images developed in their formative period. Many practices still abound from infanticide, suicide of educated women and the cont importance of dowries. Domestic violence is also coming to light and any if not most of the victims are women of India's elite.

Judaism - Jewish women lived in a patriarchal society. It was assumed that men were in charge of all affairs from leadership to teaching to legislation. Women were considered lesser than men and were to follow them. This was pattern, although there were famous biblical exception in which women were heroines and leaders. Inferior status of women was general model in ancient world of Middle East. Women were second-class citizens without power or prestige. Misogynism (hatred of women) was expressed in writings Rabbis praised women for being supportive, resourceful and self- sacrificing and were sad and dark upon death of one's wife. Menstruation - not enter synagogue, forbidden if menstruating or within 7 days of cycle. Women were separated in synagogue. Woman unclean from beginning of menstrual period until seven days passed. After child born, considered unclean for 40 days after boy, 80 days after girl. Whatever menstruating woman touches or sits on impure; intercourse with woman menstruating he shall unclean for 7 days and every bed lies on unclean.

POLYGAMY PERMISSIBLE FOR MEN

Across centuries concepts of Jewish women undoubtedly internalized so women accepted inferior status. NOW-feminists involved in all branches working to make transformation acceptable; Women ordained as rabbis and cantors in Reconstructionist, reform and Conservative Judaism, have not been able to do so in Orthodox Judaism. Divorce strictly controlled by men in Orthodox Judaism and apparent increase in domestic violence among orthodox groups. Jewish women still feel that until changes made in laws of rabbinic Judaism, women still deal with patriarchal structure in which women no equal to men in capacity for religious part.

Christianity – Jesus healed many, including women, dealt compassionately with all kinds of women among them prostitutes and women "unclean" (menstruating) according to the law who were to be shunned. He was accepted and welcomed by women due to this. Christianity granted women together with men, not segregated, equal right to participate fully in family of faith. This was a right that women did not have in contemporary Judaism or in many pagan cults. What is the fundamental prayer for the Christians? The Lord's prayer Catholicism - Throughout 20 centuries of Christianity, part Roman Catholicism, there has been conflict between two motifs in theological understanding of male-female relations: equivalence and subordination.

Conflict between two views, one affirmed equivalence as human persons and other defined woman as subordinate to men socially and ontologically. Paul wrote to Galatians the equivalence position: no such thing as Jew and Greek, slave and free, male and female; for you are all one person in Christ Jesus." Post Pauline period, social order demanded men as husband have authority over women, both as wives and children. Subordination has been maintained by insinuating women are, morally, ontogenically, logically and intellectually inferior to man; therefore less capable of independent life.

Woman's inferior status can lead to sin when she acts independently. Paul's letter of equivalence suggests early Pauline Christianity accepted radical egalitarianism of Jesus and his movement. The church did not accept Paul's vision and intent to define Christian community on egalitarian basis. Virgin Mary - only mortal born without original sin, virgin, conceived and gave birth to Jesus Christ son of God. Known as principal saint, Blessed Virgin Mary, our lady, mother of god (from Greek theotokos) name in Hebrew is Miriam.

This non-profit, 501(C) 19, national organization was established in New York in 1990 to function as a liaison between the government and female veterans and to provide a support group for women who have been victims of sexual harassment and sexual assault (including rape) in their military workplace. WVA achieves these aims in part by educating female veterans on their benefits (primarily access to the Veterans Administration medical centers), by helping them make VA claims, and by legislative lobbying on behalf of female veterans.

Both major goals of this organization are laudable. Our female veterans are both deserving of and entitled to the same benefits as our male veterans. Sexual harassment, sexual assault, and rape in the workplace, especially the military, are as old as history. Men have always felt free to use political and economic power to force women into sexual affairs.

From the slave owner, to the nobleman exercising his "right of the first night", to the conquering army, to the local factory owner promising a woman a job for her husband in return for her sexual favors, to drunken soldiers at a convention groping and fondling, men have always demanded sex from women as a condition of employment. It is nothing short of rape. The women in Women Veterans of America are willing to help all women, military and civilian, who have been forced to trade sex for a job or a career.

VIOLENCE AGAINST WOMEN AND THE MEDIA

Here the media makes the story about the woman's sexual history not about his violence. Concluding that if only women "more tolerant," "more understanding," "obedient," "stayed out of the wrong neighbourhoods," "obeyed the rules of some social sub-group" etc., then men wouldn't be "forced" or "provoked" into using violence. In other words, men can beat their wives, assault their neighbours, rape their colleagues, etc. with impunity if only they have the "right" reason. For women the message is "Step out of line and you will be beaten, raped, or murdered" and for men the message is "You can beat, rape, or murder women with impunity if you have the "right" reason." The messages should be: "Men will be held accountable for their actions and women must not allow themselves to be abused, assaulted, raped, etc. by men."

Here the story gets written before the writer has any facts. How many times have stories appeared that a serial killer stalks prostitutes because of some psychological sexual problem when it is probably closer to the truth to say that the killer stalks prostitutes because they are relatively easy victims for the beginning killer? Would a mugged man be told, "Well, he had an irresistible urge to take your wallet and beat you up," when raped women are told, "Well, he had irresistible urge to have sex with you?" When you read a story about violence against women, change all female references to male references and vis-a-versa and see how the story reads. Would such a story ever be printed?

Stranger violence and rape: Giving young, white, virginal female victims front page coverage while relegating stories about African-American women and other women of colour, older women, married women, etc. to the back pages in a few short paragraphs being obsessed with the sexual purity of the victim. Violence by "friends": Giving front page coverage to young, rich, successful, photogenic, white women while relegating coverage to victims who are African-American or women of color, older women, poor women, or average women to small briefs on the back pages.

Refusing to acknowledge that violence against women is a continuum beginning with verbal put-downs and moving on to verbal abuse, physical abuse, sexual abuse, rape, sexual slavery (as in many instances of prostitution), torture, and finally to femicide, the murder of women as women. Patriarchy uses the actual violence of some men against some women to instil the knowledge in all women that they can at any time become the target of violence by the men around them.

While investigating physical violence against women, I discovered that physical violence against women is only one type of violence on a continuum of violence that men use to oppress and subjugate women. Over the next few months, I will be investigating some of the many other ways that misogyny has manifested itself in various times and places. A summary of some of these methods is given below:

- Economic Violence Against Women: using the power of the purse (the ability of a woman to find food, clothing, and shelter) to subject women to other forms of violence.
- Emotional Violence Against Women: using words and gestures to undermine a woman's self-confidence or deprive her of intellectual space to control her behaviour.
- Intellectual Violence Against Women: stunting women's intellectual development as a method of control, depriving women of education as a way of establishing economic control.
- Legal Violence Against Women: using the law to condone or enforce violence or discrimination against women.
- Medical Violence Against Women: performing unnecessary medical treatments on women or refusing medical treatment to control their behaviour.
- Physical Violence Against Women: using raw physical power to control women.
- Religious Violence Against Women: using religious teaching to invoke "God's will" to control and to justify controlling women.
- Reproductive Violence Against Women: controlling women's reproductive decisions as a way of controlling women's behaviour.

- Ritual Violence Against Women: using torture as part of religious ritual as a way of controlling women.
- Sexual Violence Against Women: reifying women as sex objects.
- Spiritual Violence Against Women: using a position of religious authority as a tool in controlling women.
- Verbal Violence Against Women: using words that sting and burn to control women.

WOMEN'S SPIRITUALITY

As the fall harvest season draws to a close, as the winter solstice approaches, heralding the onset of winter, as the current year ends and a new year begins, many, indeed most, of us give praise and thanks to Goddess for her his bountiful gifts of life, health, family, friendship, and love. Anthropologists speculate that the earliest images of Goddess were female images based on women's miraculous power to give life. Surely, goddess must be female since she created a world so full of life. Her leading servants were priestesses, not priests and her message was one that celebrated life, not death. Gradually, as men acquired more power, the female Goddess was replaced by a male God and her female servants became his male servants.

Yet even in the times and places where patriarchy was strongest, a few, often quiet, almost silent voices, remembered that women were made in the image of Goddess. Today, feminist theologians in all religions, Christianity, Judaism, Islam, Buddhism, etc., are reclaiming the female/ feminine aspect of Goddess. By returning the female to the godhead, soon it will no longer be accepted as intellectually honest for men to rule women with divine sanction as the kings of old ruled by divine right for all will accept that women, like men, were created in the image of Goddess. A time will come when all will say, Goddess is neither male nor female and Goddess is both male and female because Goddess both transcends and encompasses our limiting concepts of male and female.

Hopefully a time will come when God is not defined as Christian or Jewish or Muslim or Hindu or Taoist for all these images of Goddess are just that, fleeting glimpses of the one all encompassing Goddess. Hopefully a time will come when we see Goddess in the innocent young maiden, in the mother with a babe at her breast and another at her feet, in the face of a wise old woman, in the back and hands of a strong, virile young man working to support his wife and child, in the balding, middle aged man studying Goddess's creation, and in the wise old Grandfather playing with the child in his lap.

All of us, women and men, white, black, brown, yellow, red, blue and green, rich and poor, young and old, of all intellectual abilities and philosophical bents (yes, even the fundies) were created in the image of Goddess. All religions agree that we honour Goddess when we honour her/his handiwork. So may the holiday season and the year to come find you healthy, warm and safe in the company of friends and family with all the necessities and comforts of a happy life, including the respect that you deserve as a creation of Goddess.

FEMINIST FAIRY TALES

For a holiday present for the special girl in your life, try Barbara Walker's *Feminist Fairy Tales.* Gone is a comatose Sleeping Beauty waiting for Prince Charming to kiss her and bring her to life. Many of the old classics were rewritten to give women the starring roles. Meet Snow Night, Gorga the Dragonslayer, Cinder-Helle, The Littlest Mermaid, and Jill and the Bean Root. I've given several copies of the book to preteens as presents and their fathers, dreading the term FEMINIST Fairy Tales decided to read the stories to their daughters. Well, even they liked them. So, for some tales of dynamic women, try Barbara Walker's *Feminist Fairy Tales.*

FEMINIST FOREMOTHERS

Many of us have Judeao-Christian roots and the Bible is a sacred book to us. To honor our spiritual heritage, this month Feminist Foremothers brings us the rather obscure Biblical story of two dynamic women, Deborah and Jael. Their story is found in Judges 4 - 5 of the Common Testament. The Israelites were a conquered people, under the dominion of King Jabin of Canaan with Sisera as the military commander. The Canaanite army had 900 chariots, the Israelites had none. It seemed as foolhardy for the Israelites to battle the Canannites as it would seem today for an infantry battalion to engage a tank battalion.

Yet, Deborah, wife, mother, prophetess, and judge of Israel summoned Barak and commanded him in the name of God to assemble an army at Mount Tabor to fight against Sisera. Barak refused unless Deborah would herself lead of the army. So Deborah led the army which Barak assembled and successfully defeated Sisera. As Sisera was fleeing the battle scene, he came upon the tent of Jael. Some speculate that Sisera had been a regular visitor to Jael, that he had taken her as his concubine. She recognized him, greeted him warmly and gave him food and drink. He bade her to keep watch while he slept. While he was sleeping, Jael drove a tent peg through his head. (The Bible gets a bit gory, now and then.) When Barak arrived at her tent, she showed him what she had done. In the victory feast following the battle, the heroines Deborah and Jael were celebrated in song.

We notice that even in this patriarchal age, women were religious leaders (prophetess), powerful political leaders (judges) and army commanders in Israel. Women played important roles in all aspects of society including on the battlefront and in the home. Women used their wisdom and cunning to overcome men's raw physical force, delivering their people from subjugation. These women were not willing to let events control their lives but they did everything they could to control the events that shaped their lives. I do find some parts of the Bible truly inspirational.

THE INTERFACE BETWEEN FREEDOM OF RELIGION AND WOMEN'S RIGHTS

As we all know, certain fundamental human rights are sometimes in conflict which each other (such as the freedom of the press and the right to privacy), and - although both concepts are equally important and universal - it becomes necessary to decide where the one ends and the other begins. This is also the case with the freedom of religion and women's human rights. I think there is no European state which still has discriminatory laws on the statute books that clearly violate women's human rights, although there are, unfortunately, plenty of states in the world which still do.

But general discrimination against women is a reality also in Europe - for example, our Committee has recently presented reports to the Assembly on discrimination against women in such diverse areas as the workplace and sport. It is a fact that much of this discrimination is inspired by the dominant culture of the respective country, which, in turn, is often influenced by (or justified by) religious teachings or sentiments. Thus, discrimination against women and violation of their rights is often trivialised and tolerated even in our European societies.

Of course, depending on the relation between the church and the State, such attitudes are often not openly attributed to religion, but to culture and tradition. Thus, as explains an excellent 2002 study by the then United Nations Special Rapporteur on freedom of religion or belief, Mr Abdelfattah Amor, on freedom of religion or belief and the status of women as regards religion and tradition: " The problem stems from the fact that a number of practices detrimental to women's health or legal status, or to their status in general, are upheld by individuals and communities, and also states, which engage in these practices or perceive them as a component of freedom of religion and as a religious obligation to which they and their ancestors have been subject since time immemorial; they see these practices as having nothing to do with issues relating to the universal protection of women's rights".

For decades, the United Nations has combated this "cultural relativism" argument put forward by a number of states to justify violations of women's rights. I think it is clear to us all in Europe that such cultural relativism is unacceptable, and that women's rights are universal, just as human rights are universal. But it is, unfortunately, sometimes difficult to separate cultural traditions and religion as such – which means that some ostensibly religious practices violate women's universal rights (female genital mutilation, crimes of honour, certain practices linked to marriage and its dissolution, lack of access to education or certain professions, and the preference of boys, being just the most obvious examples).

And it is not only men who insist on continuing such practices: paradoxically, in particular in times of conflict or crises of identity, the victims themselves – women – play an important role in perpetuating these practices. In Europe, such practices are rare outside certain minority religions or immigrant communities. However, this does not mean that European societies necessarily fully respect women's rights.

As the former United Nations Special Rapporteur pointed out in his study: "In every society there are informal customs and traditions which can play a part – sometimes a greater one than legislation – in controlling women's lives", "The persistence of patriarchal culture and the importance still assigned to women's traditional role as mothers and wives responsible for childcare and to men's role as breadwinners legitimise and reinforce the prevailing stereotypes. Most cultures, including those of some industrialised countries, are exposed to these patriarchal behaviour patterns". Thus, for example, Article 41 paragraph 2 of the Irish Constitution reads: "In particular, the State recognises that by her life within the home, woman gives to the State a support without which the common good cannot be achieved. The State shall, therefore, endeavour to ensure that mothers shall not be obliged by economic necessity to engage in labour to the neglect of their duties in the home."

Liechtenstein, Spain, Germany and Luxembourg have also recently been criticised by the CEDAW Committee for their lack of *de facto* equality between women and men – but I do not expect the situation to be much better in other Council of Europe member states, including my own. As the Special Rapporteur writes: "The most horrifying and obvious examples of discrimination committed in the name of religion should not divert attention from more subtle and less spectacular forms of intolerance and discrimination which are just as effective in achieving the subjection of women, such as the refusal to adopt positive measures in favour of women, for example in parliamentary elections, and the refusal to initiate a public dialogue on sex equality".

The interface between the freedom of religion and women's rights has now been made clear: freedom of religion must end when violations of women's rights begin, be they open, subtle, legal or illegal, practiced with or without the nominal consent of the victims - women. It is the duty of the member states of the Council of Europe to protect women against the violations of their rights, and promote and fully implement gender equality. States must not accept any cultural or religious relativism of human rights, they must not agree to justify discrimination and inequality affecting women on grounds such as physical or biological differentiation based on or attributed to religion. This is especially important in those states which permit religious education in schools: it is important for those states to ensure that all religious teaching in schools fully respects gender equality principles.

VIOLATIONS OF WOMEN'S RIGHTS IN THE NAME OF RELIGION

Until today, women's rights are violated in the name of religion all over the world. The most extreme violations - those which touch such vital human rights as the right to life, to bodily integrity, to freedom of movement and choice of partner - are, thankfully, not common in Europe, but they, too, are on the rise, in particular in some immigrant communities and communities which have fallen under the spell of religious extremism. The worrying increase in cases of so-called "honour crimes" (murders, attempted murders and the persecution of girls and women refusing to abide by certain religious and/ or cultural norms by members of their family and community) and of forced marriages, and the failure to eradicate the violent practice of female genital mutilation are all cases in point.

However, the main violations of women's rights which can be attributed to religion in Council of Europe member states are more subtle, and stem from the fact that the dominant monotheistic faiths in Europe (with the exception, perhaps, of the Lutherans) do not genuinely support gender equality. As Ms Sallé from the Pontifical Council for the Laity at the Vatican explained during our second Committee hearing, in the view of the Catholic Church men and women had been given specific and non-interchangeable responsibilities by God. In other words, while women and men may be equal before God, they are meant to fulfil different roles on earth. Traditionally, thus, the Catholic Church has emphasized the role of wife, mother and housewife for women, as has the Orthodox Church.

Over the centuries, such religiously motivated gender stereotypes have conferred a sense of superiority upon men, and have thus led to discriminatory treatment of women. They have even been used to justify violence against women "to keep them in their place". That women may want to shoulder other responsibilities instead of or as well as such "caring" responsibilities, including decision-making responsibilities, was vilified as recently as last year by the Congregation for the Doctrine of the Faith of the Catholic Church, which wrote in its letter to the bishops of the Catholic Church "on the collaboration of men and women in the church and in the world" of 31 July 2004: "Faced with the abuse of power, the answer for women is to seek power. This process leads to opposition between men and women, in which the identity and role of one are emphasized to the disadvantage of the other, leading to harmful confusion regarding the human person, which has its most immediate and lethal effects in the structure of the family."

The Catholic Church considers that "woman, in her deepest and original being, exists "for the other"" – women are seen as living "the dispositions of listening, welcoming, humility, faithfulness, praise and waiting...with particular intensity and naturalness". This religious stereotyping of women's character and role is not compatible with our modern understanding of gender equality and equal opportunities for women and men, because it reinforces women and men's traditional positions in society and deprives them of the opportunity to take on responsibilities traditionally reserved for the other sex: men are not encouraged to take on "caring" responsibilities (such as looking after their children or elderly parents, or taking on more household chores), while women are relegated to the "three Ks" (in German: "Kinder, Küche, Kirche" - "children, kitchen, church") and are not encouraged to work outside the home or take on positions of responsibility in the political or economic sphere.

It should thus come as no surprise that societies in which the Catholic and Orthodox Churches exert a lot of influence are amongst those in Europe in which the labour participation rates of women and the number of women in parliament are amongst the lowest (Spain being a notable exception). Islam is, in general, not any better than the Catholic and Orthodox faiths at promoting gender equality. On the contrary, traditional and extremist interpretations of the Islamic faith both curtail women's rights to an alarming degree, and are often used to justify severe violations of women's human rights.

The Koran is, in fact, quite explicit about women's rights - but while women are seen as equal before God (just as in the Catholic and Orthodox Church), the Koran also contains a set of instructions and "laws" regarding women. These can be seen as progressive for the time they were written, but no longer correspond to a modern understanding of gender equality and women's rights. Thus, for example, polygamy was limited to four wives (beforehand, there was no limit); a woman's testimony was considered as having half the weight of the testimony of one man (beforehand, women's testimony was worthless), women were given half the inheritance rights of men (beforehand, they had none), etc. In Europe, these "laws" are not directly applied to women (as they are in countries like Iran, Pakistan, Afghanistan, Saudi Arabia, Jordan, Sudan, and the Mahgreb to varying degrees). However, a number of immigrant women indirectly still suffer from their application, as some countries (e.g. France) have concluded treaties with some of these countries (e.g. Morocco) recognising their personal status laws. It is thus possible for Moroccan women resident in France, to be, for example, unilaterally repudiated by their husbands, or to have the guardianship of their children over the age of seven taken away from them.

Needless to say, these are very severe violations of these women's rights, and France (and all other countries) which have entered into such treaties would be well advised to discontinue the ill-conceived respect of other countries' personal status laws which violate women's rights, even if this means renegotiating entire friendship treaties. In fact, the most widespread - and visible - problem in Europe concerns the Islamic dress code for women, i.e. the headscarf (or, in some cases, even more covering garments, such as the chador, the niqab and the burka).

There is a vivid debate in many countries on whether the headscarf is simply a symbol of piety which deserves the same respect as other religions' symbols of piety (be it the Sikh turban or the Jewish kippa), or whether it is rather a symbol of the submission and the subjection of women, of their "purity" or humility. The debate is made more difficult by the fact that it is often impossible to determine whether the wearing of a headscarf (or of even more covering garments) is imposed, self-imposed or a matter of free choice, in particular where young girls are concerned.

Different European countries have found different ways of dealing with the headscarf. Thus, France recently adopted a law which outlawed the wearing of all ostentatious religious symbols in schools (including the headscarf), while Turkey forbids the wearing of headscarves in state institutions (such as universities or the civil service). At the other end of the spectrum, Great Britain allows the wearing of all sorts of headscarves, veils, etc. everywhere, including by pupils and teachers in schools. Personally, I do not find any of these solutions wholly satisfactory. Coming from the point of view of gender equality and women's rights, I do find it slightly shocking that some girls attending school in Great Britain are forced to wear very restrictive and covering clothing from the age of four or five by their parents, and that this is accepted by the authorities. On the other hand, I can understand that the authorities in some countries do not want to "make an issue" of the headscarf, for fear of increasing its popularity even further; after all, while Muslim girls may not don the headscarf in French schools, as soon as they leave the school gates, they are subjected to so much pressure (from both their parents and elder brothers, but also from their peers) that most end up wearing a headscarf – for fear of otherwise not being respected, being branded as "easy", or worse.

The reason why I find it so difficult to respect the headscarf as a religious symbol like any other is that there is so much baggage that comes with it, a sense of submission to the control by men of a girl or woman's destiny and the way she leads her life. Allowing young girls to wear headscarves in school can quickly lead to other demands by certain Muslim communities, such as separate swimming or sports lessons for girls in schools, or even the banning of co-education altogether. Where do we draw the line?

Bibliography

Abbot, Franklin, Ed. Men and Intimacy: Personal Accounts Exploring the Dilemmas of Modern Male Sexuality. Freedom, Cal.: The Crossing Press, 1990.

Bakan, David. And They Took for Themselves Wives. San Francisco: Harper & Row, 1979.

Brevard, Aleshia. The Woman I Was Not Born to Be. Philadelphia: Temple University Press, 2001.

Brod, Henry. The Making of Masculinities: The New Men's Studies. Boston: Allen and Unwin, 1987.

Brooten, B. J. Women Leaders in the Ancient Synagogue. Chico: Scholars Press, 1982.

Brown, Theron. Nameless Women of the Bible. Boston: American Tract Society, 1905.

Carmichael, C. M. Women, Law, and the Genesis Traditions. Edinburgh: Edinburgh Univ. Press, 1979.

Chappell, Clovis G. Feminine Faces. Nashville & New York: Abingdon, 1942.

Connell, R.W. Gender and Male Power. Palo Alto: Stanford University Press, 1987.

Deen, E. The Bible's Legacy for Womanhood. Garden City, NY: Doubleday & Co., 1969.

Dennis, Trevor. Sarah Laughed: Women's Voices in the Old Testament. Nashville: Abingdon, 1994.

Doane, Janice. Nostalgia and Sexual Difference: The Resistance to Contemporary Feminism. New York: Methuen, 1987.

Dworkin, Andrea. Women Hating. New Tork: E.P. Dutton and Co., Inc., 1974.

Emswiler, S. The Ongoing Journey: Women and the Bible. New York: United Methodist Church Board, 1977.

Engelsman, J. The Feminine Dimension of the Divine. Philadelphia: Westminster Press, 1979.

Ewart, A. The World's Wickedest Woman: Intriguing Studies of Eve and Evil through the Ages. New York: Taplinger, 1964.

Ferguson, Frances and R. Howard Bloch. Misogyny, Misandry, and Misanthropy. Berkeley: University of California Press, 1989.

Forward, Susan, and Joan Torres. Men Who Hate Women and the Women Who Love Them: When Loving Hurts and You Don't Know Why. Bantam Books, 1986.

Fraine, J. ed. Women of the Old Testament. De Pere, WI: St. Norbert Abbey Press, 1968.

Gerstenberger, E. S. and W. Schrage. Woman and Man. Translated by Douglas Stott. Nashville: Abingdon, 1981.

Gilmore, David D. Misogyny: The Male Malady. Philadelphia: University of Pennsylvania Press, 2001.

Gilmore, David. Manhood in the Making: Cultural Concepts of Masculinity. New Haven: Yale University Press, 1990.

Hobbs, Lottie Beth. Daughters of Eve. Fort Worth: Harvest, 1963.

Hurley, James B. Man and Woman in Biblical Perspective. Grand Rapids: Zondervan, 1981.

Jewett, Paul K. Man as Male and Female. Grand Rapids: Wm. B. Eerdmans, 1975.

Jukes, Adam. Why Men Hate Women. London: Free Association Books, 1993.

Lake, Patricia. "New Men's Movement or Old Boy's Network." Off Our Backs, April, 1992, p. 14. Are men's groups pro-feminist or promoters of masculinity?

Leidholdt, Dorchen. "Where Pornography Meets Fascism." WIN Magazine, March 15, 1983, pp. 18-22.

Loewe, Raphael. The Position of Women in Judaism. London: SPCK, 1966.

Lord, M.G.. "The Greek Rites of Exclusion." The Nation, July 4/11, 1987.

Messner, M., and Sabo, D., Eds. Sport, Men and the Gender Order: Critical Feminist Perspectives. Champaign, IL: Human Kinetics press, 1990.

Michalowski, Helen. "The Army Will Make a Man of You." WIN Magazine. March 1, 1980.

Nannally-Cox, Janice. Foremothers: Women in the Bible. New York: Seabury Press, 1981.

Patai, R. Sex and Family in the Bible and the Middle East. Garden City, NY: Doubleday & Co., 1959. 282 pp.

Patai, R. The Hebrew Goddess. New York: KTAV, 1967.

Penelope, Julia. Speaking Freely: Unlearning the Lies of our Fathers' Tongues. Toronto: Pergamon Press Canada, 1990.

Plaskow, J. and J. A. Romero, eds. Women and Religion. Missoula, MT: Scholars Press, 1974.

Pomeroy, S. B. Goddesses, Whores, Wives and Slaves: Women in Classical Antiquity. New York: Schocken, 1975.

Radclyffe, Megan. Lesbophobia: Gay Men and Misogyny. London: Cassell Academic, 1995.

Riley, W. B. Wives of the Bible: A Cross-Section of Femininity. Grand Rapids: Zondervan, 1938.

Russell, Letty M., ed. Feminist Interpretation of the Bible. Philadelphia: Westminster, 1985.

Smith, Joan. Misogynies: Reflections on Myths & Malice. New York: Fawcett Columbine, 1991.

Stoltenberg, John. Refusing to be a Man. Portland: Breitenbush Books, 1988.

Swindler, Leonard. Biblical Affirmations of Woman. Philadelphia: Westminster, 1979.

Williams, James G. Women Recounted: Narrative Thinking and the God of Israel. Sheffield: Almond, 1982.

Index